JIMMY TWO GUNS

THE LIFE AND CRIMES OF
A GANGLAND LAWYER

James J McIntyre

Black&White

Black&White

First published in the UK in 2023
This edition first published in the UK in 2024 by
Black & White Publishing Ltd
Nautical House, 104 Commercial Street, Edinburgh, EH6 6NF

A division of Bonnier Books UK
4th Floor, Victoria House, Bloomsbury Square, London, WC1B 4DA
Owned by Bonnier Books
Sveavägen 56, Stockholm, Sweden

This book is a work of non-fiction, based on the life, experiences
and recollections of the author. The author has stated to the publishers
that the contents of this book are true to the best of his knowledge.
Some names, places and events have been changed to protect identities.

The publisher has made every reasonable effort to contact copyright holders
of images in the picture section. Any errors are inadvertent and anyone who
for any reason has not been contacted is invited to write to the publisher so
that a full acknowledgement can be made in subsequent editions of this work.

A CIP catalogue record for this book is available from the British Library.

ISBN: 978 1 78530 522 1

13 5 7 9 10 8 6 4 2

Typeset by Data Connection
Printed and bound in Great Britain by Clays Ltd, Elcograf S.p.A.

www.blackandwhitepublishing.com

JIMMY TWO GUNS

To my mother, upon whose prayers I constantly rely.

'If I were hanged on the highest hill,
Mother o' mine, O mother o' mine!
I know whose love would follow me still,
Mother o' mine, O mother o' mine!'

Foreword

'Hi, Paul, I'm James McIntyre,' said the young man in a pinstriped suit, with lapels so wide Al Capone would have thought them over the top. All James ever wanted was to be an outlaw, like Jesse James, Billy the Kid, John Dillinger. As a wise man once said, 'Be careful what you wish for.' We first met back in 1988, just after the prison riot at HMP Shotts, where I was banged up. James, my new defence solicitor, had recently been released from 'the Digger', aka the punishment block in Edinburgh prison, after being cleared of a charge of attempting to murder a detective inspector in the drug squad.

Calling James a maverick is an understatement, like saying Jimmy Hendrix played guitar. Razor sharp, with an analytical brain, what mattered way more was that he was one of us. To ask if James sometimes crossed the line would be to assume he was aware there was a line to cross, or that he cared: all he wanted to do was go head-to-head with the Crown and win.

A paradoxical character, devout Catholic, devoted family man, yet seen as the 'consigliere' in his extended family circle (I gave him his first nickname, 'Tom Hagen', after the character in *The Godfather*). To other top figures in organised crime in Scotland, his office was called 'the Confessional'. We clicked that first time we met, and I became his client, remaining one of his closest friends. In our world, loyalty is everything, and James was and is loyal, in spades.

While a hero to us on the streets, he became a real threat to the judicial system. As one cop put it, 'McIntyre had to go. Far too many were getting off, including McIntyre.' After a number of close calls, 'Tom Hagen' eventually took a fall when he was arrested by an Armed Response Unit and convicted of firearms offences.

James would never flip on his friends, whatever the inducement. He did his jolt, with the result that the status and respect he'd earned rose even further, gaining him a new name – Jimmy Two Guns.

This book will take the reader on a roller-coaster ride through James' early life, some of the strokes he pulled, plus a lot of laughs along the way. One Johnny Cash song states his mother cautioned him, *don't ever play with guns* – if only James and I had taken that advice, things would have turned out a lot differently for both of us. But, by the Grace of God, I'm delighted to say James is once again my partner in crime. The difference is this time we're only writing about it.

PAUL J. FERRIS

1

'Methought I heard a voice cry, "Sleep no more!"'
                            – *Macbeth*, William Shakespeare

July 1996. A battering sound beat the air, dragging me from a deep sleep. I woke, in bed, at home: so far so good. Suddenly, I sat bolt upright, pulling the pillows to one side. Both pistols were still there. Head hammering, I glanced around the room. Empty. I checked my watch: 8.30 a.m. Evelyn must've taken the kids to school.

The racket outside was coming closer. I kicked off the covers, stumbled to the window, drew back the curtain and screwing my eyes against the summer sunlight, pushed open the glass pane and glanced out. A police helicopter hovered overhead; a gust of dust from its blades slapped my face. They don't send copper choppers to recover rent arrears. Some poor sod was bang in trouble.

Over the clatter, I could just make out the sound of the telephone in the kitchen: how long it'd been ringing I hadn't a clue. Truth is, I hadn't much of a clue about anything just then, but the receiver was ready to jump off the hook.

'I'm coming,' I yelled at absolutely nobody, as I thundered down the stairs and grabbed the phone.

'Hello?'

'It's Dad. Look out the window.'

'What?'

'Just do it.'

With the phone cord at full stretch, I crossed the kitchen. As I did so a crackling voice blared from a loudhailer.

'James McIntyre, the house is surrounded. Come out with your hands on your head!'

It's not every morning you get an alarm call like that.

'James McIntyre, I repeat, the house is surrounded. Come out with your hands on your head.'

Pushing a couple of fingers through the Venetian blinds, I peered out between the slats. Police cars and vans lined both sides of the street, lights flashing, sirens sounding. Helicopter blades beat the air as armed officers crouched behind parked vehicles.

Then I clocked him. A plain-clothes cop, crouched, half hidden by a car door, loudhailer in hand, calling out above the clamour in front and clatter overhead. My eyes raked the street, which ran at right angles to the house. Armed officers scurried from cover to cover, coming closer and closer. To my left, a couple of uniformed cops in peaked caps, carrying Heckler & Koch machine guns, crept forward.

I put the phone to my ear.

'Dad?'

'See them?'

'They're hard to miss.'

'You've really done it this time, son,' he said, and hung up.

I stared at the phone for several seconds, replaced the receiver and turned back to the window. Everything seemed so surreal. 'Surreal' is a word vastly overused these days, nearly always incorrectly by people who haven't a clue what it means, and normally about something utterly mundane; but, this time, the word fitted perfectly. Despite the seriousness of the situation, for a split second, a scene from one of my favourite films, *Heat*, came to mind: the one where Pacino plays the dedicated detective and De Niro the professional bank robber. But this was no movie, this was real life. My life. Once again, the cop's voice crackled from across the street.

'James McIntyre! You are surrounded. Come out with your hands on your head. I repeat, you are surrounded. Come out with your hands on your head!'

I'd been right about one thing that morning. Some poor sod was bang in trouble. Me!

2

'Simple Simon said, put your hands on your head.'

– Children's game

The helicopter still hovered and the guy on the ground with the loud-hailer grew more insistent. Mind working overtime, I bolted back up to the bedroom, pulled the pillows aside, grabbed the guns and shot down the stairs. Both pistols were small calibre. One was a double-barrelled derringer, the kind poker players on paddle steamers kept up their sleeves, as seen in films like *Maverick*; the other, a Spanish-made semi-automatic, had a clip that held nine bullets and a barrel adapted to allow a silencer to be screwed onto the end.

Recently, there'd been a so-called amnesty, when the police offered people the chance to hand in any unlicensed firearms, claiming no charges would arise as a result. I say 'so-called' as, once the weapons were handed over to the authorities, what were the chances the cops would destroy them without first checking if they'd been used to commit further crimes, and if so, by whom? I'd more faith that there was a tooth fairy.

The night before, when, as a defence lawyer, I'd been given the guns to hand in, the idea hadn't seemed out of order, though the amnesty was now at an end. However, with armed cops about to kick the door down, my view changed dramatically. Time was running out fast. The crackling voice continued, demanding I leave the house, my hands on my head.

For a moment it crossed my mind that perhaps, as both were small pistols, I could slip them round the S-bend in the downstairs bathroom. A couple of flushes and a bit of luck could see them shooting down the sewer pipe, headed for the North Sea. But suppose they jammed and got stuck? My defence of handing them in would be down the toilet too, and I'd look guiltier than ever.

I glanced about, spotted a laundry basket, grabbed the first piece of clothing, a pair of my girlfriend's pyjamas, wrapped the guns in them, and headed for the garage adjoining the house. Unlocking the door, I opened the drawer of a small cupboard, put the package containing the pistols inside it, and left.

Crossing the porch to the front door, I opened it and stepped outside. A dozen or so red dots danced on my bare chest, proof positive that police snipers were pointing straight at me. On top of the garage knelt the two cops in peaked caps I'd clocked from the kitchen window. They'd climbed onto the roof, it being the best vantage point, and now trained their machine guns on me. More red dots ran down my left arm.

'Put your hands on your head,' one cop called out.

I remembered listening to the car radio one day on the way to work. A former member of the SAS was talking about a time he'd trained police officers in the use of firearms. He described the cops as highly unprofessional, a bunch of silly schoolkids, who kept asking how many people he'd killed. I was taking no chances with this trigger-happy lot, and immediately did exactly what I was told.

'That's it. Now turn and go out the back door, keeping your hands where they are.'

I turned, recrossed the porch, opened the back door and stepped out onto the lawn.

'On your knees, hands still on your head.'

How many times did they have to repeat that order?

'Whatever happened to "Simon said",' I replied, attempting to appear as cool as possible in the circumstances.

'Think this is funny?' asked the nameless cop.

'It's not been a lot of laughs so far.'

The pair of peaked caps climbed down from the roof: guns trained on me as they came. One cop frisked me while I knelt, found I was clean and told me to stand up. I stood.

At that point a po-faced, but more senior policeman with the personality of a lamp post took over proceedings. I was led from the back garden into the living room, while uniformed cops searched the house and garage from top to bottom. Before long, they found the guns, wrapped in my girlfriend's jammies, and took them away. Apparently now convinced he wasn't getting clipped, this senior cop accompanied me upstairs to my bedroom so I could get dressed.

This officer and I were now the only two in the room. While dressing, I pointed to a chair in the corner, where lay a charcoal-grey suit I'd worn the day before. There was a gravy stain on the lapel of the jacket, which I'll explain later, but I realised this may provide evidence as to where I'd been earlier, perhaps even support an alibi, in case the cops came up with some further crime they fancied pinning on me.

Accordingly, I said I wanted to keep the suit as a production, and the cop told me I'd better check nothing was in the pockets that I wanted to keep, as it would be months before any court case. So, we both began to search.

I took the trousers but found only some loose change. The senior cop discovered a single wooden bead in my jacket pocket, broken off a rosary I'd carried, and on the lapel there was a Celtic badge. He suggested this could be evidence the guns were destined for the IRA. Remember my reference to the lamp post? He wasn't that bright.

Having satisfied ourselves there was nothing else in the suit, the officer handed me the jacket he'd searched, we left the house and I was placed in the back of an unmarked police car.

By this time, my girlfriend, Evelyn, had returned from taking the kids to school. She saw me seated in the back seat of the cop car, and though used to my antics, was clearly confused about what was going down. However, I signalled to stay shtum and asked for some cigarettes. Evelyn took the hint, went inside, returning with four menthol ones and, with that, the cops drove me off.

I chain-smoked the cigarettes on the way to Livingston police station, tipping the ash into each pocket of the suit, to contaminate any forensic findings that may have pointed to me having the pistols in my possession for any other purpose.

Although the senior officer had already been through the suit with me and found nothing incriminating, still I rechecked each pocket of the trousers and jacket, to satisfy myself they were completely empty.

Arriving at Livingston cop shop, I was taken to what's called the 'Custody Suite' (clearly named by someone with a sick sense of humour) where I was searched again and informed the duty sergeant that I wanted my suit tagged, bagged and kept as a defence production. He assured me this would be done, and promptly stuck me in a cell.

3

'Something cannot come from nothing.'
> – Newton's First Law of Thermodynamics

I was lying on a wafer-thin object which masqueraded as a mattress, when the cell door opened, and a plain-clothes inspector came in and looked down at me.

'Hi Mac.'

I recognised the guy as he'd been a couple of years below me at school. His father had been the local police sergeant in Linlithgow. I won't mention his name, but he was very kind and had gone out of his way to look in on me, though it wasn't his case.

'How are you?' he asked.

'Living the dream,' I said.

He smiled grimly, took out a packet of cigarettes, gave me one, put one in his mouth and lit us both up. At this point the uniformed cop who'd opened the door said to the inspector that smoking was not allowed inside.

'Piss off and leave us alone,' said the cop.

PC Jobsworth's face reddened as he quit the cell. My schoolmate and I chatted for a while, until another woodentop came along to tell me I was to be interviewed on tape. With a handshake, my friend wished me good luck and left.

Shortly after, I was taken to an interview room, where the same cop who'd searched my suit sat behind a table, on top of which rested a recording machine. He began firing all sorts of questions about the guns at me, but, as I'd been asking for my lawyer since the second I'd arrived, I refused to answer anything that could incriminate me. At this point the cop produced a small plastic capsule and placed it on the table between us.

'Guess what I've found?' he said, grinning.

'A personality?' I ventured.

His grin vanished.

'That contains a 0.22mm bullet. It was discovered in the pocket of your suit jacket.'

He was, of course, referring to the same suit he and I previously searched in my girlfriend's house, which yielded nothing incriminatory, and which, to be on the safe side, I'd polluted with cigarette ash. Yet, hey presto, this clown could now produce a bullet which fitted both the pistols I was charged with.

The trouble that faced the cops was they had only one witness, a girl doing her paper round, who I'll refer to later, who stated she'd seen me holding a gun as I crossed the canal bridge earlier that morning. She in turn must've told her mum and dad, and clearly these solid citizens had quite rightly called the cops. But, apart from this young lady, nobody else claimed they'd seen me with anything.

Both guns had been found in the garage of a house rented by my girlfriend, not in my house, nor in my possession. This meant the police were short of the necessary evidence to secure a conviction and required corroboration from some other source, something, anything to link me with the firearms.

They searched the car they alleged I'd been driving, but, alas for them, this too proved pointless, as on checking the documents, they discovered the vehicle wasn't in my name.

The police found a file about a forthcoming case I was conducting for a client and close friend, Paul Ferris, apparently hoping the mere fact I knew him and his penchant for firearms may provide some sort of connection between me and the guns. Talk about clutching at straws!

So, it seemed the police, like Darwin, were left looking for a missing link; however, unlike the author of *On the Origin of Species*, the cops had apparently soon found theirs, as despite the cop having searched my suit with me, despite his insistence that I personally take it to the police station, despite my second search of the suit and antics with the cigarette ash in the cop car, there it was sitting on the table in front of me.

I looked at the bullet, then the cop. 'We both know that wasn't in my suit,' I said. 'I want my lawyer.' And, shortly after, I was taken to my cell, where I later met with my solicitor, who advised me to say nothing.

'I don't think the cops need any evidence from me,' I said, 'I think they're providing their own!'

Monday morning eventually rolled round, and I was placed in the back of a police van and driven off to court. One of the worst things about being arrested, and there are very few good ones, is you're stuck with a lot of others in the same position. Some are solid guys, but many are cardboard gangsters who, caught with a couple of grams of coke, think they're Pablo Escobar. I was sat beside some tube who, taking it for granted I was remotely interested, told me he'd been done with a dozen car thefts. Having established himself as something akin to a character from *Grand Theft Auto*, he asked what I was in for.

'Possession of firearms,' I said.

'You mean, guns?'

I nodded.

'What did you have them for?'

'To shoot the dick who stole my car,' I said. This put paid to further conversation and peace reigned through the remainder of the journey.

Back in 1996, Linlithgow still had its own sheriff court, which was later moved to Livingston, ten miles away. For those who've never had the pleasure of being locked up in old Linlithgow Court, the practice was to simply stick everyone into the same cell, a room roughly fifteen by twelve feet, with damp sandstone walls and a black iron gate.

The whole scene could have been enacted back in the days of Mary, Queen of Scots. Approximately two dozen prisoners, depending on how busy the weekend had been, were crammed into this tiny space to while away the hours talking about what they'd done, what they were denying, and who had the best brief.

Evelyn came to court to see me, but due to the serious nature of the charges, my case was being dealt with by solemn procedure, on petition, so would initially be heard in private. I managed to get a message to her through my lawyer, who saw me in the holding cell, telling her there was no point hanging about and to go home.

However, hoping for a quick word with me, but aware it'd be a while before my case was called, Evelyn left and returned to court a few hours later. I'd just been remanded in custody and was being taken down the corridor, cuffed to a cop. Still, with a stretch I managed to get a quick peck from her in passing. 'See you in seven days,' I said with as much bravado as I could muster, winking at her, before being whisked off to Edinburgh Prison in a van.

4

'No one really knows a nation, until one has been inside its jails.'
– Nelson Mandela

I'm told today Edinburgh Prison has TV sets in the cells, PlayStations and various other creature comforts to help cons pass the time. Back in 1996, the place was very different, and conditions appalling. You arrived at reception, gave your name, stripped, showered on the spot in front of the screws, who stuck you in what was called a 'Dog Box', which was unfair, as no one with a shred of humanity would keep a dog in such a confined space.

Readers roughly my age, born mid-twentieth century, will recall the wee changing cubicles at the public swimming baths, the tiny space, with a bench to sit on, and a half door. The dog boxes were a similar shape, but smaller. New inmates sat for what seemed an eternity before being taken to whichever hall they were going to.

Back in 1996, untried prisoners were locked up two or three to a cell, for twenty-three hours out of twenty-four, and allowed one hour for exercise. This meant untried prisoners were kept in a cell for forty days if on summary complaint, or a hundred and ten, if on petition (these periods are even longer now) yet, paradoxically, if proven guilty, they were allowed far more freedom than when presumed innocent.

Prisoners were provided with a plastic potty, locked up overnight, in pairs, in cells measuring approximately twelve by eight feet, with bunk beds, two chairs, a table and no privacy. Untried prisoners were required to urinate and defecate into those plastic potties in

11

front of each other, with no hand-washing facilities, then keep the crap in the cells overnight, and next morning go through the process of standing in the slopping out line, to empty the remains of the previous evening's deposits down the toilet.

Most prisoners made sure they went to the loo before being banged up for the night, but if caught short, rather than keep the smell in the cell, would do the business on a sheet of newspaper, wrap it up and push the lot through the bars of the window, littering the ground below. Next day, some poor prisoner who'd fallen foul of the screws would be taken out on 'bomb patrol' and forced to pick up these parcels.

Slopping out's been stopped now, and conditions improved; but still, in my respectful opinion – actually, forget the respect – those who choose to prosecute or sit in judgement on others, be they judges, sheriffs or justices of the peace, lords advocate, procurators fiscal or deputes, should be required to spend a month locked in a cell twenty-three hours out of twenty-four, with a minimum of one other person, not of their choosing, before ever being allowed to order someone else be locked up in that fashion; especially those as yet presumed to be innocent of the charges against them, who may well be acquitted. Of course, this will never happen, as any prosecutor or judge I've known would coco their kecks at the prospect; consequently, nobody would ever apply for the job.

You learn a lot of clever little tricks in custody; how to spread butter on your roll without a knife, or set light to a shoelace so it smoulders for hours, letting you light a cigarette without wasting precious matches or lighters; how to stash a stack of phone cards way above the amount allowed, and so call home whenever you wish; how to smuggle things into prison, from hall to hall, cell to cell, and basically become expert at preventing every attempt by the powers that be to enforce their ridiculous, petty rules on prisoners.

The learning process begins the second the cell door slams behind you, and it's wonderful to see this spirit of survival among so many. Things are made easier as prison officers aren't the brightest. I recall passing one on the landing who was struggling to complete a crossword in a tabloid paper. As I passed, he turned to me and said, 'How do you spell canoe? I know it starts with a K.'

However, soon my short period of remand was over, I was brought to court, bailed, released and returned to doing what I did best – fighting the forces of the Crown. But, hang on, let's leave me on bail for now, and go back a bit. Way back . . .

5

'The supreme adventure is being born. There we do walk suddenly into a splendid and startling trap.'

– G.K. Chesterton

November 1956. Eight o'clock, Sunday morning, and already the sun beat down from the blue Sierra Leonian sky. A big black rat sat on a shelf, staring at the bed where I lay in the arms of the most wonderful woman in the world. I was ten minutes new. She was thirty-two years old. The night before, a radio evangelist had referred to a young woman in West Africa having a hard labour but prophesying all would be well with her and the baby. My mum prayed he meant her.

In May 1925, while giving birth to my mum, my grandmother suffered complications, made much worse by a doctor too drunk to cope with the delivery. My mum and her twin brother were six weeks premature, weighing a total of five pounds between them. Both were placed in the same shoebox, packed with cotton wool, and put in front of a coal fire. My grandmother asked that her daughter be named Hope, saying there was none for her, but she hoped her babies would survive. They did, and she didn't, haemorrhaging and leaving this life moments later. She was twenty-six years old.

My mum had faced the same fate as her mother. She'd been in labour for seventy-two hours with no sign of me making an appearance. No blood was available for a transfusion if things turned out badly, so Caesarean section was never an option. As my mother grew weaker it was decided enough was enough. As cutting was out of the question, I was pulled into the world with forceps, wielded by a German doctor named Anna. As I write, I wear a medal of Santa Anna with her daughter, the Blessed Virgin Mary, round my neck.

Connaught Hospital in Freetown, Sierra Leone, was still under construction, so my mum and I were put in a small hut on site. We were the sole occupants; apart from the big black rat sitting on a shelf above the bed, licking its whiskers, looking down with apparent interest at the new arrival.

Afraid to let me sleep in my cot, my mum kept me in bed with her. In my mother's arms I was completely safe. So formed the closest bond of my life: one which would often be put to the test but never broken in the years to come.

My dad came from what may be referred to as 'humble beginnings' – a council house comprising two bedrooms, a living room, bathroom and scullery – but like many from a similar background, he was determined to succeed. His dream was to become a doctor. My mum used to tease him, telling us kids he was a swot at school, unlike her, who'd been belted on a daily basis.

My grandad, a fitter in the local foundry, couldn't afford to send his son to medical school, so my old man went to work on the fishing boats in the North Sea to finance his university fees. My mother, on the other hand, despite nailing her exams and being offered a scholarship, hated school, left at fourteen, and went to work in the local laundry with her pals, a bunch of women I've always called my aunts: Prudence, Mamie and Bunty. Sadly, they're all gone, leaving my mother, now nearly ninety-eight, as sole survivor. My mum and her mates cleaned and repaired the uniforms for the troops fighting overseas in WW2. They'd write love letters to the soldiers, leaving them in the pockets and socks, before sending the clothing back to the front.

My mum and dad started 'walking out' together when they were just teenagers: my mother was his first and last girlfriend: she made sure of that. Shortly after graduating from Edinburgh Medical School, with the medal for excellence, he began work as a doctor in Falkirk Infirmary, before marrying the woman who'd be his partner for the next sixty-eight years.

In 1950 my parents travelled to the West Coast of Africa, known as 'White Man's Grave', where my father took up the position of Chief Medical Officer for Sierra Leone, a country with a population at that time of seven million people. He'd just turned twenty-six.

Taking that job was a massive leap into the unknown for my parents and six years later I arrived on the scene. Those early, formative years in Sierra Leone were unforgettable. I made friends with local children of every colour, clan and creed, including my best mate, Kabe Koroma, of the Timne tribe, and Lynda Moonie, the daughter of my mum and dad's friends, Jim and Elsie, who were missionaries there.

We kids led a wild, carefree life, though a good deal of inter-tribal unrest and violence was taking place around us. The country was already riven with political problems, even prior to its independence from the UK, albeit on a far smaller scale than now. But none of that was on my radar then. All I knew was my own blissful existence with my family, my friends and the hot African sun which made playing outside so much fun.

In November 1960, the Queen's arrival on a state visit coincided with my birthday. As my dad showed her round Connaught Hospital Her Majesty passed on her best wishes to me, but I'd assumed all the bunting, bands and warriors performing traditional dances in her honour were because I'd just turned four.

The following month, my parents returned with me to Scotland for a few weeks, where I first felt the freezing cold winter, with its wind which cut you in two; though seeing snow, which I'd never come across before, was some compensation.

However, I was happy when we returned to our life in Africa, unaware that only two short years later we'd return to the cold, dark land of my ancestors, this time for good.

6

'Education is painful, continual and difficult work to be done in kindness.'
– John Ruskin

The summer of 1962 saw me start first year at West Port, Linlithgow. This was the only local primary school back then; now there are five. I remember my mother waving goodbye to me at the gate, then leaving, and later Mrs Baird, the headmistress, providing a warm welcome by grabbing my ear before belting me for 'carrying on' in the playground.

I'd foolishly presumed the playground was a place for playing, hence the name, but Mrs Baird's interpretation of 'carrying on' covered a multitude of sins, and, though she wasn't specific as to which one I'd committed, insisted I was taught a lesson.

My generation, and many others, will recall teachers' belts were made of leather, about three feet long, two inches wide, half an inch thick, with a split running about eight inches straight down the middle, for maximum effect. I walked back from the headmistress' room, my wee hands red, stinging, still unaware of what I'd done to deserve being assaulted by an elderly woman with a weapon and white moustache. All it taught me was a deep and lasting dislike and distrust of authority, which I have to this day.

I'd been attending school from the age of three back in Africa, so could read and write, and as a result was put straight into primary two, making me the youngest in class. In sunny Sierra Leone, school shut at noon, due to the unbearable heat. I was so used to the former routine that, despite the difference in temperature, when the clock on the wall struck twelve, I headed for the door. Mrs Healey, our teacher, a tall, handsome, dark-haired woman, would haul me back to my desk time after time, yet still I couldn't get it into my head that I had to stay till four o'clock.

One day, she'd had enough, and brought a thick tow rope to class, which she tied around my ankles, meaning I could no longer make a dash for the door at noon, which practice by now was turning into something of a game. Like many children, I enjoyed being the centre of attention, and revelled in my new-found celebrity, jumping here, there, everywhere, till Mrs Healey realised roping me like a calf at a rodeo wasn't such a great idea after all. On occasion I'd be put into a class by myself and left alone for the day. Perhaps I was to pass the time practising sums, or something equally riveting. Nobody ever said and I never asked. Personally, I think they just wanted a bit of peace and quiet.

At that time, it never seemed to occur to any of the teachers, at least none I encountered, to inspire or encourage pupils. If you weren't bright, you were ignored; if you were clever, unless you were a teacher's pet, the response was always 'could do better'; and the smallest infringement of any rule brought out the belt.

One frosty winter morning, I lined up in the boys' playground, at the bottom of the stone steps leading up to the school, waiting for the bell to ring. In front of me was my classmate, George. He had his back to me, and I whispered to him over his shoulder.

'Alright, Geordie?'

'Okay, Mac,' he replied, but didn't turn round.

'Did you see the . . . ?'

'You two!' a voice barked from the top of the stairs.

George and I started in surprise. Glancing up, we saw the headmaster, Mr Anderson, glaring down from the top of the steps, dwarfed by the huge hulk of Mr Gault, the deputy head, stood next to him. For reasons best known to the school, although the bell hadn't yet rung and we were outside in the playground, still we weren't allowed to talk in the lines.

'Come here this instant, both of you,' Anderson bawled.

We left the line and headed upstairs.

'I know you were talking,' said Anderson, as if he'd just discovered the Higgs boson. 'And do you know how I know?'

He waited, a tight smile almost cracking his face. There was no way to answer without admitting the offence.

'I could tell,' he announced, 'from the steam from your mouths in the frosty air.'

'We were breathing,' I said.

'You were talking. Talking!' he repeated, in a tone indicating just how serious an offence had been committed. 'Feeling cold, were we?' enquired the creep, his smile even colder.

'Yes, sir,' we said, our young voices sounding shaky.

He turned to the deputy headmaster beside him.

'Warm them up, Mr Gault, warm them up.' And, with the laugh of the damned, left to slink back to his lair.

Mr Gault marched us to his room, but stopped at the door, stating he'd something to do before dealing with us, ordered George and me to remain where we were and took off down the corridor. I remember that wait, probably five minutes at most, to us, an eternity. On his return, finding us outside his office door, Mr Gault, looked puzzled.

'What are you two doing here?'

'You asked us to wait, sir.'

'Did I?' He smiled knowingly and shrugged. 'I can't seem to remember why. Run along to your class.'

We ran. Fast. Mr Gault was one of the good guys, but they were few and far between, much like most figures in authority, as I was to discover later.

7

'Education is what remains after you have forgotten everything you learned in school.'

— Albert Einstein

Having had what could best be termed a mixed relationship with authority in primary school, it was time to attend what was known as the New Academy. This recently erected building, its big glass windows filling the classrooms with light, opened its doors at the beginning of term 1968, was found to be full of asbestos and promptly closed them again.

Once the cleaning-up operation had been completed and the authorities relatively certain nobody would die as a direct result of asbestosis, the New Academy reopened, and with the holidays over, the serious business of my friends and I skiving off school at every opportunity began in earnest. Having survived primary and the relentless attention of the teachers, secondary school promised to provide a freer existence if I played it right.

We were split into classes alphabetically, by our surnames. By this method, the Ms were put into class 1A2. Miss Rena Gray taught English and was our form teacher, an ancient lady, at least twenty-six years of age. She was blonde, wore specs, and would perch on the edge of her desk, wrapped in a black gown, licking red lip-sticked lips. She once described me as the devil incarnate, but said this with a sort of reluctant smile, and I felt sure she liked me, as she was the only teacher I ever had, throughout both primary and secondary school, who didn't belt me. Even though I was consistently late, requiring me to sneak in the teachers' entrance by the technical drawing department, Rena would listen to my excuse and, after imploring her forgiveness, pardon me, for 'the very last time'.

We had a mixed bunch of teachers as we progressed through secondary school, Noddy, Ghandi, Twitch, Big Bob, Breezy Bill, to name but a few, each with their little quirks. However, their eccentricities were tolerated by the education authorities, even allowed to flourish, far more so than they would be today.

On a Friday afternoon, we had a double period of music, which followed immediately after swimming. We were always in the act of adjusting ourselves, drying and combing our hair, as we hurried to the music rooms on the other side of the school or else be late.

Our music teacher, Mrs Mclean, was a rather rotund woman. Had I been a motorist I'd have treated her as a roundabout, but due to the confines of the corridor, required to get too close for comfort. This woman considered Friday afternoons as golden opportunities to humiliate members of the male sex. She'd stand outside the classroom, her bulk blocking the way and most of the sunlight, watching as we boys approached. This was 1970, and many lads had longish hair; however, if she spotted anyone holding a comb, tidying themselves up, she'd snatch the offending article from the person, snap it in half and toss it in the bin.

After two of my combs met this fate, I decided enough was enough. Next time my comb was demanded and destined for destruction and the dump, I refused point blank to hand it over, leaving her flabbergasted at my insubordination, and claiming to never have been so insulted in her life (I found this hard to believe) she immediately marched me off to Mr Ross's room.

Mr Ross, or 'Rosco', was the head of music, and a favourite of mine: a tall, powerfully built, charming man, immaculately turned out, with exquisitely manicured nails, and gayer than a balloon on a stick. He would sit at the piano as we sang, tinkling the ivories, which he did expertly, then, during the final verse or chorus, leave us to continue a cappella as he conducted with one hand, strolling around the class, holding a heavy hymnary, hitting every boy hard on the head with his book in perfect time to the beat.

It was before this awesome individual I was brought by Mrs McLean. Again, my comb was demanded of me. Again, I refused. So it was that, at McLean's insistence, rather reluctantly, Rosco was required to drag me down to the rector's room. At the time, the top teacher's position was held by a Mr James Liston, known as 'Sonny', after the heavyweight boxing champion, but believe me, this guy wouldn't have taken a dive for Mohammed Ali.

Sonny was a huge, heavyset man, with unruly tufts of hair sprouting from each ear, though I considered it unwise to offer him the use of my comb at that time. He asked Mr Ross what I was doing there, and on being advised, I recall the rector exchanging a quick look with the head of music, which clearly conveyed, 'Are you kidding me?' and Rosco, in return, offering a slight shrug that said, 'I know. But what could I do?' This passed between them without a word being uttered, and after a moment's deliberation, the rector turned to me.

'How about, I don't belt you,' he stated, a shade too matter-of-factly for my liking, 'but you give Mr Ross your comb, and at the end of the period, he gives it back to you. Eh?'

'In one piece?' I looked at Rosco.

'Obviously,' replied Mr Ross, as if the question seemed strange, and the fate of combs, at least in his hands, was not to be broken in half and binned. Accordingly, I gave him the comb, and received it back as I left music class, much to the chagrin of Mrs McLean. So it was comb-gate ended, and no boy had his comb confiscated by the she-devil again.

One day, later that year, Rosco called the class to order, and announced a fourth-year outing abroad. Excitedly, he informed us each summer there was a festival in Salzberg, the Salzburger Festspiele, which transformed the entire town into one glorious stage and a musical extravaganza. This news was greeted by an enormous amount of glee by many who considered Bach as the opposite to front, and Wolfgang Amadeus as Dracula's enemy in a *Hammer House of Horror* film.

However, whatever the joys to be found in that Austrian town, I was never to taste of them. My parents (who considered, quite correctly, the whole idea a complete waste of time and money, and merely a skive) were advised by the rector that he and the music department had decided my behaviour on the trip would likely prove too great a distraction to other pupils (little lambs that they were) and accordingly I was not allowed to go. Apparently, combgate hadn't been quite as firmly closed as I'd thought.

Clearly, my card had been marked by this stage in my school career. And that was the way it stayed until the day I left, doubtless to a collective sigh of relief from those teachers who had survived the challenges I set them. But now there was the even greater freedom of student life to look forward to, a far less strict world which would present tremendous new opportunities to flout authority and live a life I could formerly only dream of. Finally, the time had come to get my own back.

8

'I was educated once. It took me years to get over it.'

– Mark Twain

Despite my teachers' lack of support and forecasts of doom regarding my future in academia, my exam results turned out way better than expected – than they expected, not than I did, or my dad demanded. I revelled in sticking two fingers up at the school authorities, as I knew I'd do okay academically, whatever they thought.

I'd always enjoyed English and, wanting to make a living as a writer, saw journalism as the route to take. However, on hearing of my journalistic aspirations, my father dismissed the idea as ridiculous, advising me to become a doctor, lawyer or civil engineer. His logic was unimpeachable. People need to visit their lawyer or doctor and require roads and bridges to reach said destination, so civil engineers were also necessary.

'Just think! If you failed at journalism!' My old man looked horrified. 'You could ...' He struggled hard to get the words out, picturing the scene in his mind. 'You could ... You could end up writing for the *Linlithgow Gazette*!'

He had a point. Eventually we compromised. My dad agreed to me reading English and History if I agreed to also read Business Law. So it was, with no intention of darkening the door of the Business Law lecture room, I started at the University of Stirling in the autumn of 1974.

I had been allotted a room a prisoner on remand would have considered small, in the Andrew Stewart Hall of Residence. There

24

was no student union as such; instead, a short walk from the halls stood a small hotel called the Grange, comprising a foyer, a games room and a saloon type bar which became a second home to many, myself included. Tables and chairs were scattered about randomly, joints smouldered in every ashtray and The Rolling Stones, David Bowie, Roxy Music and, later, The Sex Pistols and other punk bands blared from the big speakers on the wall.

I enjoyed History, though not enough to attend many lectures. English was by far my favourite subject and sole reason for attending university. Business Law bored me rigid, with the result I whiled away the time in class distracting my pals, which didn't prove difficult as most found the subject as tedious as me. However, my antics left the lecturer livid.

Come the end of my first semester, although my essay on James Joyce's *The Dubliners* was marked as excellent, my score of 10% in Business Law left my dad distinctly displeased, and he decided I should change course. By then I'd caught the student bug, and was supremely disinterested in what subjects I studied, lectures I'd never attend and tutorials I wouldn't turn up for so long as wherever I wound up I had access to alcohol, amphetamines, snooker tables and women.

Adopting his previous strategy when picking my profession, my father suggested I apply to the Law Faculty at Dundee, on the grounds that someone was always suing someone else, or getting into some sort of trouble, and to increase my chances of admission I should approach my former business law lecturer and obtain a reference to forward with my application. As a back-up position, he suggested I apply for dentistry at Glasgow. Anything but write for a living.

To my amazement, my business law tutor told me she'd write a glowing report, painting me as her star pupil, destined to go far, urging Dundee Law Faculty to take me on board. However, as I picked myself up off the floor, she added all this was predicated on me promising her one thing: whatever happened, should I be refused admittance to Dundee, I had to swear to her by all I held holy I would never return to Stirling University. I agreed, we shook hands and I never saw her again.

Shortly after, I received a letter from Dundee University offering me a place to study for a Bachelor of Law Degree, and there was, no doubt, a collective sigh of relief from Stirling University that I'd no longer be their problem. A week later, a letter arrived accepting my application to study dentistry at Glasgow, but by that time I'd taken Dundee's offer. Had I received Glasgow's first, I could've spent a career pulling teeth, instead of pulling strokes.

So it was, in 1974, I arrived at the University of Dundee to study law. On the morning I arrived, I was hanging about the foyer of Belmont Hall of Residence, where I was staying that term, looking lost, keen to meet someone, anyone, maybe even make a new mate. Suddenly, I spotted a young guy dressed from top to toe in denim with a mop of curly blonde hair and a moustache looking like an eyebrow come down for a drink. He was trying to heave a heavy bag into the hall, and, recognising a fellow newcomer, I held the door open for him. He thanked me with a shy smile and a hand-shake, and we got chatting. The guy's name was Moray, another prospective law student, as keen on studying the subject as me. Had we both been earthquakes, we'd have failed to register on the Richter scale.

Moray dreamed of becoming an actor and a writer and went on to be successful as both. But back in the day, his dad, like mine, had different ideas regarding his son's future and, as Moray wasn't too crazy about being a lawyer, and I didn't believe being a lawyer could ever be too crazy (how wrong was I?) we spent most of the time in the student union.

The Law Faculty was situated, rather inconveniently, across town in a building named after former British Prime Minister Andrew Bonar Law, who held office for only one year. He remained the record holder for the shortest-serving PM, until very recently. I hadn't heard of him prior to my arrival, nor indeed had much acquaintance with the building named after him, as in four years I doubt I visited the place more than half a dozen times.

The faculty building was a grim, foreboding place, a granite and marble mausoleum, where no fun was to be found. I have few recollections of this fortress of doom and gloom, but an occasion I do recall was an oral exam I had in a subject for which I'd sat the written test and thought I'd done well. It turned out I had answered all the questions satisfactorily – bar one. However, my answer to that question had been so far off the mark they dragged me in front of a panel to discover what on earth I could possibly have been talking about.

The three examiners sat in a row, I stood facing them, while Walter Kamba, Dean of Faculty, a South African, and good guy, sat out of sight, a short distance behind the panel. Things kicked off and various questions were fired at me. However, as I answered, if I veered from the correct course, Mr Kamba, unseen by the examiners, would quietly close his eyes, shaking his head slightly, causing me to pull up and change tack. Once I'd successfully stumbled back onto the right road, still with his eyes closed, he'd smile and nod gently. In this way, the Dean helped steer me safely to a pass in Jurisprudence 3, and so, unwittingly, played a vital part in my future fight against the forces of the Crown.

As anyone who's read for a Bachelor of Law Degree knows, and for those who haven't I can confirm, there are a host of different subjects: Constitutional Law 1 and 2, Jurisprudence 1, 2 and 3, Contract, Criminal, Family, Commercial, International, Accountancy, Taxation, and others even more riveting, but by far the worst, way out in front of the pack in my opinion, was Conveyancing.

Our lecturer, a man named Professor McDonald, had, it was said, previously been in the SAS. I don't know if that's true. This guy's motto was more like 'Who bores wins'. These conveyancing classes were held at the perfectly ridiculous time of 9.00 a.m., every day, including Saturday mornings, in Andrew Bonar Law Hall. I only ever attended one of these bore-a-thons during my entire time at Dundee, but Moray attended religiously in the firm belief that by turning up, across town, at that unspeakable hour, somehow the act of simply being there would result in some of what the mad old paratrooper was banging on about seeping into his brain and remaining until the end of term exam. Fat chance.

Moray's notes were not the best, but fortunately our friend Jem, who never missed a lecture, took notes which were the dog's bollocks.

Moray would copy out Jem's, believing that by doing so and attending lectures the facts would become firmly fixed in his head.

My approach was rather different. It involved a pocketful of change, borrowing Moray's handwritten copies of Jem's notes and photocopying them. (It would have been cheaper buying that Xerox machine!) When the end-of-term exams rolled round, I'd rarely sit them, aware of what the results would be after the time I'd spent on the union's snooker tables, and thought it best to swot up over summer, then take the resits. However, when it came to conveyancing, I now had Jem's notes, and they were dynamite.

I crammed and crammed and crammed! Not so Moray, who took the conveyancing test only to discover that turning up for lectures, copying Jem's notes by hand, or indeed liquidising the pages and drinking them for breakfast immediately before the exam kicked off, did not guarantee any kind of success, with the result that he failed, and I passed.

This, however, was a one-off, and before long I found myself back in Airlie Hall of Residence (where we resitters resided) with Moray, after he'd flunked Commercial Law and I'd dodged it first time round. It was three o'clock in the morning. Moray and I were poring over our notes prior to taking the exam at ten o'clock that same day.

At one point I looked up from my labours and my eye caught sight of a book on Moray's desk, entitled Company Law. I nodded towards the tome.

'What's the book?'

Moray glanced at the volume, then at me. 'Company Law.' He shrugged, turning back to his notes.

Puzzled, I paused for a moment, then asked, 'Any danger that'll come up in the exam?'

'Obviously,' said Moray. 'After all, that's what the exam is about.'

I reflected on this remark, then enquired, 'Do you think I'll have time to read it before the test kicks off today?'

Moray turned to me again, this time doing me the courtesy of affecting to think before replying.

'Eh . . .' Then, shaking his head, he added, 'No.'

We stared at one another for a moment, then both doubled up and dissolved into desperate, helpless, hysterical fits before falling to the floor, laughing the laugh of the utterly insane.

Amazingly, later that day, we both sat the exam, and both passed. Such was the state of my brain after several weeks of continual cramming, it must've slipped my mind which books I'd read and which I hadn't, and, with the help of Heaven I was able to recall some of the subject matter and, apparently, answer the questions correctly.

During my first year in Belmont Hall of Residence, readers will doubtless not be astounded to discover I paid the odd visit to the Principal's Office and University Court, mostly for minor matters, at least I saw them as such, though the powers that be weren't always in complete agreement.

On one occasion, a dental student reported me for banging into and breaking a glass door while chasing my mate down the corridor. Okay, I did, and yes, it was a daft thing to do, but in my defence, I was running at full speed, and it was in no way deliberate.

Nobody likes a grass, and my mates all agreed the guy was bang out of order for sticking me in. Accordingly, I went to see this student, taking with me my Luca Brasi, a big guy, Mark, who hailed from Croydon, and we discussed this dentist's dental plan, leaving shortly after with a statement explaining my breaking the door had been purely accidental. Ah, dear reader, the lengths one sometimes requires to go to in order to arrive at the truth.

Another time, a group of mums, dads and prospective students were gathered in the quad outside Belmont Hall, being given the guided tour by our hall governor, a black-bearded, balding biochemist named Dr Stansfield, who could have been the long-lost triplet of the incompetent twin detectives, known as the Dupont Brothers in *The Adventures of Tintin*.

It was a warm summer's day. Some friends and I were standing at a first-floor window observing the proceedings taking place below. We thought it'd be a hoot to turn a fire hose on this gathering, and duly did, drenching everyone. Unfortunately, we were spotted by an eagle-eyed student, and hauled up in front of the university court.

The other two pled not guilty, whereas I frankly admitted my part, as it was merely a prank. However, the court considered it a heinous crime, but as there was no corroboration, the case was dropped against my co-accused. Yet I, who had confessed, made a clean breast of things, was fined forty quid, the equivalent of £150 today, and was told by the court in the most high-handed manner that they hoped I had learned my lesson.

I most certainly had. That was the first and last time I ever pled guilty to anything.

9

'Never put off till tomorrow what you can do the day after tomorrow.'
– Mark Twain

I've always been a fan of Tom Sawyer's creator, his sayings such as, 'Put all your eggs in one basket, and watch that basket'; 'A clean conscience is the sign of a bad memory'; 'It's not the size of the dog in the fight, it's the size of the fight in the dog'; and a host of others have always been a source of inspiration to me. However, I confess to taking his advice on procrastination rather too literally when it came to arranging accommodation for my second year at Dundee. So it was, as the sun rose on the last days of the third term in my first year, it dawned on me I'd nowhere to stay when we returned after the holidays.

I immediately attempted to arrange residence in Belmont Hall, but that proved to be a no-go as it was, apparently, already fully booked, though the fact the hall governor had no great love for me may have had some bearing on that decision. I tried to find a room in Airlie Hall, then Mayfield Hall, but met with no success. Next, I tried for a university flat, finally any flat, but failed to find anywhere as there was nothing available. It happened that one day while making these futile attempts, I was playing snooker with a mate of mine, Hugh Grant. Hugh was a mountain of a man and rejoiced in the nickname 'Huge Grunt'. As I bemoaned my lot and Hugh sank one pot after another, he happened to mention that the president of Belmont Hall was assured accommodation. Not only that – it was *free*. Further, Hugh informed me, pocketing the money he'd just won from our game, the election for the new hall president was to take place in a matter of days.

Facing the possibility of spending the next term in a tent, I decided nothing ventured, nothing gained, and threw my hat into the ring.

The hall president that year was a guy named Geoff. I don't recall his second name, he was rather a forgettable figure, but I remember him as a lanky individual, a daddy-long-legs, with a public-school voice, though he had, rather impressively, filed his room key in such a fashion that it served as a skeleton key to every other room and cupboard in the hall.

I approached this Ichabod Crane type character, enquired about the forthcoming election for the presidency and was advised there were currently three other contestants. The first was a medical student, Tony Hill. This guy couldn't have been more than eighteen or nineteen years old, the same age I was, but unlike me, with my high-waisted bags, Doc Martens, and denim jacket, he dressed like a middle-aged man in sports jacket and flannels. Due to his appearance, I referred to him as Tony 'Over-the-Hill'. He was continually found in the company of another medical student, a drab-looking, sycophantic female who fawned over him, believing him to be just the man for the job. Soon to be past president, Geoff and Tony were big chums, and Ichabod clearly wished to pass on the baton to Over-the-Hill.

The second runner in the race for hall president was named Richard, known rather inevitably, but no less appropriately, as Dick. He was a public-school boy with even more of a Hooray Henry accent than Geoff What's-His-Name and a member of the Officers' Training Corps. I recall those halcyon summer evenings, on our way back to Belmont from the student union on a Friday, hurling half bricks through the OTC windows, in the firm belief we were striking a blow for freedom, though freedom from what, we were never quite sure.

Dick, unlike Tony, was blessed with a loud voice and strong personality, but so was Italian dictator Benito Mussolini, and look what happened to him. The only difference between Il Duce and Dick is that Dick would have been booted out of the fascist party for being too far to the right.

The third contestant was a young woman, and, unfortunately, I forget her name. Clearly, she made even less of an impression on me than Geoff did, and that was no small feat. Accordingly, for the sake of the narrative, rather than constantly referring to her as Ms Can't-Remember-Her-Name I'll simply call her 'Belinda Bland', which makes her sound like a character from Cluedo, but infinitely more interesting.

These then were the three opponents I faced for the position of hall president (although the hirsute hall governor was to prove a fourth obstacle) and each had been canvassing for some time, and consequently had a considerable start on me.

This was the 1970s, and though Xerox machines existed, as mentioned earlier, the cost of using them to print off any large amount proved astronomical, and being almost the end of term, I was brassic. However, the hall possessed a kind of printing machine called a 'Banda', which I understand was first invented in 1923. Going by the one in Belmont, it may well have been the prototype. The Banda was an ink-filled monstrosity which, when fed paper and the handle turned over and over like a bacon slicer, dashed out copies of the document you wished printed, but all in all it was a messy business.

The person in charge of this contraption was the then hall president, Geoff, who was also responsible for printing off the flyers, posters and other propaganda for the proposed candidates for the future presidency. Each candidate was allowed 312 copies, that being the number of people residing in the hall and so entitled to vote.

Accordingly, I wrote out my manifesto long hand, on a sheet of A4 paper, putting forth my plans for the future running of the hall, then went along to the president's room and presented him with the document, asking him to provide me with 312 prints, so that I could put a copy under each student's door, as all the other candidates had already done.

However, on hearing my request, I was advised by the outgoing president that, although the election was still a week away, the day before had been the cut-off point for all printing on the Banda, and that was that. I can be forgiven for thinking this scenario smelt about as fishy as a kilo of kippers, and immediately beat a path to the hall governor's door.

Blackbeard answered in a chunky Aran sweater and slippers, puffing on his pipe, and, after pretending to listen sympathetically to my printing problem, advised me that sort of thing was entirely up to the president, and he could be of no further assistance. With that, he promptly shut the door, leaving me in something of a predicament.

I needed a place to stay next year; in order to get that place, I needed to be president; in order to be president, I needed to be elected; in order to be elected, I needed people to vote for me; in order for people to vote for me, I needed them to know I was a candidate; in order for them to know I was a candidate, I needed to tell them. But how? I had no access to a printing machine, therefore was unable to advise anyone of anything about my campaign, and the forces of darkness were clearly conspiring against me.

I was desperate, I had to do something to get the message out, but what? Suddenly, my mum's words came to me. 'When you're feeling down, son, it's time to look up!' So, I prayed. People may accuse me of using God as a genie, praying when I was in difficulty while otherwise not living a very devout life, and banging on about my bad behaviour. But thankfully, as King David tells us in Psalm 103, '*He hath not dealt with us according to our sins: nor rewarded us according to our iniquities.*' If God did that, the world would have stopped spinning a long, long time ago.

Belmont Hall was, and doubtless remains, the largest hall of residence in Dundee, and a significant percentage of students living there came from abroad. As I paced the floor, trying to figure out my next step, there was a knock at the door. I opened it to find the Chinese guy who occupied the room next to mine. He was studying engineering and had some fellow countrymen round for coffee, but he'd run out of mugs, and asked if I'd any spare.

I fetched a couple of cups, and as I handed them over, one of his pals called from next door, and my neighbour replied in the same language. Aware that China was, and apparently still is, rather a large place, I asked what dialect his mate was speaking, and he advised me though there are many, this was Mandarin, the official Chinese language, and the only one which could be properly written using traditional Chinese characters. After this, he thanked me for the mugs and left. However, what he told me had, as Hercule Poirot would put it, 'caused me furiously to think'.

As mentioned before, Belmont was blessed with a broad range of students from around the world: India, Pakistan, Lebanon, Greece, Chile, China, and elsewhere. The plan was simple. I'd ask a member from each country to write out my manifesto for becoming president in longhand in their own language and make it known that a vote for me would be a vote for a better, more peaceful future, something very different than many foreign students who lived and studied in the hall were used to experiencing.

My cause was helped immensely, not that they intended to assist me, by members of the University Rugby Club, most of whom didn't stay in Belmont Hall, but would stagger across from the student union, filled to the brim with beer, drinking carry-outs, get even drunker, let off a few farts and then some fire extinguishers, as a sort of finale to the evening's frolics, before heading back to wherever they came from.

The trouble was, unlike letting off one of the fire hoses (which, I admit, I'd been fond of doing from time to time) attached to the main water supply, and so costing nothing to turn off and on, the fire extinguishers once emptied by these idiots not only constituted a safety hazard until they were refilled, but said refills by the manu-facturers came at a considerable cost, and were paid for by monies taken from the hall residents' deposits.

I had noticed during my first year at Dundee that foreign students were rarely, if ever, seen behaving badly, causing trouble, or stag-gering about steaming drunk. Rather, they preferred to concentrate on their studies, wanting to do so without being disturbed by the riotous behaviour of others. Knowing this, at the hustings I prom-ised all those present that, if elected, I would do everything in my power to ensure there was no trouble in the hall, no undue racket interrupting their studies, and no student would have their deposits affected detrimentally by the antics of any outsiders. Everyone knew the rugger buggers and other idiots I was referring to, and this announcement was received with loud whoops.

The actual voting took place either the next day or shortly after. When the votes were counted, doubtless much to the chagrin of the past president and Dr Stansfield, I received more votes than the other three candidates combined. So it was that I took my place as President of Belmont Hall and became the grateful receiver of free bed and board for that year.

10

'Uneasy lies the head that wears a crown.'

– *Henry IV*, William Shakespeare

Okay, so it wasn't a crown, but being president had its share of problems. Before reaching these dizzy heights, the only difficulties I'd had to deal with were my own: now, I had everyone's. Also, some were desperate to criticise the way the new president was running the hall – in particular, those who'd stood for election and their pals.

I'd made the residents two firm promises: firstly, they'd be able to study in peace; further, the deposits they'd paid in case of any damage being done to the hall during their stay would not be deducted due to the bad behaviour of a few clowns, nearly none of whom lived in Belmont. Sinner though I admit to being, breaking promises is one of the few things not to be found among my many faults.

As I've said, the most common complaint made by students was about other students making too much noise, playing music too loud, partying, basically disturbing their studies. The trouble was, when the students who complained weren't studying, many of them made a racket, so the ones they complained about complained about them, then everyone moaned at me. I realised all this rapidly required nipping in the bud.

As president it was impossible to be everywhere at once, and so I turned to those few, firm friends who'd helped in my presidential campaign. Among these were Mark, who was so big he could've been the jolly green giant, if you left out the bit about being green, or jolly. Another good friend, Lloyd Kersh, was a muscly medical student who hailed from Clarkston. Accordingly, I made Mark, Lloyd and some other mates members of my newly established Subcommittee for Security.

The purpose, or perhaps more properly the mission, of this subcommittee was to deal directly with the cause of the continual complaints I received. As each complaint came in, I'd give it to a member, who would be dispatched to deal with it, or I'd deal with it myself.

On one occasion a young female student studying hard for a forthcoming exam complained of continual noise coming from the room next door, occupied by a guy named Johnny. The young woman told me she'd repeatedly asked Johnny to turn the music down a bit, but he ignored her, so could I have a word. Accordingly, I set off to deal with the matter. As I approached the room in question the music got louder and louder. I had to knock hard to be heard, but eventually the door was opened by a big guy dressed in jeans and a T-shirt with the figure of Chuck Berry playing a guitar emblazoned across the front. I explained the girl next door was swotting for an exam and politely asked him to turn down the volume.

He shrugged and made to close the door, and assuming this to be some sign of agreement, I smiled, thanked him, and left. It turned out my friendly words had fallen on deaf ears; perhaps the decibel level in his room had left him hard of hearing. In any case, ten minutes later the same student presented herself at my door to inform me nothing had changed on the noise front.

As a result, I retraced my steps, banged on Johnny's door, and when he eventually answered told him firmly, but again politely, to please turn the music down. This time, he added a slight nod to his shrug, and again, taking this to mean he agreed, I smiled and said, 'Thanks, and remember, Johnny, be good.' I recall this incident clearly, not because of what happened later, but because I remember chuckling at what I considered a clever little quip. Pride is one of my many sins.

Ten minutes later there was a rap on my door. I opened to find the same student. I stopped myself from saying, 'We have to stop meeting like this,' but truthfully, I've had girlfriends I've seen less frequently. Obviously, you've guessed why she came back: Johnny-be-good was still being bad.

At this juncture I wish to make it crystal clear that I do not consider myself in any way to be what's known as a 'hard man'. Some guys are born scrappers, square-go experts, who come out of the womb that way. I'm by no means one of them. However, I am a believer in doing what is required in specific cases, when and if the occasion calls for action. In this case Johnny on the second floor was begging for it.

Accordingly, I turned up at his door and hammered loudly to be heard above the din. To my surprise, this time I had no need to wait as the door was yanked wide open, to reveal Johnny stripped to the waist, shouting at me above the noise, 'What is it now?'

You may recall that rather than attend law lectures while at university, I preferred playing snooker. I must also mention that Johnny was on the biggish side, whereas I'm only five feet nine inches, and at nineteen years old weighed in at around nine and a half stone. I had therefore come prepared for all eventualities.

As Johnny opened the door, I jammed the butt of a snooker cue under his jaw, causing his eyes to pop as he staggered back. I heeled the door shut, told him the story of the three bears in the most unmistakable terms and left. The direct approach had the desired effect, and the music was lowered to a level in which one could hardly hear Chuck Berry playing on his ding-a-ling.

Of course, I'd made a second promise, namely no student's deposit would be reduced because of damage done to the hall by outsiders setting off fire extinguishers and the like. This affair was far more easily taken care of. Belmont was a mere drunken stumble from the student union, with the inevitable result that, especially on weekends, some students would stagger across half-cut, or full-cut, carrying on, play fighting, getting up to pranks, none of which I'd any problem with. I've always liked a laugh, but with great power comes great responsibility. Someone had to pay the piper, and it wasn't going to be my students who footed the bill.

I adopted what I considered a positive procedure, and when some drunken idiots set off a fire extinguisher, or broke a window, the members of my subcommittee for security and I would approach those responsible, advise them what it would cost the hall to refill or repair the damage, and have them pay up on the spot; a practice now adopted by the authorities both here and abroad, which merely illustrates how far ahead of the times I was.

Of course, there were times those who had run amok were unwilling to pay up, and consequently a modicum of force was applied to ensure their compliance. However, my efforts to fulfil my electoral promises to residents as regards keeping their deposits intact came to the attention of Dr Stansfield, who in due course drew the Law Society of Scotland's attention to the matter, in a letter stating, as I recall, that: 'McIntyre ran Belmont Hall with a reign of terror, with the assistance of his barbaric subcommittee for security.' This was totally untrue. The students I made my promises to were delighted with the way I handled matters, meaning they were left in peace to study, with their deposits intact. What is true is that the bullies didn't like the consequences of doing whatever they wanted, and Blackbeard wished rather to complain about me and jeopardise my future career (something I was perfectly able to do myself) than concern himself with the welfare of the students in his care, many from abroad, who paid a great deal of money to live in Belmont Hall.

To misquote Al Capone, on the occasion involving Johnny-be-bad, I found I got further with a pleasant word and a pool cue than just a pleasant word. Truth be told, I couldn't have cared less what Stansfield said. When my tenure ended, the hall's finances where firmly in the black, whereas under all past presidents the bank balance remained in the red. Even the hall's annual ball, which I based on an underwater theme, was a swimming success, as opposed to past years where outlays exceeded income, but we turned a tidy profit.

My hall presidency delivered exactly what the voters wanted – peace and quiet to study, plus financial solvency; but, though effective and well received, especially by foreign students, my unorthodox methods of achieving these goals would come back to bite me.

11

'Don't tell me the moon is shining; show me the glint of light on broken glass.'

– Anton Chekhov

'Twas a moonlit night, towards the end of my third year at Dundee uni, after an evening at what was known as the Barracuda Night Club, I was walking home with a few friends, and we'd all had a fair bit to drink. As usual, in the past when I over-indulged (I no longer drink alcohol at all) Dr Jekyll had retired for the day, and Mr Hyde was out for the night.

On the Perth Road stood an antique shop, displaying in its window items of Nazi memorabilia. Rumour had it the owner held racist views, sending his kids to school with leaflets stating 'Blacks Out' and similar slogans. Whether true or not, my young, befuddled brain took it to be so. At the time I had participated in various left-wing student marches against Nazism and fascism and had been photographed doing so by the powers that be.

The items in the window, combined with the rumours and the alcohol coursing through my veins, caused me to lose the plot and, along with a friend, I kicked in the shop window, shattering the glass. For some reason, we pulled out a fireplace, which we placed on our shoulders and proceeded to march down the Perth Road to the student flats, singing heigh-ho, and sounding like the seven dwarves setting off to work.

By this time the shop alarm had been ringing for some time, and the surrounding area was buzzing with the boys in blue. I recall running into a dental student's room, trying to hide. Dental students, as opposed to medical ones, were meant to be the wild bunch, but I only ever met a couple who'd dare to open a box of After Eights if it was only half past seven; plus, this guy was meant to be a bit of a ticket. However, when I asked for a change of T-shirt, to make identifying me more difficult, his bottle flashed, he refused and seconds later the cops crashed in, cuffed and stuck me in the back of a panda car.

I woke next morning wondering where I was, to discover it was the cells in Bell Street police station. Next came court, and unluckily the sheriff was a conviction-minded bully named Cox, who enjoyed throwing his weight about on the bench.

Despite the efforts of my solicitor, the judge refused to reduce the single charge against two drunken law students from theft by housebreaking to malicious mischief; accordingly, in my hopelessly hungover state I agreed to plead to the complaint as libelled, which was to make a massive difference to my future career.

Sheriff Cox, par for the course, disregarded all mitigation put forward on our behalf, fining my mate and me the sum of £75 each (£360 today) for a first offence, payable at £5 per week (£18 today). I worked collecting pint glasses in the union to pay my fine, desperate to keep the conviction from my parents, but my dad worked in the Scottish Office in Edinburgh and one of his colleagues from Dundee spotted the report in the local rag and told my old man.

My father wasn't furious, which was just as well, as my mum was angry enough for them both. However, he was deeply disappointed, which hurt far more than any sentence that clown handed me. Of course, my smash and grab activities on the Perth Road quickly became common knowledge among the other students, so that every time I walked into a disco in the union, the DJ would play Nick Lowe's hit, 'I Love the Sound of Breaking Glass', which seemed funny at the time, but it would turn out to be no laughing matter.

12

'When I was a lad I served a term, as office boy to an attorney's firm.'
— *H.M.S. Pinafore*, Gilbert and Sullivan

Graduation day grew ever closer, requiring me to look for a future position in a legal firm. Back then, there was no diploma in legal practice. You left with your degree and dived straight into an apprenticeship, but at that time the pool of opportunities was rather dry.

As has been the case since mankind crept out of the caves, it's not a matter of what you know but who, and how well they know someone else. Through a friend of a friend, my parents arranged an interview for me with a man named John Bell, senior partner of Russell and Dunlop, Writers to the Signet (originally Clerks to the Signet, dating back centuries) with offices in South Charlotte Street, Edinburgh.

Mr Bell was a heavily built man in his seventies and wore pinstriped suits, the lapels and waistcoats stained with coffee and tea and covered with crumbs from digestive biscuits. When out and about, he sported a bowler and carried a cane or brolly. I can't remember much about the interview, but as he was doing an old friend a favour, he agreed to take me on as office boy, court runner and general dogsbody. So began my glittering legal career.

Mr Bell confided in me that when he'd started in the law business, many moons before, he had in fact been on the way to Haymarket Station to apply for a situation as a clerk with British Railways. On the way, he'd spotted a notice outside the offices of Russell and Dunlop, Clerks to the Signet, for an office boy, and rather than take the trouble of walking any further, stepped inside, applied, got the job and sixty years later was senior partner.

The arrangement arrived at with old man Bell was I'd travel down from Dundee by train and work two days a week, Monday and Friday, for no pay, but in return he'd keep open a position for me as an apprentice, which I'd then take up once I had graduated: the other three days I would attend university.

Making it to Edinburgh in time to start work on a Monday and Friday morning meant having to catch the train from Dundee at 6:30 a.m. The train after this got into Edinburgh a few minutes past the hour, and since it was six and two threes whether I walked from either Waverley or Haymarket to Charlotte Street, I'd arrive at work at about twenty minutes past nine – not the way to impress the person you hope to become apprenticed to in the future.

Russell and Dunlop W.S., as it was then called, was a very old, well established and highly respected legal firm before I arrived. I don't mean because of my arrival it ceased to be well respected, but rather by the time I started there its glory days had come and gone, as had most of the solicitors, including Mr Bell's two sons, leaving the old man as the senior and sole surviving partner. The staff comprised two secretaries, one named Jean, a lady of about forty who'd been with the firm since she was sixteen years old, and another slightly older woman, who Mr Bell referred to as Mistress Marshall. Captain John Audis, a military gentleman in his eighties, was responsible for the post room, readying all the court processes and any other documents for lodging in Edinburgh's Court of Session.

Captain Audis had spondylitis in his shoulders, causing him to stoop, and had served as a professional soldier for thirty years, fighting in both World Wars. As such he felt qualified – indeed thought it his duty – to slag off the British Army at every opportunity. Recounting to me his arrival in Berlin during the last days of World War II, he said, 'They talk about the liberation of Berlin, and they're right, we liberated them of everything we could lay our hands on.'

He would laugh his schoolboy laugh and state that if the British soldiers were thirsty in the desert and found water, the army thought it more important to 'blanco' their white uniform belts than drink and stay alive. He was the oldest member of staff; I was the youngest. Together we formed our own army of two.

My duties, as with the character of the Rt Hon Sir Joseph Porter in Gilbert and Sullivan's HMS Pinafore, required that I 'polished up the handle on the big front door', along with the brass plaque stating the firm's name. I also spent hours hand-stitching legal documents together with a large needle and thread, tying them into bundles with red tape (hence the expression 'cutting through the red tape') before carrying them up the Mound to be lodged in process in the Court of Session.

Mr Bell was old school and used to being obeyed immediately, without question. He could be very quick tempered, and this, coupled with the fact he was forgetful where he'd put things, often caused problems. He constantly lost files, then instigated office-wide searches for them. We'd look inside cabinets, between them, under them, on shelves, on tabletops, everywhere a file could possibly be. After some considerable time and effort, we invariably discovered the object of the quest lying on Mister Bell's desk, under a cup and saucer, or in his briefcase, or that he'd been sitting on it the entire time.

Jean was the only one brave enough to confront Mr Bell, saying, 'There it is, right in front of you.'

However, no apology was ever offered, the old man would merely nod and grunt, 'Why, so it is,' then ask for a cup of coffee and a digestive biscuit.

Russell and Dunlop's practice was concerned with civil litigation and divorce. Accordingly, counsel was instructed in these cases and, apart from going across to McVitie's Tea House for lunch every day, Mr Bell rarely left the office during working hours. However, there were a couple of times he attended court, taking me with him, to sit behind counsel in a particularly important motion.

Counsel, both senior and junior, clerks of court, advocate's clerks, indeed anyone we came across in the court corridors, were all scared to death of Mr Bell. The old man was hard of hearing, not quite corn beef, but on the way there. When, if sitting behind counsel, he couldn't make out what was being said, he'd hit the advocate on the shoulder with his walking stick and bark 'Speak up, man!', which resulted in counsel talking at the top of his voice for Mr Bell's benefit while deafening everyone else, including the judge on the bench.

On one of only two occasions I accompanied Mr Bell to court our counsel moved a motion which was refused by the judge. However, as we left the courtroom, it became clear Mr Bell assumed our motion had been granted. Outside court, our terrified junior counsel apologised profusely for failing to get the motion passed, with the result the true position dawned on the old man for the first time.

Mr Bell stopped in his tracks, turned on his heel, and spotting the clerk of court sneaking off behind him with a bunch of papers, waved his cane, crying aloud, 'Bring him back on the bench.' By 'him' he meant the judge.

As this was completely unheard of, the clerk was initially extremely unwilling to do as requested, but after being bellowed at a few more times, he beat a retreat to the judge's chambers. While this was going on, the advocate and I were trying, without success, to explain to Mr Bell that the judge had made his decision and that was that. But the old man was having none of it, merely barking out, 'Nonsense! I've known him since Noah wore shorts. We were at school together!'

It sounds incredible, I'd never seen it happen before, nor have I seen or heard of it since, but the judge at the time, Lord Wylie, was brought back on the bench, the clerk of court called the case again, our counsel moved the exact same motion in identical terms as before, only this time the judge performed a U-turn and granted it. Mr Bell rose to his feet, and with a loud, satisfactory sigh of, 'Now, that's more like the thing,' left the courtroom.

13

'Woe to you, teachers of the law and Pharisees, you hypocrites!'
— Gospel of Matthew, Ch. 23 v 27

I graduated Bachelor of Law in July 1980, on the highly auspicious day of Friday the thirteenth. It was now time to apply to the Law Society for admission, as I required to be indentured to Mr Bell as soon as possible, so my apprenticeship could officially start. Accordingly, I filled in the relevant form and sent it off.

I received a reply from the Law Society telling me I required to attend before a subcommittee of the Legal Education Committee, which I did. At this meeting the three members of the board questioned me about the criminal conviction I'd received in Dundee, treating it as if it were the most heinous crime they'd ever come across in their careers.

These individuals wouldn't know a criminal if they found one in their soup, and probably the first time they come across an accused person is when they're made sheriffs in later life, as a reward for 'playing the game'. Once elevated to the bench, they tend to consistently believe the police, even if the cops claim the Earth's flat, so desperate are they to convict and keep in the Crown's good books. This subcommittee had been provided with a letter from Dr Stansfield of Belmont, describing my presidential term as a 'reign of terror' – sheer nonsense, as any student back then would testify – but, after taking me to task for some time, they refused my application for admission on the grounds that I was not a fit and proper person to be a solicitor.

This came as quite a blow, but it upset my father far more than me. Okay, I got drunk, broke some Nazi's window, pulled some stuff out, but I'd been prosecuted, pled guilty, fined, worked to pay it off, and had no previous convictions. To bar me from being a solicitor at the start of what I'd hoped would be my future career was way over the top.

To try and have the matter reconsidered, my dad and I went to meet a woman named Slater, who dealt with admission applications, and asked what we could do next. I've met many slaters before, the majority live under rocks, but personally I've found them infinitely preferable to the individual in question. I took with me a letter from my director of studies at Dundee, Robert Ramsay, who'd recently taken up the post as Head of Legal Studies in Port Moresby, Papua New Guinea. As my director of studies, Mr Ramsay was the lecturer who knew me best, and wrote a full report by no means whitewashing me but giving all the pros and cons. He explained exactly what happened during my time at university, advising that, in his view, I had been dealt with unduly harshly by the Law Society, recommending they reconsider their decision and allow me to be admitted.

However, far from being impressed, Ms Slater was furious I didn't accept the decision and go away. She advised my father and me there was no appeal and that was that. She added, had it been up to her she would personally have seen to it that I never became a solicitor.

It looked like we were up against a brick wall, but my dad, normally a mild-mannered man, was also an incredibly determined one, as his success in his chosen field clearly demonstrates. He contacted a solicitor, the son of a friend of his, and we met and explained the situation. This solicitor was and remains highly respected, and kindly undertook to help, advising us 'though it had never been done before, it was possible to appeal the Law Society's decision to the Court of Session'. He then went ahead and prepared the case for counsel, and I'm eternally grateful to him for what he did for me.

14

'With man this is impossible, but with God all things are possible.'
                    – Gospel of Matthew, Ch. 19 v 26

I continued working at Russell and Dunlop W.S., until eventually a date was set for my appeal. As counsel was required to conduct my case in the Court of Session, we instructed John. L. Mitchell, then a junior advocate, who later went on to take silk and become a Queen's Counsel. Mr Mitchell had also been apprenticed to Mr Bell some years before, and very kindly charged me no fee. The case kicked off, I waited nervously, and then to my delight, the three judges on the bench decided the Law Society had dealt with my application and appeal in a fashion which was not in accordance with the rules of natural justice, and accordingly overturned their decision and sent the matter back to them.

Obviously, I was over the moon. The organisation whose sole purpose was to properly regulate the actions of solicitors in Scotland had itself been accused by the highest court in the land of acting unfairly and unjustly in my case. This was a resounding result, not to mention a massive embarrassment for the Law Society of Scotland.

However, this was far from the end of the matter; we were merely beginning again. But, this time, when my application was heard, I'd be appearing before all forty-three members of the Council of the Law Society of Scotland, the same body whose Committee for Legal Education had been criticised by the High Court and held to have acted unjustly.

I didn't expect a lot of friendly faces. My solicitor kindly appeared with me at the hearing. The Law Society had chosen the procurator fiscal for Edinburgh to cross-examine me when I went before the council; clearly putting a heavy hitter in to bat from the off. As we took our seats, I saw a solicitor who lived in Linlithgow, a partner in a prestigious Edinburgh firm, who had been one of the members of the subcommittee which refused my initial application. I pointed him out to my lawyer and will never forget his response. He nodded to where the man was seated, saying, 'Don't worry. Look at the number of empty seats next to the man. People normally sit next to someone if they like them.'

The hearing commenced. My lawyer examined me as he would a client in court, and I answered calmly and clearly, trying to come across to the council as best as I could. After putting forward my case it was the turn of the procurator fiscal for Edinburgh to cross-examine, and this man was an expert, which of course is why he'd been handpicked.

My criminal conviction was dealt with relatively quickly, but then I was quizzed about my so called 'reign of terror'. I explained that 312 students resided in Belmont, many from abroad, the vast majority of whom wished to study in peace and quiet. My actions and those of my subcommittee, everything we'd done, was for the greater good and any force used had been required to restore order and prevent damage to the hall. I pointed out my success as president was reflected in the hall's financial accounts and students' deposits. However, the prosecution ignored the fact the residence had been run to the great satisfaction of nearly all students, as the fiscal banged on and on about my barbaric behaviour.

About halfway through, we broke for lunch. I headed to the gents' toilet and standing at the sink was an elderly solicitor. Careful not to make eye contact with him, only too aware of the way my behaviour had been scrutinised to date, and not wanting to be accused of trying to curry favour or interfering with the process in any way, I ignored him.

However, as this gentleman finished drying his hands, I went to wash mine, and he turned to me, saying, 'Waste of time, all this carry-on over a few boyish pranks. Some people forget they were young once.' And with a smile and a nod, he left.

His remarks lifted my spirits slightly. However, I reflected that while some people may forget they were young once, there are others who apparently were never young in the first place, and I felt sure the council had its fair share.

Following lunch we reconvened and, shortly after, the fiscal at long last ran out of bullets and closed his case, leaving my lawyer to finish by addressing the council on my behalf.

The hearing was over. Council members withdrew to consider their verdict, and my solicitor told me that as we probably wouldn't get their decision that day, not to hang about but to go back to the office and he'd be in touch. I headed back to Russell and Dunlop and was on tenterhooks for the rest of the day. Shortly before five o'clock my lawyer called the office and told me the decision of the council.

My application had been granted, by a vote of twenty-two to twenty-one. I don't remember leaving the office that day, but vaguely recall running down the platform at Haymarket station to catch the train home bursting with joy, desperate to tell my parents the miraculous news, and I mean that literally. To say both were delighted is an understatement, especially my dad, a devout Christian, now gone to his reward, to whom I was and am due so much. No matter how often, how badly I let him down, infuriated him, drove him crazy, he was always there for me, and without doubt still is, praying for me, as I do for him each day until we meet again.

15

It was now vital I began my apprenticeship as soon as possible. The council's decision to grant my application had been qualified, to the extent that the two years I'd spent working for Mr Bell wouldn't count, and I required to start my apprenticeship from scratch, meaning it would be at least another two years before I qualified as a solicitor.

As mentioned earlier, the firm of Russell and Dunlop was held in high esteem, and dated back centuries, but then, so did Mr Bell. Okay, not centuries, but he'd a few decades under his belt, and the workload was becoming way too much for him. The old man's two sons had been partners, but apparently hadn't seen eye to eye with him, and both had left the firm before I joined; one for another legal practice, the other to become an advocate.

As a result, Mr Bell decided to amalgamate his firm with that of another sole practitioner, and as the old man was soon to retire, this solicitor would take over the business. So, it was arranged that the firm of Aikman and Sons would merge with Russell and Dunlop.

I don't know about you, but if I was in an unknown one-man band who'd managed to join a group with a rep like The Rolling Stones, I'd leave the name alone, not make it a deal breaker we call the new group James and the Rolling Stones – but not Andrew Aikman.

Despite Russell and Dunlop's long-established name (there was a document referring to the Battle of Bannockburn in 1314, tucked away in a safe somewhere) this Johnny-come-lately was determined the firm would now be known as Aikman, Russell and Dunlop. You may think this was part of a crafty plan to ensure, before the world wide web, when folk 'let their fingers do the walking' through the *Yellow Pages*, or today with a Google search, they'd come upon the name Aikman as one of the first lawyers in the book, or online. But you'd be wrong. It seems he simply wanted to see his name in lights, or rather on a shiny brass plaque, in South Charlotte Street. Mad! But as my mum would say, it takes all sorts.

Mr Aikman arrived with his staff, consisting of his apprentice Graham, secretary Nan and his cashier whose name escapes me, though not a penny ever escaped her. Graham and I shared a tiny room with two desks jammed in it. As Aikman's firm involved mostly conveyancing, Graham spent a great part of the time 'noting title', poring over piles of dog-eared deeds, looking for any burdens a future buyer may have been landed with.

Luckily for anyone purchasing property, this job was never given to me, or else people all over Scotland would have had mines dug beneath their homes, canals flowing through their front rooms or bridges built in their backyard, from which they could watch ramblers making their way across what should have been their private property.

Back in the dark ages, no matter how hot it became in the office, Graham and I required to request permission to remove our jackets and work in shirt sleeves: such was the respect demanded by the old school. However, Mr Aikman's secretary had her own way of dealing with her boss. I'd be talking to Nan and Aikman would come through to the typing pool, almost on tiptoe, as if frightened to approach her. No matter how quietly he came, she'd clock him, roll her eyes and without turning exclaim loudly, 'What is it now?'

Her boss would gingerly hand her a Dictaphone tape, telling her he needed it typed for such and such a time. Nan would glance at her watch, sigh heavily and say, 'I'll see what I can do,' and as her boss retreated, she'd toss the tape onto a pile and proclaim loudly, 'Now where were we, James, before we were so rudely interrupted?!'

It would be fair to say old man Bell wasn't over keen on the new boy, as became evident when Aikman made an offer to buy Mr Bell's library. This library was by no means large, merely a few shelves, but contained the public statutes affecting Scotland from the 1745 Jacobite rebellion till the 1980s, a set of encyclopedias on Scots law, plus various other books. I don't know how much Mr Bell had been offered but suspect all the money in the world wouldn't have sufficed, for a day or two before he retired, Mr Bell told me to take the lot, refusing to accept a penny, as he was making a present of them to me.

I always got the train home, but that day called my dad, had him pick me up in his Datsun Cherry, and we jammed the books in the boot and were homeward bound before anyone knew they'd gone. Don't get me wrong, Aikman wasn't a bad guy, in fact I liked the man, he just lived in his own wee bubble; but then so does everyone to some extent.

Time was ticking. Still, I'd not officially started an apprenticeship. Mr Bell was about to leave, and it was too late to become indentured to him. I asked Mr Aikman if, as Graham was soon to finish his apprenticeship, he would then take me on. True to form Aikman advised he had to mull it over and asked me to work on while he thought about things. Two months later, still without an answer I pushed the question and again Aikman claimed he wanted me to work on a little longer, while he made up his mind. It was then I made up mine. I was offski ASAP. But where could I go?

Moray, my mate from Dundee uni, still longed to be a writer, or an actor, anything other than a lawyer, but was serving an apprenticeship with Drummond & Co, Solicitors in Moray Place, Edinburgh, near where I worked. One afternoon, while hand-delivering some documents as one did in those days, I met him in the street and told him I was desperate to get indentured. He said the firm Laird and Wilson Terris, SS, where his brother, Willie, was a partner, were looking for someone and I should try giving him a bell.

The minute I was back in the office I rang Moray's brother, and he told me he'd have a word with his bosses. A day or so later, Willie called back. He'd arranged an interview for me and gave me the date and the time. I thanked him warmly, hung up and shut up, as obviously I didn't want anyone at work to know.

A few days later found me attending for interview in front of Alex Laird, joint senior partner with the firm of Laird and Wilson Terris SSC, at 22 Hill Street, Edinburgh. Mr Laird was a tall, distinguished, grey-haired gentleman in his mid-sixties. Before embarking on a legal career in his father's business, he'd seen action in World War II, and was parachuted into Normandy, behind enemy lines, twenty-four hours before the invasion in 1944.

Despite his military bearing, Mr Laird was a mild-mannered, softly spoken man, a member of the SSC (Solicitors to the Supreme Courts) and very much the embodiment of the monied, middle-class Edinburgh solicitor. His was a civil and commercial law practice, and he had his own set of clients, but his wife was the heiress to some tea company and had a right few quid.

Mr Laird began by asking me the usual questions, then, after a few moments, the internal door linking his spacious office to that of his partner's, Mr Corbett, opened and in came the man, cigarette in hand. Ian Corbett was a completely different bottle of bass. His practice was purely criminal. Pure is perhaps not the appropriate word, but criminal certainly is. He too had a particular set of clients who, in many respects, weren't too particular.

Average height, dark-haired, with a sallow complexion, Corbett wore a suit that screamed expensive and was echoed by the solid gold Rolex on his wrist. Alex Laird made the introductions, stating he'd been over the relevant initial matters and was perfectly happy. Corbett didn't mess about. He turned to me, drawing deeply on his cigarette.

'They tell me you were expelled from school,' he said, not elaborating on who 'they' were. However, I was used to 'they'. 'They' always had something to say, normally never anything nice, and 'they' are still doing it today.

Still, this sudden statement caught me on the chin, but I adopted honesty as the best policy, a novel approach for any lawyer as I grew to understand. I nodded.

'Yes, I was.'

Corbett drew hard on his cigarette, then blew out a thin, blue stream.

'So was I,' he said. 'Start on Monday.' And with that, he left the room.

16

'You have to learn the rules of the game, then you have to play better than anybody else.'

– Albert Einstein

'Cross-examination, Mr Sutherland?' enquired the sheriff.

I was sitting in on a sheriff and jury trial, watching my mentor, the one and only Walter Sutherland, defend a client charged with numerous car thefts. Walter was a legend, a truly amazing defence lawyer, devout Hibs supporter and dedicated drinker. He had had his own firm, but due to some discrepancies in his accounting or some such thing came to work at Laird and Wilson Terris several years before I arrived on the scene. Today, this was the man teaching me the ropes about criminal procedure.

Grunting in the affirmative, the bold boy rose to his feet, apparently deep in thought, studying some notes he'd scribbled on the back of a beer mat. He glanced briefly at the bench and, seeing the man in the wig's mind was obviously elsewhere, turned to the uniformed police inspector in the witness box, looked at him and barked loudly: 'That's just shite, ya lying bastard!'

Everyone inhaled sharply. The fiscal, in this case, a keen gardener, looked like she'd just contributed to her own compost heap. Even the part-time sheriff, sensing something wrong from the silence, sat up and started to take notice. Pulling off his half-moon specs, de rigueur for a floating sheriff, selling his soul for a shot on the shrieval bench, he looked about, desperately trying to work out what had just happened.

'I object!' screamed the fiscal, rocketing to her feet.

'Mr Sutherland . . .' began the sheriff automatically, though still at something of a loss as to what had occurred.

Walter ignored all attempts to interrupt his flow and fixed a rheumy eye on the red-faced witness.

'Are those not the very same words my client used when you charged him, Inspector?'

The silence which followed was deafening and seemed to last forever. Jurors glanced nervously at one another, the cop gripped the edge of the witness box, his knuckles white, irate, but impotent; meanwhile the fiscal sank slowly to her seat, sighing as the wind left her sails. The sheriff, realising Walter had been up to his usual antics, replaced his spectacles and stared over the rims.

'Careful, Mr Sutherland, careful.' He shook his shrieval head in warning.

Walter adopted what I later found to be his infamous *what's all the fuss about* look. No further censure forthcoming, the jury tittered slightly, the fiscal and inspector exchanged dark looks, and Walter began again.

'Well, Inspector, we're waiting.'

The cop hissed from between clenched teeth. 'I can't be expected to recall exactly what your client said, it was some time ago.'

'It certainly was. And my client's been counting the days.' Walter looked at the jury meaningfully. 'All one hundred and ten of them, while locked up in custody.'

He turned back to the inspector. 'You told my friend the fiscal you cautioned my client before charging him, correct?'

'Yes.'

'Kindly tell the ladies and gentlemen what happens when a person is cautioned at common law.'

'A suspect is advised that they are not required to answer any questions, but anything they do say, will be taken down and may be used in evidence.'

'So, you took down what the accused said.'

'It had no bearing on the charge.'

'Maybe not. But obviously, you still noted it, as per the caution,' Walter said, fully aware that the cop hadn't.

'As I have already stated, his remarks were not relevant.'

Walter, seemingly shocked by this statement, turned to face the jury, and continued cross-examining the cop with his back to him.

'Are you telling these ladies and gentlemen that, despite what the common law caution requires you to do, you didn't take down what my client said?'

Walter appeared incredulous, as if finding it impossible to comprehend any police officer could act in this fashion, shaking his head to clear the very idea from his mind. The sheriff looked up momentarily, in time to witness Walter's award-winning performance.

'You've made your point, Mr Sutherland, move on,' he said, and returned to his reading material.

Walter ignored him.

'Basically, Inspector, to use my client's words, you took it upon yourself to decide what was shite and what wasn't.'

The fiscal was back on her feet.

'I object . . .'

Walter ignored her too.

'Deciding what's shite is a job for the jury, and, after hearing you, I doubt it'll take them too long?'

'That's a yellow card, Mr Sutherland!' said the sheriff.

'My client's words were a clear denial of his involvement, a denial you decided to ignore,' continued the bold boy, completely undeterred.

'The accused called me a lying bastard,' said the cop.

'Whether you are is also up to the jury to decide, his reply still should have been recorded as per the caution.'

The jury members looked sideways at one another, smothering smiles with limited success.

'Let's call that yellow card a red one, shall we?!' barked the sheriff. 'Sit down, please.'

'Don't worry, I'm done,' Walter replied, and sat, fully aware that at this stage in his long legal career he was more-or-less fireproof.

'That concludes the Crown case, my lord,' said the fiscal, rising and sitting in a single motion.

'That's all they've got!' Walter informed the jury, in a stage whisper that could be heard halfway down the High Street.

'I beg your pardon, Mr Sutherland?' said the sheriff.

'Don't mention it, my lord,' said Walter, standing up. 'I lead no evidence.' And, winking almost imperceptibly at his fifteen new friends on the jury, sat down again.

The Queens Arms public house, 49 Frederick Street, Edinburgh was Walter's second, and unofficial office. The barman placed another rum and pep in front of him, as we both sat on bar stools that had seen better days.

'I can't believe your guy walked,' I said, and sipped my Guinness.

Walter shrugged and swallowed half his rum and pep.

'He was bang to rights, Wattie. Look at the evidence.'

Walter snorted, placed the glass on the table and patting his pockets, produced a pack of cigarettes and lit one up, a luxury still afforded to customers back in the day. He sucked the smoke deep down into his lungs, before blowing it out through his nose as he turned to me.

'The last thing a jury ever bothers about is the evidence.'

'Don't talk daft,' I said.

Walter shrugged. 'Okay. So, how come he got off?'

My turn to shrug.

'Exactly,' said Walter.

'Close thing, mind you,' I muttered, unwilling to concede the point; not proven.

At the time of writing, there are currently three verdicts available to a jury in Scotland, guilty, not guilty and not proven, though there are moves afoot by people whose experience runs to defending clients who've received a parking ticket, and have no clue about criminal defence, to do away with the not proven verdict. Apart from being older than the not guilty verdict, it seems to me, and many others, a matter of common sense that a case is either proven beyond a reasonable doubt or not proven, and to state someone is not guilty of a crime because of a lack of evidence or because the evidence is dubious seems to say much more than one is entitled to. Either the Crown has proved the case by corroborated evidence which the jury find credible and reliable beyond a reasonable doubt, or they haven't.

However, the not proven verdict is now looked upon as a verdict delivered by a jury where they are pretty convinced an accused is guilty, but they're letting him or her off, which, as it often occurs in cases where juries can envisage themselves sitting in the dock, isn't a bad thing. In my view, as the saying goes, if it ain't broke, don't fix it.

Anyway, back to the Queens Arms.

'The client didn't complain about the not proven,' said Walter, and produced some banknotes from an inside pocket. 'In fact, he was most appreciative.' He took a tenner and laid it on the bar. 'Same again,' said Walter to the barman. 'And one for the boy.'

The barman nodded and turned to the optics.

'Even so, the truth is . . .'

'The truth?' Walter looked at me as if I'd just fallen from the sky. 'What's that got to do with anything?'

I tried not to look lost. I failed, miserably. Walter saw this.

'Forget the truth, son, whatever that is. Concentrate on what counts, which is?'

I maintained my vacant look. I was getting good at that.

'The jury,' sighed Walter. 'The fifteen folk who decide your client's fate. Connect with them, get them on your side, become their sixteenth member, and they're less likely to hand you a guilty verdict. Make it seem like if they did, they'd be betraying a pal. And never, ever talk down to them, like the Crown do calling jurors ordinary individuals, living ordinary lives, and the peers of the accused. The Crown think they're paying them some kind of compliment, but who the hell wants to be ordinary, or compared to some dick in the dock?'

He had a point.

'And,' continued the bold boy, 'never put the accused in the witness box, unless they're definitely going down. Think about it. Your client is in court because he got caught. He got caught because he's no good at being a criminal. What makes you think he's going to be any better as a witness?'

I took a moment to digest this now obvious fact, which till then I confess had never crossed my mind.

'The fiscal depute was desperate my guy took the stand, but I told the jury everything they needed to hear in my speech.'

'But that wasn't evidence. The sheriff told them as a matter of law to disregard your version of events.'

'He'd have been as well letting one rip in the jury room and telling them, as a matter of law, to disregard the smell. Besides, I couldn't risk my client going in and cocking things up!'

'But the facts . . .'

'Forget the facts. Find a hole in the Crown case, any hole, no matter how small, find it, focus on it, until it seems to the fifteen good citizens that's the only fact that matters. There's always a hole. In this case, it was that clown not noting my client's reply, all because he called him a bastard.'

'Lying bastard,' I corrected. 'And the accused's reply made no difference to the case.'

'It made all the difference. It got the inspector angry. It gave me the chance to make him out to be a man who didn't do his job properly, refusing to note the accused's reply. I made him seem unreliable, then made the jury laugh at him. And finally . . .'

Walter downed the remainder of his drink and laid the empty glass on the table.

'I made a reasonable doubt.'

'But we both know he was stealing cars. He told us when we saw him in prison.'

'Did he?' Walter shrugged. 'I must've missed that. Still, he wasn't guilty.'

Walter inspected his empty glass as he spoke, holding it up to the light in an annoying manner, that meant it was my round next.

'And why wasn't he guilty?' asked Walter, turning to me.

'Because the jury didn't convict him?' I ventured.

He nodded. 'You're beginning to learn the game, son. Because that's all it is, a game.'

Walter waggled his empty glass in my face. The rum and pep had clearly kicked in, as at this point the bold boy launched into one of the three songs in his entire repertoire, which were, 'The Gambler', 'I Recall a Gypsy Woman' and 'Una Paloma Blanca'. I tried to catch the barman's attention, as Walter began his Kenny Rodgers impression.

Walter was no singer, but he was right. I was beginning to learn the game. And one thing was certain: this was the game for me.

17

'A hole has been discovered in the wall of a local strip-club. Police are currently looking into it.'

– Old music hall joke

I knocked on the door of the cubbyhole Walter Sutherland called his office and entered to find him in consultation with a client. Platinum blonde, painted face, pelmet skirt, black stockings with white stilettos. Her roots needed doing and her red nails were bitten to the quick.

Stubbing her cigarette out on an overflowing ashtray Walter had recently acquired from the Queens Arms, she crossed her legs, revealing a ladder running the length of her thigh.

'You rang?' I said, in what I assumed was a droll manner.

Walter grunted and nodded to a seat. I sat. He looked at the woman.

'Don't mind, do you, Greta? He's learning the ropes.'

'Is what I say still confidential?' She appeared anxious, as if keeping some state secret, or in possession of plans for a nuclear submarine the Russians were desperate to get their hands on. Upon being assured anything she said would be taken to the grave, she relaxed and shrugged her assent.

'This is Ms Cant,' said Walter. I later found out that in fact Greta could, and often did.

'Pleased to meet you.' I smiled.

'You Wattie's understudy, aye?' she asked.

For some reason, Walter's clients insisted on referring to me in this fashion, as if I was somehow waiting in the wings, ready to run on stage and take over, if something untoward took place. Of course, with Walter leading, anything was possible.

'Assistant,' I corrected.

'Apprentice,' said Walter, telling the truth for the first time that week, and handed me a complaint.

A complaint is what most people know as a summons, in a summary criminal case, served on an accused person by the procurator fiscal, ordering them to appear in either the sheriff or district court.

'Greta's been done with lewd and libidinous behaviour,' said the bold Walter.

She turned to me. 'Can you believe it, son? It's getting so a girl cannae take her top off without getting into trouble.'

I shook my head in what I hoped was a sympathetic sort of a 'what on earth is the world coming to' type of way.

'It's me you're talking to, Greta.' Walter sighed. 'You must've gone further than that. A good bit further.'

'That's what the punters are paying for, Wattie. It's not a fashion parade.'

It was 1984, and whatever Orwell's prophecies for the future, they hadn't yet materialised. Lap dancers with G-strings and supersized silicon breasts, lips like pillows, performing acrobatically round poles, were still a long way off. Instead, Go-Go Girls strutted their stuff in the seedier bars of the city of Edinburgh. Three of these – The Western, The Burke and Hare, and The Lord Darnley – formed an area known by those who frequented these establishments, called the Hairy Triangle.

In these pubs, young women, some not so young, stood atop bars, tables, stages and astride customers, grinding their hips, stripping in time to preselected tunes they'd put on the juke box at their own expense, before giving way to the next girl, and so on.

'The thing is, Wattie . . .' The woman lowered her voice. 'It was a private party, a stag night for some guy on the rigs who was getting married, and things just got a bit out of hand.'

'How much out of hand?' asked Walter.

'Well, at first, it was just me and another lassie, dressed as a traffic warden, and I was done up like a French tart.'

'And?' enquired Walter, reaching for his cigarettes and lighting one up.

'We started stripping to the music. Like I said, it was a private do, so the landlord let us have a lock-in. I'd had a good drink and ended up dancing about almost starkers.'

Walter blew a stream of smoke out each nostril. 'Go on.'

'Well, the groom's pals kept shouting for more, egging us on, so I got the guy on the stage and started taking his clothes off.'

'While you were still naked?'

'Not at all.' She sounded almost offended. 'I kept my stilettos on.'

'Then?'

'The usual: I undid his buttons, took his shirt off, then unbuckled his belt, unzipped his fly and let his trousers fall to the floor, till he was standing there in his boxers.'

'I see.' Walter drew hard on his cigarette.

'Then, I got down on my knees, my hands on his hips, took hold of the waistband on his boxers between my teeth and pulled them down. Next thing, he's starkers, standing bollock naked, with his thing in front of my face.'

Walter looked at her.

'This guy, the groom, did he have an erection?'

Greta seemed puzzled.

'A hard-on?' said Walter.

Greta cast her mind back, then, sensing a legal loophole, she shook her head.

'Not that I remember.'

'Must've been a ginger beer,' said Walter. 'I've got one just listening to you.'

What Greta hadn't realised was that it seemed among the revellers on the night was an off-duty copper, who had wormed his way into the audience, witnessed her adaptation of the dance of the seven veils, without apparently appreciating the cultural content of the performance. As a result, she'd been arrested leaving the bar in the early hours, charged and banged up in a cell overnight.

'I told the turnkey I wanted you right away, Wattie,' said Greta, entirely au fait with the process of being in police custody, 'but they couldn't get hold of you.'

'I had a locus inspection in connection with a case,' said Walter.

This, to some extent, was true. What the bold boy didn't say was that the locus was the Hibs Club in Easter Road, and the case contained a dozen bottles of Old Navy Rum.

Mobile phones being a thing of the future, Greta had been forced to accept the services of the duty lawyer, a real hit-or-miss affair, but who, that morning, by the grace of God, was a good friend of Walter's, one of the sharper defence solicitors in the Scottish courts. Bail being granted, Greta headed off to discuss matters with her own brief, Walter, who had brought me down from my perch in the attic to listen and learn.

However, so far, all I had gleaned was the client was guilty as sin. But, as I was to become increasingly aware, Walter was no mug: behind those bloodshot eyes, his brain fired on all cylinders. A big fan of Burns, he'd toasted many a haggis, but the bard's warning about drink and cutty sarks went as unheeded by Walter as it had by Tam O' Shanter, indeed by Burns himself.

The bold boy had become suspicious. Why, instead of spending his evenings off duty with family and friends, would a policeman waste precious hours working overtime, undercover and unpaid?

Whether true or not, I don't know, but I'm told that during Walter's usual liquid lunch in the Queens Arms a few days later, his fellow lawyer and drinking buddy, Donald, stated, and I don't know if this is true, he'd had a female client arrested for an identical offence, in a Go-Go bar, by the same police witness.

Apparently, further enquiries revealed more arrests by this off-duty crusader. Finally, it seemed that Walter phoned the Fiscal's Office and enquired if they were aware one of Edinburgh's finest had taken to spending his leisure time lurking in the shadows at the back of pubs, watching women take off their clothes, while playing with his baton? Did the Chief Constable and the Crown Office really want that coming out in court, when Walter called each woman involved in the officer's voyeuristic activities as witnesses in his client's case? It came as no great surprise, Walter told me after, the charges against Greta were dropped faster than her scanties.

18

'The Moving Finger writes; and, having writ, Moves on'
— The Rubáiyát of Omar Khayyám

I was newly qualified, fresh out of the gate, and so my boss, Ian Corbett, decided to break me in with some district court cases. My first ever trial was acting for someone who was a KT. KT stands for 'known thief', and this client had climbed four floors up the side of a tenement and was trying to force open a window when he was spotted by the police, ordered to come down and arrested. His excuse was he'd been caught short, so scaled the scaffolding to find a place to relieve himself, which sounded rather a tall story. Despite my best efforts, the magistrate convicted my guy of housebreaking but at least the fine was only £50, which wasn't too bad a result in the circumstances.

My next venture into the District Court was for a client of a completely different calibre. This character was a heavy hitter: as a young man of sixteen, he'd been convicted of culpable homicide and spent ten years in prison. On this occasion, he'd been charged with minor assault on a member of another crime family. My boss told me there was no way the guy who'd been hit would identify my client, as that'd be breaking the code. This proved to be the case, as when the complainer was giving evidence, he had a sudden attack of amnesia, couldn't remember being assaulted, never mind being able to identify his attacker. The matter lasted about five minutes before the fiscal dropped the charge.

The reason I mention this case isn't because I put forward some clever defence, as I hardly had to open my mouth; rather, it's because my client insisted on taking me out to lunch after. We were sitting at a table in a restaurant somewhere up Lothian Road, Edinburgh, and I ordered a steak. When the waiter enquired how I wished it cooked, I said blue, and remember feeling very sophisticated.

The food came, and as we ate, we chatted about this and that, and for some reason the talk turned to the topic of literature. People often get the impression that those who are involved in the underworld are not well educated, but many of my clients, especially those in organised crime, were often extremely clever, well read and could have easily been the CEO of some company or corporation had they chosen that career path. Certainly, they had the killer instinct required – quite literally.

During our discussion, I mentioned some poem or other I was fond of. At this, my client put down his knife and fork, looked me in the eye and quoted:

> The Moving Finger writes; and, having writ,
> Moves on; nor all thy Piety nor Wit
> Shall lure it back to cancel half a Line,
> Nor all thy Tears wash out a Word of it.
>
> And that inverted Bowl we call the Sky,
> Whereunder crawling coop't we live and die,
> Lift not they hands to It for help – for It
> Rolls impotently on as Thou or I.

Then he smiled and said, 'When I go out to take a life, I like to quote Omar Khayyám to myself.'

Even now, some forty years later, I can recall the chill running down my spine on hearing these words. Without doubt the person who'd experienced his bout of amnesia in court made a wise decision to remember to forget.

This client spent a lot of time in London, doing what he described as 'some bits of work down the road' for a heavy firm there, and was well connected. Once, when paying a visit to the Big Smoke, my client had put me up in a five-star hotel, round the corner from

Piccadilly Circus. I could never have afforded this, but my friend knew the concierge well. But then, who didn't he know. We became very friendly and would go out occasionally for a night on the town.

One evening we were standing in a bar at the bottom of Morningside Road in Edinburgh, with another man, a friend of my friend, about fifty or so years of age. This guy originally came from Edinburgh, but ran away to London when he was fourteen, where he'd enjoyed a successful criminal career as a high-class shoplifter, targeting places such as Harrods, Selfridges, and the like.

My client was an impeccable dresser, and this evening was sporting a smart, charcoal-grey suit. The three of us were chatting, when an elderly gentleman approached our group and, after politely excusing himself for interrupting, addressed my client, saying, 'Excuse me, but my wife and I are sitting at the table over there –' He turned and nodded in the direction of a woman sat in the corner, before turning back to us. 'We couldn't help noticing how smartly dressed you are and had a bit of a bet between us on what it is you do for a living. My wife thinks you're perhaps a fashion designer, but I'm sure you're an undertaker; is either of us correct?'

At that point, my client's old friend from London leaned over and said in a loud Cockney accent, 'You're both wrong mate, but one thing's for sure, he's buried a few.' He followed this with a guffaw of laughter, while my friend merely smiled quietly. The old gentleman, looking mystified, made his way back to his wife. He hadn't got it quite right, but his guess was the closest.

19

'One fears that so called "Pious Perjury" of this nature from young officers can lead to even more serious perjury on other matters later in their careers.'

– Sir David McNee, Commissioner, Metropolitan Police 1983

In 1988, I was going out with a young female lawyer; a stunning blue-eyed brunette, but being a gentleman, I won't mention her name. Her father, a well-known sheriff, concluded each case by stating he'd no reason to doubt the police were telling the truth and was apparently incapable of pronouncing the words 'not' and 'guilty' in succession. Whenever I, or any defence agent I know, appeared before him, there was only one verdict: guilty.

A client of mine, a respected member of the Travelling community, did me the honour of asking me to be best man at his wedding. On reading the guest list I noticed several people, including the legendary 'Diamond Lil' – at that time undisputed queen of the shoplifters – were unable to attend.

Though at liberty when the invitations were sent out, they'd been arrested in the interim. I duly attended the church and reception with my raven-haired girlfriend, who wore a striking if rather revealing red dress and danced the night away.

Some months later, this same client was stopped by the cops and charged with driving under the influence of drink. This was unusual, as he was normally out of his box on hash. It turned out that the trial called before my girlfriend's father, in the old Sheriff Court Number 6, now the site of the High Court at the top of the Mound.

Heading upstairs, I passed the prosecution witness room, glanced round, and suddenly stopped in my tracks. The three police officers due to give evidence for the Crown in my client's case, were huddled in a corner, clearly in collusion with one another. This guilty group comprised two young constables, one male and one female, and a sergeant, a man in his mid-fifties. I made a mental note, entered the courtroom and soon after the trial commenced.

After the first Crown witness, the female cop, had given her evidence in chief, it was my turn to cross-examine. I rose with the solemnity that suited the situation and addressed her.

'On my way to this court, I passed the Crown witness room, and on glancing through the window, could not help but notice that you and your colleagues . . .'

'Is there any possibility of this ever becoming a question?' asked the sheriff, without bothering to look up.

'Any moment now, my lord.' I smiled and turned back to the witness. 'As I was saying, on my way into court, I noticed you and your colleagues were apparently comparing notebooks, is that correct?'

'Yes, that's right,' she answered in a manner as refreshing as it was astonishing.

'And had this comparison any connection with the case before this court today?'

'Of course.'

I steadied myself with a hand on the table, her honesty over-whelming me, as she continued, unabashed.

'You see, it was so long ago, I needed to ask my colleagues what had happened when the offence was committed.'

'Allegedly committed,' I corrected her, still recoiling from the shock of such innocence displayed by a cop in court.

'Is that also to become a question, eventually?' asked the sheriff.

'No, my lord. That's simply a fact.'

'I'll be the judge of that,' he replied.

I squeezed a smile at the bench as we both pretended that he hadn't made up his mind before he came into court.

'Indeed, my lord.'

I turned back to the witness.

'So, basically, you all went over your statements together in the witness room, because you couldn't recall what happened that night, is that right?'

I asked this, as if it was the most common thing in the world for police to do, which of course it is, only no cop ever confesses to it. However, clearly this young woman had been absent from Tulliallan Police College the day they taught recruits about perjury, and the art of committing it.

'Yes, that's right.' She smiled.

I could have kissed her, but I turned to the bench.

'No further questions. Perhaps my lord would instruct the witness to remain in court at this stage.'

'Why would I do that?' asked the sheriff, pretending he didn't know the exact reason for my request.

'My lord, clearly there's been enough collaboration in the witness room without the witness leaving to mark her colleague's card as to what questions he will be asked.'

The sheriff looked up from the notes he was pretending to take and turned to me with a withering look.

'Are you suggesting this officer would leave this courtroom to relay her evidence to the next witness?' he asked, as if someone just told him the Earth was flat.

'Not so much suggesting, my lord; rather expecting,' I replied.

The sheriff glared at me, and feeling the need to continue the dance, like Nelson lifting his telescope to his blind eye and stating, 'I see no ships' (did you know, dear reader, Nelson never wore an eyepatch?), he stated: 'I see no reason why the witness may not stay or leave, as she wishes.'

Fortunately, this female recruit to Lothian and Borders' finest had evidently also missed the lecture instructing police officers that, after giving their evidence, they should immediately leave the courtroom, so they could pass on what they just said to the next cop about to go into the witness box. Instead, my motion flew straight over her head, and bless her little blue uniform if she didn't take a front row seat to watch proceedings.

Her innocence was intoxicating. I beamed up at the sheriff, who studiously ignored me.

The second cop, young, male, keen as mustard, took the oath, and proceeded to describe the events of the evening my client was arrested in the exact same detail as the earlier witness. Satisfied, the fiscal took her seat. I stood to cross-examine.

'Constable,' I said, sounding suitably friendly. 'You seem to quite clearly recall exactly what happened in this case?'

The officer smiled confidently, nodding. 'Indeed, sir.'

'Even though the events of that night took place twenty months ago.'

'Yes, sir.'

'Really? How remarkable. Then why did you bother to compare notes with both your colleagues in the Crown witness room?'

The cop recoiled as if hit with a right hook. Ten seconds in and already I had him reeling on the ropes.

'That's not a proper question,' the sheriff cut in, sending me to a neutral corner and buying the witness a standing eight count while he gathered his wits.

'I asked why he compared notes; surely that's a question, my lord.'

'Your question should have been, did you compare notes with your colleagues? But you presented his past actions as established fact. You'd be as well asking the witness if he'd stopped beating his wife!'

'I'd no idea he was married, my lord.'

'Rephrase the question,' said the sheriff, I thought, rather brusquely.

By now, the cop in the box was giving his colleague in the front row a 'what the hell's happening?' look.

'I'm over here, constable,' I called out, attempting to make it clear to the bench what he was doing, though why I bothered, as the sheriff didn't give a toss. 'Did you, or did you not, compare statements with the other Crown witnesses before court today?'

'No, well . . . I mean, we . . . We obviously chatted about the case, but I can't really remember . . .'

'You can't remember?' I cut in. 'Do you honestly think the court will believe you can recall what occurred twenty months ago, but can't remember what took place in the past twenty minutes?'

By this time, the cop was sweating like a snowman in a sauna. He looked desperately to the bench for support. He wasn't disappointed, as the sheriff turned to me.

'I'll decide what I believe, and frankly I fail to see the relevance of this line of questioning.'

Well, at least the old goat was acknowledging these were questions, though experiencing his usual difficulty in seeing anything from the defence's point of view.

'The line and question both go directly to the credibility of the witness, my lord.'

The sheriff didn't bother to reply but rather glanced at the clock and picked up his pen with a sigh. I turned back to the witness.

'You know perfectly well you compared notes with your colleagues, as the WPC has already testified.'

The cop turned to his colleague, then back to me. He started to stammer an answer, as I cut in:

'Yet, despite this, you decided to come into this courtroom, tell a pack of lies and commit perjury, isn't that correct?'

And without waiting for his answer, I sat down as if quite disgusted, leaving the witness with his mouth open. But the sheriff, entirely nonplussed, didn't miss a beat.

'Re-examination, madam fiscal?' he asked, in a tone that said, 'There's no need to bother.'

'No, thank you, my lord.' The fiscal beamed, her head so far up the shrieval backside that her fake tan was beginning to melt. She turned to the bar officer. 'The final Crown witness is, Sergeant . . .'

The witness's name escapes me now, but I looked up to see a rather rotund figure wearing a uniform with sergeant stripes waddle into court and raise his right hand to take the oath. I ducked, fearing this effort may cause his buttons to fly off and ricochet round the room like shrapnel. Having been sworn in, the sergeant trotted out his evidence, which was identical to that of the last two woodentops. The fiscal sat. I stood to cross-examine.

'Sergeant, your evidence to this court entirely corroborates that of your younger colleagues, isn't that, right?'

'Correct.' He smiled smugly, as if expecting some sort of prize for exemplary behaviour. I looked at him, puzzled, then threw a jab.

'How would you know? You weren't here when they testified?'

It was an old trick, but it caught him out. Realising I wasn't playing the game, Piggy's eyes narrowed. This wasn't a defence solicitor merely going through the motions, refusing to rock the boat, rather rowing with hope towards an eventual place on the shrieval bench.

Straightening to his full height, he said, 'I assumed their evidence would be the truth, as is mine.'

And with that he glanced at the bench, looking suitably offended. I continued.

'Tell me, as a self-confessed lover of the truth, sergeant, while in the Crown witness room, did you and your fellow officers compare statements and discuss the evidence you would give in court today?'

The sergeant acted as surprised as if he'd suddenly been black-balled by his local masonic lodge.

'I most certainly did not!'

His offended tone turned to outrage, and his head once more to the bench.

'Then,' I asked, 'perhaps you can explain why the WPC the court heard from earlier testified she had conferred with both you and the other constable in the Crown witness room about my client's case?'

The sergeant looked like he'd been hit with a hammer, but before he could attempt a reply, the fiscal leapt up.

'My lord, whatever another officer may or may not have said earlier in this court cannot be known to this witness, nor affect his testimony.'

'But it does mean one of them is committing perjury,' I added.

'The other officer's evidence is irrelevant as far as this witness is concerned,' bleated the fiscal, perfectly aware it was vital to the overall case, and were there any justice in this sheriff court, could sink it.

'Irrelevant?' I half laughed. 'The question goes directly to credibility and reliability. Both the witnesses can't possibly be telling the truth.'

'I'll decide all matters of credibility and reliability, Mr McIntyre,' said the sheriff, as if he hadn't already done so. 'Do you have any further questions for this witness?'

'I'm waiting for a response to my last one, my lord.'

'That question's been asked before, and answered,' declared the sheriff. 'Move on.'

It was clear I was flogging a dead horse.

'One last matter, my lord.'

The sheriff sighed as I turned to the witness.

'I note from your statement that you have several years of service, have you not, sergeant?'

'Twenty-nine,' he replied.

So, only twelve short months away from the magic number, thirty, after which he could retire, be handsomely rewarded with a significant lump sum and handsome pension for his years of perjury in the service of the Crown.

'Meaning you'll be eligible for your full police pension very soon?'

'That's correct.'

'Did you know it profits a man nothing if he gains the whole world and loses his own soul?'

The fat man's face reddened.

'That question's also been asked before, but there's no need to answer,' I said and sat down.

The Crown closed their case. It was now the defence's turn. The sheriff turned to me.

'And what do you say?' As if it was of the slightest importance.

The general rule of thumb for defence lawyers is, as Walter Sutherland told me: never put your client in the box unless absolutely necessary. Knowing the sheriff would sooner believe a tale told by the Brothers Grimm than my client's testimony, I advised the court, 'I lead no evidence, my lord.'

In my opinion there was a clear presumption of innocence, each officer having given a different version of what took place in the witness room. Their evidence, at least in my book, was neither their own recollection, nor could be called credible, nor reliable, and accordingly my client should be acquitted.

The sheriff didn't pretend to deliberate, but performed one of his legendary legal somersaults, and, before my bum hit the seat, pronounced his verdict.

'I have no difficulty in believing the police evidence in this case and find the accused guilty.'

I put forward a plea in mitigation, which, as any defence lawyer who has gone to trial knows, can no longer involve an explanation of the facts, but only amount to a statement of one's client's financial means, family circumstances etcetera. This I duly did, and my client was disqualified for a year and fined £200.

The evidence from the police witnesses had been as different from one another as the temperature of the three bears' porridge in the Goldilocks story, yet despite this the sheriff ignored the fact and decided there was no reasonable doubt, which says so much about the Scottish legal system and those elevated to the bench, there's no need to emphasise further.

The sheriff rose. The fiscal bowed, until her head almost touched her toes, and both left the court. I didn't bow, having as little or no respect for the court or the Crown then as I do now.

Outside in the corridor, I found my client, unconcerned, leaning against the wall, lighting up a cigarette, by striking a match on the NO SMOKING sign. As I approached, he slipped his hand inside his jacket, pulled out a pile of twenties, peeled some off and tucked them into my top pocket.

'Sorry we lost,' I said, and nodded to the banknotes. 'Still, there's no way you're getting a lap dance.'

He smiled, and put his hand back inside his jacket, this time drawing out four driving licences.

'Pick one,' he said.

I stared at him, but he insisted.

'Go on.'

I made my selection and handed it to him. He considered my choice a moment, then shrugged.

'Barry McPherson, fair enough.' Looking up, he clocked my puzzled face and smiled.

'No disrespect. But I had a friend of mine make me up some snide licences, you know, in case I get a tug over the next twelve months.'

'But . . .' I began.

78

'Forget it,' he said. 'That old fecker was always going to convict me.'

'True but, another day, another sheriff . . .'

'Would've done the same. Call the cops liars, y'kidding? You know the score with most of that mob.'

I did.

'Course,' he said, 'you dating his daughter probably didn't help.'

And, slapping me on the shoulder, he whistled his way downstairs.

20

'Be humble when you are victorious.'

– Old Viking proverb

I had a client from Leith, a sixteen-year-old boy, who had previously exhibited a particular talent for breaking into warehouses and other locked commercial premises without being apprehended. Being small and slight, he was custom built for this type of enterprise, and had once more managed to squeeze himself through a minute window, giving access to a storehouse containing stacks of designer denim gear.

Once inside, he passed piles of jeans and jackets to an accomplice outside before quitting the premise by the same means he had entered. They started selling the denim jeans and jackets at a third of the normal bat, and not surprisingly, sales were brisk, with the result lots of local lads were wearing so much denim they looked like they were on their way to a rodeo, or a cowboy convention. Word got about, the cops found out, and my client was captured with the remaining loot.

Being bang to rights, a trial requiring the Crown to prove my boy was in possession was pointless; however, as there was no direct evidence that he'd committed the break-in, I did a deal with the fiscal depute, and my client threw his hands up to a lesser charge of reset.

Accordingly, he appeared in front of Sheriff MacVicar, an old-school type, who ordered social enquiry reports. Three weeks later, back in court, with the reports provided, the sheriff placed my client on probation, following my heartfelt plea in mitigation, during which I advised the court my client and his parents planned to leave Edinburgh and start a new life in Shetland.

And start a new life he most certainly did. About six months later I received a copy complaint, sent to me by the same client, alleging not theft or reset this time, but rather a total of eight charges of assaulting police officers on the island. Though still aged only sixteen, the Crown was apparently concerned if given bail, he'd offend again (though they hadn't proved he'd offended at all yet) and, clearly worried he may pose a flight risk, and make a break for freedom by swimming the North Sea to the mainland, decided there was no other option than to remand him in custody in the adult prison of Craiginches in Aberdeen.

Apparently, the thinking behind this idea was that sticking this youngster in the same nick as a bunch of hardened cons for forty days until trial would no doubt do him a world of good and help put him back on the correct path in life: either that, or the procurator fiscal and sheriff remanding him were a pair of pricks. You decide.

Anyway, on receiving the copy complaint and being advised, admittedly to my surprise, that they had telephones in Shetland, I enquired with the clerk of court as to possible trial dates, the number of Crown witnesses, etcetera, and whilst on the phone asked why no solicitor from Shetland had been instructed in this case.

I wondered if perhaps some annual sheepdog trial, or important Shetland pullover knitting competition was taking place simultaneously with the date of trial, requiring the mandatory attendance of all the local lawyers, or perhaps an important personage had recently passed and the Shetland solicitors were involved shoving a blazing boat containing the corpse of some councillor or other, into the North Sea, bound for Valhalla, as otherwise I thought the Scottish Legal Aid Board would be rather unwilling to fork out the cash for an Edinburgh agent to travel all the way to Viking Island to conduct the defence case.

However, I was reliably informed that each of the local defence agents were, if not pushing a boat, pushing this case away with proverbial bargepoles, refusing to be associated in the matter, as each of them had attended school with the police officers involved and weren't willing to represent anyone charged with assaulting their former classmates. This spoke volumes about the local briefs' belief in the presumption of innocence and clearly things had changed dramatically since the warrior-spirited Viking days of yore.

So it was I headed for sunny Shetland. Now, the thing was, I'd never flown before, so my first taste of flying was to take a tiny plane, looking like it was powered by a wound-up rubber band, holding half a dozen passengers, to make the short hop from Edinburgh to Aberdeen.

On arrival in the Granite City, I boarded yet another plane, with propellers, marginally bigger than an Airfix model, which flew us to the Isle of Orkney. Amazingly, Shetland was surrounded by a sea mist, caused by the heat! The result was we required to fly back to Aberdeen to take the ferry to Shetland and meanwhile wait in the hut which Orcadians, rather amusingly in my view, referred to as 'the Airport'.

This building was slightly larger than a standard garage, but with fewer amenities, and it was there we whiled away the time, waiting for our return flight. A couple of hours later we boarded another wee plane and arrived back in Aberdeen, where I caught the ferry, a far more pleasant experience, and we set sail for Shetland.

The journey was to take place overnight, so I dumped my bag in my little cabin, found a bar on deck, and ordered myself a drink. As I sat sipping a pint, I looked across and was surprised to see my young client entering the bar, in the company of two prison officers. He was obviously being brought from Craiginches Prison, on the mainland, for his trial the next day in Shetland.

I decided not to let on, but merely watch proceedings from a distance and noted my client wasn't handcuffed. But then, unless he intended to dive into the North Sea, his avenues of escape were non-existent. The three took a seat at a table at the other end of the deck, then, to my astonishment, and amusement, I saw one prison officer hand my client some money. After this, this sixteen-year-old boy, whom the court had demanded be remanded in custody in an adult prison for forty days, awaiting trial for allegedly assaulting half a dozen or so big burly policemen, was now being told to commit another offence, by the very officers in charge of locking him up, namely buying alcohol when underage.

I continued to watch as my client was served without any difficulty, and returned to the table, carrying a tray with three pints of lager on it. Of course, legally, the position was the prison officers were complicit in this crime, having committed an offence by providing not only an underage boy with money for the purpose of buying alcohol, but a prisoner in their care, who should not have been drinking, whether underage or not. However, I confess, I was delighted to see what amounted to an act of compassion on the prison officers' behalf, and I take my hat off to them.

Having assumed, erroneously as it happened, I'd fly over, do the case and fly back that night, I'd brought very little baggage. Accordingly, I had only an emergency change of clothes, my court gown, the case file and a copy of the book *Scarface*. So, after a few chapters of, 'Say hello to my little friend', I fell sound asleep and was woken early next morning by the sound of the ship docking in Shetland.

Shetland didn't disappoint. It was as drizzly and miserable as I'd been led to believe. I immediately enquired the way to the procurator fiscal's office, and on arrival was ushered into an old-fashioned office with a high ceiling and a large desk, on top of which sat a small West Highland terrier.

I'd been in the law game for some time, and although this trip had led me into totally unknown territory, still I was pretty sure this puppy wasn't the procurator fiscal for the entire island: a depute maybe, but certainly not the top dog. My assumptions were proved correct as moments later a gentleman entered the room from a side door and introduced himself as the fiscal (forgive me for not remembering his name, it was thirty-five years ago).

He seemed a very friendly man, and clearly assuming I was there to sort out some sort of guilty plea, offered me a seat. However, as far as any guilty pleas were concerned, the fiscal and his terrier were about to be disappointed.

'In this case, there were eight charges libelling eight separate assaults on eight police officers,' I said.

'That's correct,' he replied, presumably taking me for an idiot for stating the obvious.

'The evidence is quite overwhelming, so is your client willing to plead to all eight charges, or is he looking for some slight reduction?'

The fiscal beamed at me, clearly feeling in a benevolent mood, and, doubtless prepared to drop the odd charge, provided my client copped for the rest on the complaint.

'I can see the evidence is indeed overwhelming and corroborated,' I said, 'though I expected nothing less when it all comes from one source, one police station, on one island.'

The fiscal's face lost his benevolent smile. Even the dog on the desk drew me a 'how dare you' look.

'I hope you're not insinuating . . .'

'I didn't come all this way to insinuate anything, but rather to point out a major flaw in the charges libelled against my client.'

This was fighting talk.

The fiscal's face fell further, and I heard a distinct growl coming from the terrier. I rose and handed the fiscal my copy of the complaint.

'As you'll see, while there are numerous allegations of assault, there is no mention anywhere as to when, or where, any of them allegedly took place.'

The fiscal scanned the complaint as I continued.

'Clearly, the complaint can't stand in these circumstances. Nor can it be amended, as my client may well have an alibi for each one of these charges, but as no dates or times are mentioned and therefore were not intimated to me, and as he's been banged up in an adult prison for nearly six weeks, I've had no opportunity to properly prepare any special defence of that nature, nor advise you of one.'

The fiscal let out a loud sigh. Even the dog lay down on the desk, knowing it was all over bar the barking.

'Dates and locuses!' He slammed his fist down hard on the desk. (The fiscal that is, not the dog.) 'Damn it. How many times have I told that depute of mine to put down dates and locuses?'

As the Crown's case was vanishing down the proverbial plughole, I resisted the temptation to tell the PF that the plural of locus was in fact loci, but instead replied sympathetically in the circumstances, 'Never mind. It's a mistake anybody could have made,' not mentioning, 'if they're as thick as mince', which would merely have added salt to the wound.

The fiscal nodded, recovered and rose, politely handing me back the copy complaint.

'I'll require to drop all the charges, but you needn't stay, Mr McIntyre. I simply won't call the case, so the matter will fall automatically.'

He glanced at his watch.

'If you hurry, you'll catch the ferry back to Aberdeen. It leaves in just under an hour.'

And with that he showed me the door, clearly anxious to be rid of me and the embarrassment his depute had apparently caused.

So ended my first and only trip to Shetland. My client was cleared of all charges but had required to spend forty days in an adult prison for the privilege. I met him again years later when he was serving a sentence in Saughton, but whether being banged up before when he was sixteen had an adverse effect on him, or not, it certainly hadn't helped.

If I recall correctly, the legal aid bill for preparing the case, travel to Shetland and back, the whole caper, came to around £4,000 (none of which as a young assistant I received), which in today's money would be just under £10,000.

On top of that expense, who knows how much more it cost the taxpayer to transfer my client, under escort, to the adult prison in Aberdeen (whether this was legal or not remains a mystery), keep him there for that length of time, then transport him back by boat, supposedly under guard, but I wouldn't be surprised if the officers' bar bill was included as expenses.

Throughout my short time there, while hanging about to see the fiscal, at no time did I spot any depute, the one being blamed for not putting the dates and 'loci' on the complaint, and I suspect there wasn't one. The only other being the fiscal could have blamed would have been the West Highland terrier, and, from the growl that wee white devil could give, somehow I don't think he would have dared.

21

'Cut to the chase.'

– Joseph Patrick McEvoy

It will come as no shock to the reader when told that any gathering of lawyers is a guaranteed bore-a-thon at the best of times, but the Edinburgh Procurators Society Dinner takes first prize.

For those not entirely au fait with this annual bash, it's a black-tie affair where defence agents attend a dinner, held in an hotel, and demonstrate to other defence agents that their business is booming and rub shoulders with the odd sheriff (the odder, the better).

The plan appears to be that, by plying them with drink and smiling sycophantically, the sheriff, recalling this show of hospitality, may deal with the solicitor's client in a lenient fashion in future, and in turn these lawyers, many of whom couldn't fight sleep, hope word of their success in gaining acquittals or lighter sentences gets around the criminal circles and more clients will be attracted to the firm. The food on these occasions is the usual forgettable fare, the guest speakers tedious, and getting drunk as a skunk utterly essential.

This annual bun fight was formerly held in the Roxburghe Hotel, George Street, Edinburgh. I attended the final dinner there and recall an incredibly drunk sheriff tripping up a female solicitor as she made her way to the ladies' powder room. This woman had no sooner hit the well-carpeted floor of the Roxburghe than the sheriff in question clambered on top of her and, despite her struggles, started simulating sexual intercourse – I think the term is dry-humping her – and adopting for this purpose the missionary position. Had he not been a sheriff, he'd have been banged up and placed on the sex offenders' register.

The week following the ruckus at the Roxburghe, a friend and fellow defence agent was acting for a client charged with a minor breach of the peace, and as fate would have it, the case called in front of the very sheriff responsible for the Roxburghe episode. The offence occurred a year before coming to court, and didn't libel any physical contact, certainly no sexual assault. It was a first offence, the accused pled guilty, so obviating the need for any witness to give evidence, and an admonition appeared to be on the cards.

However, despite having himself behaved in a despicable manner a mere forty-eight hours earlier, not even a modicum of mercy was shown, and the accused was fined £200 pounds, approximately £1000 today.

Not long after his Roxburghe romp, the same sheriff was dining at an Italian restaurant in Lothian Road, Edinburgh, doubtless washing dinner down with his obligatory bucket of booze. At the end of the evening the learned sheriff discovered his jacket, containing his wallet, bank, credit cards and cash, which he claimed he'd hung on a hook in the restaurant, was missing and, after a search of the premises proved fruitless, the police were called and a search for said jacket and its contents was commenced.

As a sheriff had made the complaint, the cops pulled out all the stops, lifted all the usual suspects, plus a few unusual ones, hit lucky and caught the culprit. The accused was banged up and a solicitor, a colleague of mine, saw the client, a regular repeat offender, in the police cells.

As the guy had been caught with the wallet, he was bang to rights, and was told he'd be best throwing his hands up, to try and mitigate the sentence. However, the client said he was going to trial, because, although he admitted the theft, he'd stolen the wallet from a jacket he'd found hanging in a massage parlour, upstairs from the restaurant. The solicitor informed the cops about what his client claimed had happened, and shortly after, the charges were mysteriously dropped and the accused freed from custody.

It wasn't the last time a senior legal figure would be found acting far differently in his private life from the way he expected others to behave in theirs. In my opinion, if hypocrisy was a criminal offence, the judicial benches would be decimated.

In 1988, my partner Raymond Megson was due to sit on the top table at the procurators' bash. Aware I'd require a little livener for that evening's event, I headed off in search of same, and, having accomplished my mission, left that flat and headed back to get changed. As I did so, I glanced in my rear-view mirror. The same red Peugeot had been behind me for some time.

What I didn't realise, but have since been told, is the cops had previously caught the person I'd just visited with a substantial quantity of coke. He'd flipped and was now saving his neck by grassing others. It was summer, but when the cops got a call concerning me, they thought Christmas had come early.

I drove across town, taking left and right turns, rounding a roundabout twice, three times, still the Peugeot didn't deviate from the route I took. No longer suspicious, I was now fairly certain I was being followed by the drug squad: Edinburgh's finest, according to my clients, at fitting them up. Approaching the King's Theatre, I turned right into Gilmore Place. Seconds later, the red car turned in after me. Further on was Maxwell Street, where a friend of mine lived and I'd intended on getting dressed there before leaving for the dinner, but by now it was evident I'd better literally steer clear, because if captured, who knew what would happen, but the consequences could be catastrophic.

I glanced again in the rear-view mirror as I took a right into Maxwell Street. The red Peugeot was still there, but instead of turning in after me, it pulled up, blocking any retreat. I spotted several more Peugeot 205s, parked on the right, further down the road, and about half a dozen men stood reading newspapers outside my friend's flat.

This wasn't normal behaviour for five o'clock on a Friday. Suddenly, one avid reader dropped his newspaper and started running towards me. Ramming into reverse, I shot backwards, away from the man; then, grinding into first gear, revving the engine, I held the car on the clutch. Their charade over, the other cops tossed their papers aside and closed in. The running man reached the front of the car and put his hands on the bonnet, as if by so doing he could somehow prevent the fuel-injected Ford Orion 1.8 Ghia from going anywhere. Perhaps he could jump tall buildings with a single bound or catch bullets in his teeth; I wasn't waiting to find out.

I edged forward slowly, giving this lunatic the chance to get out of the way, but he wouldn't budge. By this time the others were pulling at the car's back doors. Suddenly, the guy in front made a dash for my driver's door. I let go the clutch, took off, wheels spinning, rubber burning; and, swerving to the left, avoided this madman, who, now the danger was over, dived dramatically to my right. Engine screaming, I slammed into second, then third and shot across the bridge.

Behind me, the horns of the pursuing Peugeots blared. One car managed to pull alongside me, the passenger pointing to a radio he was holding. This was no time to catch up on the pop charts. I cut in front of him, causing the driver to brake, gaining myself precious seconds. Reaching the junction with Slateford Road, without slowing down, I wrenched the steering wheel hard left. By the grace of God, the car skidded sideways into a gap in the outgoing traffic. Straightening up from the slide, I glanced in the mirror. The unmarked cop cars ground to a halt at the main road, waiting for an ebb in the rush hour tide flowing fast from the town. Fortunately for me, this time on a Friday incoming traffic wasn't heavy, so I pulled out, put my foot down and overtook four cars in front, then another couple, dodging in, out, weaving my way along the road.

Realising the red car that had blocked the entrance to Maxwell Street would be racing parallel to head me off at the lights, I had to make them first. I flew past cars, vans, buses, and was cutting back in when a police panda car pulled up ahead, waiting to block me. The ball was on the slates. A marked cop car meant I could no longer pretend not to realise who was chasing me, but not wanting to be boxed in, I hammered through the lights, hit the brakes, bounced the offside wheels onto the pavement opposite the Diggers Pub at the top of Henderson Terrace and jumped out of the driver's seat.

Locking the car door, I watched as a line of different coloured Peugeot 205s screeched to a halt behind one another. I walked to the rear of my vehicle.

'What's all this about?' I asked.

Two drug squad officers left their cars and hurried towards me; even undercover, in leather jackets and jeans, they blended in like a live band in a library. One of the detective constables jumped from his car, pointing at me, yelling, 'Cuff that cunt!' (Forgive the language, but the guy had clearly been dragged up.)

Two cops grabbed my arms, twisted them behind my back, threw me over the car boot and clicked the cuffs around my wrists as tight as they could.

'Good,' grunted the DC apparently in charge. 'Detain him under Section 2 of the Misuse of Drugs Act, 19 ... Who cares? That bastard knows what I'm talking about.'

22

'A lie doesn't become truth, wrong doesn't become right and evil doesn't become good, just because it's accepted by a majority.'

– Booker T Washington

Torphichen Street is in Edinburgh's West End. On the east side there was a police station, on the west, a massage parlour, where the sauna girls merely hired out their services, whereas the mob across the road had sold their souls a long time ago.

On arrival at the cop shop, my hands cuffed tightly in front, I was booked in at the custody desk, searched and taken to the cells. I glanced about the small room, with its stainless-steel, lidless toilet in the corner.

'Can't say I like what you've done with the place. For a start, the colour's all wrong, and as for the furniture . . .'

The cell door slammed, cutting off any remarks.

Banged up, I knew the only drugs that could be found in my car or on me were those the DS would have to plant themselves. According to my clients, this was par for the course during the eighties and nineties, and I've no doubt the tradition dates to the days of Sir Robert Peel and his 'bobbies' in the nineteenth century (old habits die hard) together with the rampant racism, sexism, homophobia, corruption and perjury that apparently continues to permeate every level of the police today.

I paced the tiny room, glancing at my watch, wondering how long I'd be there. After about an hour, the door opened, and two drug squad officers came in. They said they'd searched my car, even emptied the petrol tank checking for drugs but had found nothing.

'Told you,' I said. 'Frankly, I'm hurt you wouldn't take my word. Still, now you know there's nothing there, I've a dinner engagement and need to change into my tuxedo.'

At this point the DS officers looked at one another, then one of them turned to me.

'You're not going anywhere, I've a charge to prefer against you.'

Knowing from the rather glum look on their faces they couldn't have found any drugs and apparently hadn't planted any, I assumed he was talking about some sort of speeding offence, or road-traffic violation.

'If you're wondering why I was driving so fast,' I said, as straight-faced as I could, 'four car-loads of complete strangers were chasing me. I was scared stiff.'

'You tried to kill Detective Inspector McCrae.'

This was a lie. What's worse was, they knew it was a lie.

'You can't be serious,' I said.

'Sounds serious to me,' said the other cop.

Before I could protest further, one of the officers proceeded with the common law caution. Today, there are videos, tape recorders, lawyers present, all sorts of so-called safeguards put in place to attempt to make sure the boys in blue don't verbal or stitch anyone up, although it's possible to get round anything, if they put their minds to it. Back in the day, the caution should have been along the lines of 'You are not required to say anything, and that's okay, because we're going to make it all up anyway'; however, for form's sake, the cop stated, 'I must caution you that you are not required to say anything, but anything you do say will be taken down and may be used in evidence. Do you understand?'

Dumfounded, I nodded. The cop continued, to the best of my recollection, stating that:

'On 8 June 1988 in Maxwell Street, Edinburgh, you did drive a motor car, namely a Ford Orion Ghia, at detective inspector John McCrae, of Lothian and Borders Police, causing him to throw himself clear of the path of said vehicle in order to avoid being struck and you did attempt to murder him – have you any reply?'

I used to tell clients, and continue to advise anyone who asks me, that if asked this question by the police, to make no reply. None.

Niente, nada, zilch. If a person is charged with a common law crime or statutory offence, while very tempting, especially if the person charged feels themselves in the right, ill done by, or is in a state of excitement, anxiety or anger, any reply they make, no matter how innocent, can all too often backfire, providing the police with vital evidence they can and will use as corroboration.

Despite my advice to others, and the old proverb, 'He who is his own lawyer has a fool for a client', I couldn't help thinking that on this occasion, as there were about two dozen cops to witness my presence at the scene, it was best to immediately deny what they claimed had happened there, and, in the strongest possible terms; especially as they were lying, and they knew it, so accordingly I stated, 'That's simply not true, as you both very well know.'

The cop took this down, then looked up from his notebook.

'That it?' he asked.

'Unless there's something else you feel like fitting me up with?'

Apparently, there wasn't, so after clapping the cuffs back on my wrists, they brought me out of the cell and stuck me back into the panda car, bound for pastures new.

It was already Friday night and with the weekend beckoning, the drug squad drove me to the High Street cells, there to spend a delightful Saturday and Sunday before Monday morning's court appearance on a totally trumped-up charge of attempted murder.

Being banged up, anywhere, is far from a fun experience. However, the old High Street cells in Edinburgh looked like they dated back to the Dark Ages. Indeed, one almost expected the Man in the Iron Mask or the Count of Monte Cristo to be locked up next door. These dungeons formed part of the now defunct District Court, tucked away, as if in shame, behind the Cathedral of St Giles; rather ironically the patron saint of depression.

By now, I realised I'd only two chances of attending the procurators' dinner. Slim and none; and Slim had just left town.

The drug squad stuck me in the first cell we came to, and, convinced I'd swallowed a huge quantity of cocaine, desperate for nature to take its course, posted two young cadets at my open cell door to observe me continually, in case I produced a bag of Bolivian from my bottom, like a rabbit from a hat. They cover this violation of a prisoner's privacy by calling it a 'suicide watch'; odd, as I felt it unlikely my two guards might simultaneously kill themselves. Anyway, I stripped down to my boxers, stretched out on the rubber-covered mattress, and settled in for the evening.

I come from a medical family but had no personal knowledge of how long any substance one may have swallowed remains in the bloodstream or body. After ten minutes I asked for a glass of water. One of the cadets fetched this in a plastic cup. Ten minutes later, I asked for another, then another ten minutes after that, each time downing it in a oner. Shortly after, I asked to go to the toilet. Concerned I may be planning on producing the long-awaited rabbit and disposing of the evidence, one of the officers accompanied me, eyes trained as I relieved myself, and together we returned to the cell.

Then minutes later, I requested another drink. One of the cops rolled his eyes.

'Not again?!'

'It's roasting,' I said. 'You could grow tomatoes in here.'

Reluctantly the cop headed off, returning with a cup of water. I downed two more before again asking to use the loo. Each time the cadets rolled their eyes, but couldn't refuse, so took me, watched me pee and escorted me back, commenting on my weak bladder.

I was lying on the mattress, eyes closed, when a third cop burst onto the scene, breathless, waving a plastic cup at the two wooden-tops on watch, calling out, 'The PF says he's to piss into this!'

The two cadets stared at him, then turned to me on the mattress. They assumed I was asleep, but I was watching the proceedings through slitted eyes, listening intently.

'You're a bit late. He's been to the bog twice,' said one.

'Not for a crap?' asked the newcomer in horror.

'Course not! Think we're stupid?'

I smiled to myself, refraining from answering with considerable difficulty, continuing to feign sleep, adding a snore for authenticity.

'Just as well, 'cause, the DS says if he needs one, he's to do it into this.'

And through half-closed eyes I watched as he produced one of these papier-mâché bedpans they use in hospitals, the kind that look like wee bowler hats.

The cop continued, 'You've to call the DS if he does the business. The code is, "The eagle has landed."'

A few minutes later, the cop left, confirming my earlier conclusion these clowns had nothing on me, and were still clutching at straws, hence the trumped-up charge.

23

'Water, water every where, and all the boards did shrink.'
— 'The Rime of the Ancient Mariner', Samuel Taylor Coleridge

By now, I was certain I was ahead of the game, but gave it another few minutes before asking for yet another glass of water.

As the officers watching me thought I'd been asleep when the other cop turned up, they brought me two plastic cups, filled to the brim, obviously keen for me to ask to go to the loo again. I drank both cups, and after twenty minutes, told them I was hot and wanted more to drink. Rather than roll their eyes, Gunga Din couldn't have fetched the water faster.

One cop raced off, returning with another two cups in twenty seconds. I drank them down, then lay back on the rubber mattress, and pulled the rough brown blanket over my chest. The two young officers given the mission of watching me sat on chairs at the open cell door and chatted quietly as I lay apparently sound asleep.

Sometime later, these two woodentops were relieved from duty by another two cadets. During the swap-over, the order was passed on, namely that I was to pee into a plastic cup and do the business in the bowler hat. The new cops were also advised it had been about an hour since I had four glasses of water, so should be needing to go to the toilet soon.

I continued to pretend to be asleep, lying quietly in the dim light, listened to the two newcomers sat on chairs, side by side, blocking the open cell door. I watched them going over lecture notes, in connection with some upcoming exam. As they did so they bragged to one another about young guys they'd beaten up while arresting them, then charging them with police assault to cover themselves, an all too regular occurrence. They also boasted about giving people a kicking when they were off duty on nights out.

One of these young cops had apparently been in the army in Northern Ireland, and (whether true or not, I have no idea) was talking about roughing up people at checkpoints. I stayed completely silent and listened as they confessed to various violent crimes they claimed to have committed, sniggering at the fact they could get away with whatever they'd done simply because they were police officers.

I confess the boastful admission about beating up Irish and British citizens at a border checkpoint caught even me by surprise back then. However, after years of fighting the forces of darkness, any shock I experienced then has long since dissipated. It's a known fact, amongst lawyers, clients, prosecutors, judges and increasingly among the general public, that cops can be extremely heavy-handed when arresting someone, and a significant number have died in police custody in suspicious circumstances. However, when these cases are dealt with, if considered at all, the enquiry inevitably turns out to be a complete whitewash.

About ten minutes after the change of shift, a voice asked, 'Jimmy, d'you want to go to the toilet?'

Receiving no answer, the cop in question raised his voice.

'Jimmy!'

I pretended to be roused from a sound slumber, sitting up slowly, rubbing my eyes.

'What is it?' I asked.

'Need to go to the loo.'

'On you go then,' I said.

'No, not me. I mean, do you need to go?'

'No, no. I'm fine, thanks.' And I lay back down.

'Any more water? I'm getting some anyway.'

I shrugged. 'I wouldn't mind, if it's not too much trouble.'

'Course not.' The cop smiled and headed off, as his colleague continued to keep an eye on me. I looked over at him.

'If you're expecting the eagle to land, you're onto plums.'

'That's what you want us to think,' sniggered the officer.

Teaching cops how to snigger is perhaps on the Tulliallan time-table, coming right after the tutorial on how to commit perjury and plant evidence.

Cop number one arrived back with the water, again I drank both cups, and my guards resumed their watch. Time ticked by. But as Pinky and Perky prattled away to one another, they kept glancing over. Clearly, they couldn't comprehend why I wasn't desperate to take a leak. I continued to lie on my mattress, concentrating my stare at the ceiling while softly humming a song to myself written by a couple of guys nobody's probably heard of, Arthur Freed and Nacho Herb Brown, made famous by Gene Kelly, 'Singing in the Rain', for reasons that would become all too apparent very shortly.

Considering the occurrences of the last few hours included being chased by the cops, arrested, and charged with attempted murder, you'd think, dear reader, sleep didn't come to me quite as easily as normal that night. You'd be wrong. I said my prayers as usual, also asking Our Lady to pray for me and my family, and, as Coleridge wrote: 'To Mary Queen the praise be given. She sent the gentle sleep from Heaven, That slid into my soul.'

'Wait!' I hear someone ask. 'You said your prayers?' Of course. Make no mistake, I've never been under any illusion as to the sins I've committed, I've merely held different views than those held by the police and procurators fiscal: different at least from those they claim to have, not necessarily from what they do in their private lives.

The reality is the legal profession is chock-a-block with hypocrites. However, in my submission, hypocrites, as far as the practice of law is concerned, can only come from one side. Defence lawyers defend, so a defence lawyer may do what he likes in his personal life. Whilst what he does may be illegal, and he may be caught, fined or imprisoned, he isn't being a hypocrite.

I've known defence agents, advocates, QCs, who take drugs, and as I say, whilst doing these things may be illegal, they're not being hypocrites. However, judges, sheriffs, magistrates, procurators fiscal, advocate deputes, if they indulge in these activities, are undoubtedly hypocrites, due to their decision to prosecute and sit in judgement on others for committing offences that they themselves are equally guilty of committing.

So, I slept the sleep of the innocent as the function I'd planned to attend at the Sheraton hotel was in full swing. It had been arranged previously that I would welcome our guests to the annual dinner of the Procurators Society, the former name for the Bar Association, not to be confused with the procurators fiscal, whose society no one welcomes, as my business partner, Ray, was president that year.

Ray was presiding on the top table, sitting alongside the good and the great. While referring to hypocrites in Matthew 23:6, Our Lord states that they 'Love the place of honour at banquets and the most important seats', and this bash was bang in keeping with the biblical text, as among those invited to the top table was a former Procurator Fiscal, since elevated to the shrieval bench, a man once described by my dad, who'd known him some years back, as 'a stuffed shirt'. If you knew how mild-mannered my old man was, you'd realise that was him really letting rip!

It so happened the stuffed shirt was sitting at the top table, beside Robbie Burnett, a friend of mine, and a very different kind of man to the buffoon in question. Robbie's one of life's good guys, a first-class defence lawyer, now retired, whose rosy cheeks shone like a couple of ripe apples when he smiled, and doubtless still do.

As the evening progressed, my absence began to be noticed, and the whisper went round I'd been captured and clapped in irons. On hearing this, this former fiscal apparently turned to Robbie, and said words to the effect, 'Got him at last. We've been following him for years.'

If that was the case, you'd think after all that time they'd have a Scoobie Doo what they were doing, and not need to fit me up with attempting to murder some muppet.

Saturday morning brought the turnkey, who in turn brought a polystyrene box containing my breakfast. This consisted of a pile of yellow rubber pretending to be scrambled egg, and a slice of spam, microwaved to the max. I gave both a miss. Accompanying my meal was a massive mug of tea, the idea being, once I drank this I'd require to relieve myself, the police would pounce, produce the plastic cup and request me to perform. They were to be deeply disappointed.

Lunch followed breakfast, and dinner followed lunch, both meals nuked beyond belief and left uneaten, and each was accompanied by more fluid. There was no sign of the eagle landing yet, but these woodentops were bursting for me to do the business, of any kind.

Unfortunately for them, even by Sunday, I wasn't bursting. Why? Simple. As I lay on my back, eyes closed, under the cover, I'd slipped my boxers down and had been busy peeing into the rough brown blanket since the first time the plastic cup had entered the equation.

The liquid I was expressing had been soaking into the blanket, but eventually began running down the rubber mattress and continued to for a considerable time that night, forming a puddle on the floor alongside me, unseen by the cops in the dim light of the cell.

However, the stage was reached when the river broke its banks and began streaming towards the cell door into the light, finally touching the boots of one of the cadets on duty.

Suddenly, woodentop number two leapt up, as he spotted the flood at his feet.

'See that!?' He pointed to the pool of pee.

Woodentop number one, who'd fetched the water, followed his partner's finger, then turned to me, with an expression as if he'd been betrayed.

'You were meant to piss into this.' And he held up the plastic cup provided for the purpose.

I looked at him, apparently puzzled.

'Sorry, I was asleep and missed the memo.'

The police persevered with the plastic cup the rest of the weekend but got nowhere. I continued to be a wet blanket, in more ways than one, refusing to play the game, and determined not to do the business into a bowler hat, which was what the drug squad desperately desired. And so, the day drew to a close without any sign of the eagle landing.

Monday morning arrived, as did another breakfast in a box. No sooner had I declined this delicacy than the drug squad showed up to escort me to the sheriff court. This was the old court at the top of the Mound, which is now the High Court of Justiciary. My case called before Sheriff Nigel Thomson, a tall, well-built man, with a lived-in face and strong jaw that belied his benevolent nature. He was a known lover of the arts, a man of culture with a dry sense of humour, referring to me as a 'young Turk', which I took as a compliment.

The Crown advised the court they suspected I had swallowed a significant quantity of class A drugs and moved to grant a warrant to force me to swallow some sort of emetic, which would cause me to vomit, and throw up the evidence. Further, the fiscal wanted a warrant to take me to have my stomach X-rayed to see if any illegal substance was present.

After a few minutes' consideration, Sheriff Thomson stated by forcing me to drink an emetic, the Crown would be carrying out an assault on my person, accordingly he was refusing their motion. However, as the X-ray would cause no harm, he would grant the Crown's motion and allow this to be carried out. He then remanded me in custody for seven days.

I was escorted from the court back to the cells in the High Street, to await being taken for the X-ray. After a while, some cops came to collect me and I was brought downstairs to another cell, and told to wait there, not that I had much of an option.

I lay down on the mattress in the cell and promptly fell fast asleep, only to be woken a short time later and told the idea of the X-ray had been abandoned, and I was being taken to Edinburgh Prison. I don't know why they didn't bother with the X-ray but guess that after their motion to force me to throw up was tossed out, the X-ray, if it showed anything, would be unable to tell whether what was in my stomach was an illegal substance.

It had been three days, the Crown were no further forward, and, with God's help, that's how I intended the situation to stay; still, the drug squad had another card to play.

24

'Much Ado About Nothing'

– William Shakespeare

Doctor Anthony Busutill was a Malteser: not the type that melts in your mouth and not in your hands, (readers from my era may recall that advert) but a native of that fair island. Speaking of hands, fortunately for me, the good doctor had rather small ones, as he was a rather petite man, and an extremely pleasant one at that.

I'd met this gentleman several times before. Besides working as a police doctor, he also regularly appeared as a medical expert for the defence, and apparently proved very helpful. A friend of mine once recalled a case in which he was acting for the accused, where the good doctor gave evidence that in his medical opinion, rather than being struck from behind by the accused, the alleged victim had in fact backed onto the axe that caused his injuries, resulting in a not guilty verdict.

Anyway, it was to this gentleman the drug squad dragged me in their increasingly desperate attempt to find incriminating evidence, hoping if he carried out an internal examination, he'd discover a quantity of concealed drugs. Had I been older, I'd have asked him to check my prostate while he was up there.

The reader will immediately realise the relevance of my earlier reference to the doctor's hands. Small hands meant small fingers, and small fingers meant less discomfort for me. Not that I had anything to fear. I much prefer keeping things in pockets, drawers, cupboards, containers rather than up my rear-end, so there was nothing at all for the doctor to discover. However, Doctor Busutill was a kindly soul. As he snapped on the surgical latex gloves, he quietly said to me, 'You know if you have cocaine inside you, and the packet burst, it could prove extremely serious.'

He was about to expand on just how serious when I stopped him.

'Doctor. Believe me, I've absolutely nothing to worry about.'

'You seem very sure of that.'

'Because it's the truth, do you want me to lie? Now, you do what you've got to do, and be gentle with me.'

And he did. And he was. For a few awkward moments, this forensic physician felt in and round about the relevant area, finally withdrawing his fingers and nodding in confirmation.

'No, there's nothing here.'

I could have said, 'Told you so', or 'what a total waste of time that was' or 'what an affront to my personal dignity', etcetera, but refrained from doing so. After all, no harm was done, my point had been made, and though this was the first time any man ever shoved anything up my bottom, if it had to be someone, I'm glad it was Doctor Busutill.

The doctor left the room to report his findings, or lack of them, and I had just finished fastening my trousers when the door opened and some rather disgruntled, disappointed members of the drug squad reappeared.

'Cheer up, lads,' I said. 'Nobody likes a sore loser.'

But these policemen weren't of the laughing variety. They quickly clapped the cuffs back on my wrists, and took me out to a waiting car, one that would drive me not only to Edinburgh prison, but to the old 'D Hall Digger': the punishment block.

25

'Nor stony tower, nor walls of beaten brass,
Nor airless dungeon, nor strong links of iron,
Can be retentive to the strength of spirit.'

– William Shakespeare

Stretched out on a mattress thinner than a credit card, naked, apart from my boxer shorts, I stared at a cockroach crawling about the floor and up the leg of the cardboard chair. In the cooler, or as they called it in Edinburgh prison, the Digger, the chair and table were both made from cardboard, in case you threw a wobbly and smashed the cell up. You're not going to do a great deal of damage flinging a few pieces of papier-mâché about the place.

Normally, when the court remands someone in custody, you're put with all the other untried prisoners. However, the drug squad, still convinced I'd swallowed a substantial quantity of cocaine, and consequently concerned that if I was put in the untried wing I'd dispose of this, decided without any legal authority or warrant whatsoever to have me placed in solitary, where I could be watched around the clock.

Back in 1988, the Digger, or to give it its Sunday name, the Segregation Unit, was basically the punishment block where prisoners were put after a fight had broken out between them, or if they simply didn't know where else to stick someone. The building comprised three or four concrete cells, with no windows, some of which were cells within a cell, so that it was possible to walk around the perimeter.

Each prisoner was kept in solitary confinement and not allowed to talk to or communicate in any way with the prisoner through the wall from him. I remember some kid who'd been remanded in custody being given a seriously strong sedative called 'Largactil', known as liquid cosh, and locked up overnight in the cell next to mine, before being shipped back to the Polmont Young Offenders. Despite the drug, he yelled his head off for hours on end. The next day he'd disappeared.

I was watched 24/7 by a pair of guards whose job it was to catch me in the act of answering the call of nature. In school, during Physics we were told every action has an equal and opposite reaction. Accordingly, I decided not to eat anything. What doesn't go in, doesn't come out. It was late in the day by this time, and an officer arrived with some dodgy-looking sandwiches, which could have had anything crushed into the contents; therefore, I politely declined them and settled down for the night.

I couldn't sleep a wink. The white light which had burned all day had been replaced by a red one, which would burn all night. Rubbing my eyes, I looked over at the two screws sat outside the open door. I pointed up at the red light in the ceiling.

'Are you pair developing photographs or something?'

Neither gave a glimmer of a smile.

'I'm here all week,' I said, lying back, not realising how true my words would prove to be.

The days in the Digger dragged drearily by. During that time my business partner, Ray Megson, visited me. Such was his haste, he was rather brusque with the bizzies, and at first refused admission, resulting in him getting angry and nearly being himself arrested.

Next came my lawyer, Alex, who is now a KC, and a senior prosecutor with the Crown Office, but unlike others is a man of blameless character and a cert to be handed a red jersey (become a High Court judge). During my consultation with Alex, I told him I'd no intention of performing my toilet duties like a trained puppy, in the manner the drug squad wished, to which he responded, 'If you don't eat, you don't shit,' which fitted both my theory and that of Newton's laws of motions (pardon the pun). Accordingly, I stuck to my self-imposed diet.

The probability is that most of my readers will not have found themselves in prison, at least not at that time, and so will be unaware what comprised a breakfast inside one of Queen Betty's B&Bs. I can't talk about the menu today, but back then, while there was always a plentiful supply of porridge, (hence the nickname for the nick) a prisoner would be given a roll and butter, accompanied by a piece of something pretending to be bacon one morning, a bit of black pudding the next, or an egg, or perhaps a plum tomato; but, these never arrived together on the same plate on the same day. Food in Edinburgh Prison is nearly all steamed, rather than fried or grilled, which ensures that it is extremely healthy, and totally tasteless.

By my third day in the Digger, I had been fasting for six days, and I was beginning to dream of my favourite meal: a lamb bhuna curry, from Khushi's Restaurant, at that time situated in South Bridge, Edinburgh. I was roused from my thoughts by the arrival that morning of an officer coming from the kitchen, carrying a plastic plate (everything was plastic, for obvious reasons) on which were bacon, eggs, black pudding, plum tomatoes (plural) and a helping of beans, which was something of a record breaker.

'Looks good, doesn't it,' said the officer as he laid the plate on my cardboard tabletop. 'I don't know what you've done to deserve all this.'

'It's not so much what I've done, but rather what I haven't done, and the drug squad are desperate for me to do.' I smiled.

He shrugged.

'Still, smells delicious?' he said, encouragingly.

'You really think so?'

'Definitely.'

'Then eat it yourself,' I said. 'And shut the door behind you, there's a dreadful draught in here.'

The officer glared at me, picked up the plate and left. I'm sure he felt like slamming the door behind him, but that wasn't an option, as it was vital it remained ajar to enable the two officers sitting in their seats eating their breakfast to continue watching me as if I was a show on morning television.

Not eating was one thing, but not drinking was different. The heat down in the Digger was akin to that of a boiler-house, and I stood the risk of becoming dehydrated. Down the corridor stood a single WC cubicle on the left and a large Belfast sink on the right. I was allowed to wash each morning, and to drink as much water as I wished. I decided to revert to the old routine, with a twist; since it was so hot, I didn't get given a blanket to cover me during the night, only a thin sheet.

I'd request a fresh towel each morning, go for a wash at the sink, accompanied by a screw, then after returning to my cell and lying once more on my mattress, under the single sheet, wrap the towel round my nether regions, nappy fashion, and let nature take its course. The next day, I'd repeat the procedure, take the old towel and pretend to throw it into the large bin provided for the purpose, but in fact, when the screw's back was turned, I'd toss it high up on top of a cupboard, way out of sight.

The reason for this was after spending a penny or three into the towel during the night it would dry out, become rock solid, so stiff it could stand up on end, and if this had been noticed, the game would have been up. After a few days of towel throwing, which due to their increasing stiffness became more akin to tossing the caber, I received another visit from my partner, Ray, who advised me my dad had called him to say any substance I may or may not have swallowed would have changed its chemical consistency, and so no longer be correctly identified, if I wanted to pee.

But by that time, I was into a routine, and there was no danger of me urinating into a cup just because I was being told to by some halfwit in the Crown Office. Call me stubborn, but . . . No, just call me stubborn.

By now, it was my seventh day of being banged up, my fourth in the Digger, and I confess to getting even more peckish. I decided it was time for some nutrition; however, this required some planning. Accordingly, I told the screws to contact the drug squad, and tell them that I was prepared to permit the eagle to land, provided they took me to my favourite restaurant for a meal, never thinking for a moment they'd fall for this request.

Apparently, they were even more desperate for a result than I'd thought. One hour later, two of the drug squad were at my cell door, handing me a set of prison clothes as my own clothes were being forensically examined for any traces of drugs. Unlike today when prisoners are togged out in tracksuits, trainers and coloured tops, this outfit comprised a blue striped shirt: blue for untried prisoners, and red for convicted, a pair of trousers and jacket fashioned from some thick, rough brown fabric, with black shoes.

I was escorted to an unmarked car, cuffed, placed in the back between two other cops, and asked where I wanted to go. I told them to take me to Khushi's Restaurant, which at that time was situated in Drummond Street, up 'the Bridges', in Edinburgh. The restaurant has moved several times since then, and I knew the owner well, and back then it served what was easily the best curry in town.

I recall being in Khushi's on one occasion with my boss, Ian Corbett, plus Hamish Wilson and two other lawyers. At a nearby table sat four sheriffs, at another there were four plain-clothes cops, and at yet another, four members of an organised crime family I knew well. Each group treated the restaurant as some sort of neutral zone, a no-man's land, as they enjoyed the food, and the bill back in the day was as cheap as chapatis.

The unmarked car drew up outside the restaurant, and the officers decided rather than march me inside in handcuffs, I should order a takeaway, and they'd take me to Torphichen Place police station to eat it. Despite being banged up, that miserable mob made sure they got the money from my property in prison to pay for my meal, but having said that, I was delighted to be out of the Digger for a few hours.

When asked what I wanted to eat, I decided on something which would digest easily, produce very little waste, so I avoided vegetables and brown rice, and requested a simple lamb bhuna with chapatis. The cops collected my takeaway, and we headed to Torphichen Street. Once we got to the police station, I must admit the cops pulled out all the stops. They got me a plate, knife and fork, and a huge mug of tea.

I took my time, eating slowly, though it was hard to resist the temptation to simply scoff the lot, as I was starving. After my meal, the cops gave me a cigarette, and once I'd finished that, the officer in charge asked if I was ready to go to the toilet. I told them to hold their horses, nothing happens that quick, and requested another mug of tea. After this, I was asked again if I was ready to do the business. By this time, I realised I couldn't drag my time out of the Digger any longer and told the cop in charge.

'That bhuna must've bunged me up, 'cause I'm kinda constipated now.'

To say the drug squad weren't happy is an understatement. I doubt Scott of the Antarctic experienced greater disappointment when on reaching the South Pole in 1912, he found a Norwegian flag stuck in the snow. Honestly, going by the fuss they made, you'd think they'd paid for my meal themselves.

They cuffed me again, shoved me in the back of the car, and drove back to the Digger. Obviously, they didn't understand just because someone was out to dinner with you (especially if you're going Dutch) doesn't mean they can expect anything intimate afterwards, and what they wanted me to do was about as intimate as it gets.

26

'A friend in need is a friend indeed.'

– Old proverb

As mentioned earlier, the prison authorities had to come up with a rota of officers willing to work overtime to watch me. This round-the-clock observation meant six officers were required in order that two were available for each of the three eight-hour shifts. There were a variety of screws who took part in this, and all of them had volunteered.

One officer volunteered far more than any of the others. At that time, I was thirty-one years old, and he must have been just a few years older. I won't mention his name, even after thirty-four years, as I wouldn't want him to get into any trouble for what he did, affect his pension, whatever; but for present purposes I'll call him Dave.

One of the times Dave was on duty, I told him he must be a glutton for punishment, as he was constantly offering to sit in a seat and watch me for eight hours solid after already putting in a shift. He told me he was doing it because he needed the money.

During his shifts, Dave and I often ended up chatting and discussed all sorts of subjects. He was a very non-judgemental kind of guy, and we got on well. It was the day after I had been to Khushi's, and despite my best efforts, my avoidance of vegetables, brown rice or any type of roughage, I really felt myself in distinct need of a number two. The other officer who was on duty that evening didn't say much, and I can't remember anything about him, as he merely sat and read his book while Dave and I blethered about this and that.

About halfway through the shift, I heard the other officer tell Dave he was going to D Hall, to use the microwave there to heat up his dinner. The guy was obviously breaking the rules, as there were meant to be two officers with me at all times in order to corroborate matters if I was to do anything like dispose of drugs.

However, Dave happily agreed for the guy to go, and this meant the screw had to walk up the corridor, get to D Hall, use the microwave, then make his way back down the corridor to the Digger. I thought for a couple of seconds. It was tight but possible. I sprang off my mattress.

'Dave,' I said, 'I'm going for a crap.'

And without further ado, I headed out of my cell.

Dave almost fell off his chair.

'What?' he exclaimed.

'You heard me.' And I passed him, heading down the short corridor.

'But ... But you can't!' he stammered, not through fear, rather totally gobsmacked.

'I'm going, mate,' I called back, 'but if you feel you have to hit that button, hit it.'

'You can't!' he called after me. 'That's the whole reason we're here watching you!'

'There's only you, and nobody's going to know,' I called back, opening the toilet door, pulling down my boxers, planking myself on the loo seat, leaving the cubicle door open.

Dave stood, looked down the short passageway at me, turned back, but he didn't hit the panic button. Instead, he hurried to the door of the Digger, stuck his head round the corner and kept watch, then glanced back and hissed at me.

'Okay, but hurry up then!'

He didn't have to ask. I was busy squeezing with all my might, when suddenly I let off a ripper of a fart that could have been heard in the sheriff court, never mind D Hall. That was it. Nothing else. The Khushi had been completely absorbed, along with anything else I may or may not have swallowed before that, and the desire for the loo must've just been a massive build-up of gas in my tummy.

Suddenly, Dave turned and hissed again from the door.

'Quick, he's coming back!'

I pulled my boxers up and bombed along the short corridor as fast as my bare feet could carry me. As Dave retook his seat, I shot past him, skidded into the cell, onto the mattress and slipped under the sheet, just as the second screw arrived back with his hot meal. Dave and I carried on chatting, as if we were in mid-conversation on yet another topic, and Mr Microwave was none the wiser about anything that had happened. Later that evening, when Dave had his break, he gave me one of his sandwiches, which I now accepted gratefully, much to the surprise of his colleague.

Call what this officer did a result of reversed Stockholm syndrome, call it not doing his job, call it what you like; however, I call it the very kind act of a very kind man, who saw I needed a hand, and was prepared to stick his neck out for me.

I was never able to send him a thank you for what he did, as I was advised that the authorities might put two and two together – but Dave knows who he is, and I hope he knows how grateful I am to him.

Saturday morning came around and I woke to find the prison governor staring down at me on top of my mattress. Was there no privacy at all in this establishment Her Majesty had the cheek to call her own?

'How are you?' he asked, pretending he was remotely interested.

'Never better,' I replied. 'You should try it in here yourself some-time. It's like a religious retreat, most relaxing.'

'Good,' said the governor, 'because you've been here a whole week now, nothing has happened, and I can't spare the staff any longer.'

'I didn't ask anyone to babysit me,' I said.

He merely nodded, left and moments later the two officers who had replaced Dave and Microwave Man, were removed and my cell door closed with a clang.

Victorious, I settled back down onto my mattress, and was just starting to fall asleep again, when the cell door opened and several drug squad officers entered.

'Get up,' one of them said. 'You're going back to the High Street.'

By this, they meant they were taking me back to the old cells in the police station, behind St Giles' Cathedral, where I'd been the weekend before. Of course, as the court had remanded me in custody to prison, the drug squad had absolutely no authority to take me anywhere else, but when have the cops ever abided by the law if it didn't suit them? In any event, I stayed schtum. You never know when a technicality may come in handy.

Once back in the old cells, round the clock surveillance started again. I passed most of Saturday lying down, but by late afternoon, bored stiff, I came to a decision that might hasten my getting me out of there, while still retaining my dignity. As for the DS, they had no dignity, so my idea should work.

I told the young, uniformed cops who were watching me to get in touch with the drug squad, and say I wanted to see them. The DS arrived within half an hour, and I told them my idea. If they placed a bowler-hat-type container on a chair behind the cell door, I would sit on this, my body completely out of sight, but with my hands in view, and the eagle would land. The drug squad immediately agreed.

Moments later, my Hugo Boss boxers down, I was perched atop a papier-mâché bedpan, upon a chair, behind the door, my hands in view. Once again, I squeezed with all my might, and this time, thanks to the sandwich Dave had given me the night before, though not the mighty eagle the drug squad hoped for, an innocent little sparrow fluttered into the bowl. I then made myself respectable, the drug squad retrieved the bedpan and I was allowed to go to the loo alone, to clean up.

On returning from my ablutions, I admit it was with a certain sense of satisfaction I watched a sergeant poking a tiny piece of poo with a wooden spatula, before eventually realising there was nothing of interest. I've heard of shit stirring before, but only metaphorically.

At the time the sheriff remanded me in custody, he'd made it crystal clear that immediately I cooperated in the above manner, I'd be bailed. Of course, it turned out not to be that simple. The cops claimed they'd first to contact the fiscal, Ken MacIver, and I was informed all attempts to contact him had failed, as he was playing golf somewhere, so my hopes of being bailed that day ended up in the bunker.

However, early next morning, I woke to hear a voice saying, 'Right, Mr McIntyre, time we got you washed, shaved and out the door.'

I looked up from my mattress to see a uniformed policeman standing in the open doorway, holding a towel. I recognised the officer immediately as someone I'd cross-examined on numerous occasions in Edinburgh District Court. He was one of the old-school. Each time we crossed swords in a case, he lied his backside off, and every time I accused him of committing perjury, like the true professionals we were. On this occasion, I couldn't have been happier to see a familiar face.

'I've been bailed?' I said.

'That's correct, sir,' he replied.

'In that case,' I said, 'let's forget the shaving part, and concentrate on the getting me out the door bit.' And taking the towel he handed me, I made for the sink, washed and was back with him in about thirty seconds flat.

'What about my clothes?' I asked.

'I'm told they're still at forensics,' the cop replied. 'Sorry, sir, but you'll just have to go out the way you are.'

However, I wasn't about to argue over the dress code for being released on bail. Accordingly, I was quietly let out the back door of the High Street cells, into Fleshmarket Close, wearing the prison uniform: striped shirt, ill-fitting brown serge jacket and trousers and black shoes with no socks. On reflection, I realise I was slipped so silently into the street because the drug squad had no lawful authority to remove me from prison and place me in a cell in the police station, and, no drugs having been found, aware the attempted murder charge was absolute nonsense, were getting shot of me as quietly as possible.

I came out of Fleshmarket Close, into summer sunshine, and the sound of St Giles' bells pealing loudly on a Sunday morning, looking like I'd got dressed out of a skip. I headed up the High Street, ignoring the stares of people passing, and at the traffic lights at the top of the Mound, hailed a black cab and told the driver to take me to an address in Colinton.

The taxi pulled up outside the large, detached house. I hadn't a penny to bless myself with, so told the taxi to wait, walked up the garden path and rang the doorbell. After a few moments, the house door opened, and a boy, about nine years of age looked out at me.

'Tell your dad to come. I want to see him, son,' I said to him.

The young boy stared at me, taking in my shabby appearance, the ten days' worth of stubble on my face, turned and shouted back inside.

'Dad! There's a tramp at the door wants to talk to you.'

A few seconds later, my business partner Ray appeared and burst out laughing when he saw the state I was in.

'Do me a favour, Ray,' I said. 'Pay the driver.'

Five minutes more found me under a hot shower, scrubbing away the stink of D Hall Digger and the High Street cells, before scraping my face clean with a disposable razor. A quarter of an hour later, I was sat at the breakfast table where Ray put a plate of bacon, egg, black pudding, sausage, and beans in front of me. But this time, I greedily gobbled it all up, washing it down with a couple of cans of cold lager.

27

'Round and round the garden, like a teddy bear'

— Children's nursery rhyme

It was the summer of 1988, and I was back to work, but was now on bail for allegedly attempting to murder a detective inspector of the drug squad, five charges of perverting the course of justice, plus some more minor stuff the Crown had tacked on for good measure. Things were still a tad hot for me, so, going by the maxim 'a change is as good as a rest', I decided to head off to Spain for a week. While there, I got talking to a cop by the hotel swimming pool one day. For some reason he assumed we were on the same side as he boasted to me that he'd kicked the mince out of some poor guy he arrested in London, then charged him with police assault. As a result, the officer received £1,800 criminal injuries compensation, and decided to blow it on a break abroad. It seemed wherever I went, I ran into bent cops.

Speaking about bent cops, I'd been back in Scotland for a week or so after my brief sojourn abroad, and was driving along Pollokshaws Road, Glasgow, when I became aware of a car directly behind me which seemed to have been there for quite some time. Not again!

I took a sharp left at the lights, drove down to the Ivory Hotel, U-turned, and headed back up to the lights at Shawlands Cross which were then at red. The other car pulled over to the left, then a few seconds later also U-turned and drove up to the traffic lights, just as they turned green.

I took another left, and the other car came too. It was clear I was being followed, so I pulled over and parked, and watched as the other car copied my movements some fifty yards or so behind. I hadn't a clue what was going down, but as it seemed rather iffy, I thought it best to have a bit of back-up, and I knew just who to call. My mate no longer moves in that world and has done rather well for himself as a legitimate businessman. Back then he hadn't crossed over from the black market to the open one. Having said that, I've yet to be convinced there's any difference between them.

I phoned my friend and found out he was also in the southside, not far away, and I asked him to come and collect me. Ten minutes passed, still the car behind me didn't move, and a few moments later, Paul Ferris arrived. I got out of my car, climbed into his passenger seat and as we pulled away from the kerb, the car began following us.

I explained what was happening, or to be more exact that I didn't know what was happening. Paul, being Paul, decided to put some distance between us and the car, stuck the foot down and we flew along Pollokshaws Road, with the other vehicle still behind us. We headed for Busby, taking various twists and turns on the way, and when we approached the mini roundabout on the main street, I told Paul to drive round it twice. He did. The other car followed us right round both times. Clearly, they had no wish to hide the fact they were on our tail.

However, as we completed this manoeuvre, the car behind came so close I was able to recognise the driver. It was one of the detective constables from the Edinburgh drug squad who'd been involved in the high-speed chase along Slateford Road, months before.

After circling the roundabout a second time, Paul turned sharp right and started driving up the hill, but the traffic suddenly came to a halt, due to roadworks being carried out. There was a set of temporary traffic lights up ahead and these were at red.

At that moment there was a lull in the flow of traffic coming towards us, and as the car following us pulled up behind and stopped, Paul said, 'Let's overtake this line and see what that lot behind us do.'

With that, Paul, a talented motorist, pulled out into the right-hand lane, shot past the line of cars on our left and, performing a perfect handbrake turn, joined the flow of traffic now coming down the hill, so that we passed the cops on our right, giving them a wave as we went.

Once safely out of sight, I called the drug squad in Edinburgh and asked to speak to a detective sergeant, whose first name was Jimmy. Jimmy was one of that rare breed of police officer, a good guy who played the game hard, but by the rules.

'James McIntyre here,' I said. 'Any chance you can tell me why that clown,' and I gave his name, 'is driving round Glasgow, following me in my car?'

There was a moment's silence. Then ...

'There must be some mistake.'

'No mistake. I clocked him twenty minutes ago, he's been tailing me ever since, and I'm with a witness. Either that, or he's got a twin brother, and no mother's that unlucky.'

'But it can't be him, it makes no sense, that officer is suspended from duty,' said the DS. 'I don't understand this.'

'That makes three of us,' I said and ended the call. Confused? You bet. But wrong? No way. It was him alright.

Back in the day, the Edinburgh drug squad were zooming about in bomber jackets and jeans, sleeves rolled up to the elbows, emulating Don Johnson from *Miami Vice*. A few of the young female fiscal deputes fell for some of them. That didn't end well. I heard from a reliable police source that several of the drug squad lived up to the name and enjoyed using some of the drugs they confiscated, which never made it to the productions department. Enquiries I made with a retired police inspector I'm friendly with, also revealed that the cop in question who I'd clocked following me had apparently been suspended in connection with alleged mortgage fraud.

Talk about hypocrisy. But it's always the same with these guys. There's one law for them, and one law for everyone else. When, in the unlikely event a cop ever comes before a court and the judges are summing up, they almost fall off the bench, so busy are they bending over backwards trying to get the jury to acquit. The courts do this as it doesn't do for the public to lose faith in the police force. But the reason an ever-increasing number of the public don't have faith in the cops is largely because of the bias shown them by the courts, who pretend to believe their perjury, and so the vicious circle continues.

The cops who arrested me after the car chase in Slateford Road were perfectly capable of telling a pack of lies. In their statements, different officers gave different versions of the event. Some claimed rather than me pulling over and parking, they'd overtaken me in a car, cut across the front of my car forcing me to stop. One cop claimed he had dragged me out the driver's door, while another stated he had leaned across and pulled me out of the passenger side.

Anyway, I understand the detective constable following me round Glasgow that day was apparently taken to court, but unsurprisingly (after all, he was a cop) was found not proven, a verdict particular to Scotland, as explained previously. But hey, a walk's a walk, so good luck to him.

I don't know if he remained in the police force after this, or if he was quietly put out to pasture with his pension; neither do I know to this day why he was tailing me around Glasgow. My guess is he was trying to get some sort of Sam Spade, Jim Rockford, Private Eye thing going; thinking perhaps if by following me, fitting me up, he'd score points for his own case. I neither know, nor care.

28

Prosecutor: 'Did you attempt to murder this man?'
Accused: 'No, I did not.'
Prosecutor: 'Do you know what the penalty is for perjury?'
Accused: 'Yes, and it's a lot better than the one for attempted murder!'
– Old Scottish play

By now, I'd been on bail for a year, still carrying on business as usual for my clients, when I received a call from my solicitor, Alex. The Crown had eventually concluded that perhaps I hadn't attempted to kill this detective inspector after all, but rather just tried to run him over a bit, causing him to dive out of the way as my car hurtled towards him at three miles an hour.

Anyway, the Crown dropped the charade and the charge. Now, instead of the High Court, I was facing a sheriff court indictment for assault to the danger of life. This was still a load of baloney, and I told Alex so. He agreed. When were the Crown ever going to get it into their heads that I hadn't tried to run that clown down?

More weeks passed, and Alex contacted me again. It seemed that the DI involved didn't get on too well with his troops, wouldn't allow them to smoke or drink on duty, even if they were in a pub, in plain clothes, when it would make them appear more plausible, as a couple of guys in a shady boozer drinking Irn Bru was a bit of a giveaway.

Anyway, apparently, because of the inspector's Calvinistic adherence to the rule book, a certain amount of disquiet existed in the ranks, and there was a general reluctance to back up his claim that I'd tried to run him over. Once again, the man upstairs was looking out for me. In any event, Alex advised me the Crown were prepared to reduce the charge to one of dangerous driving, stick it on a summary complaint, and leave it at that. Rather than risk going to trial, as who knows what porkies the cops and the Crown would have come up with if pushed, I instructed Alex to accept the deal.

The date for court arrived and Alex in turn instructed the late Donald Macauley QC to act for me. Donald, tragically no longer with us, was a truly charming man, a terrific lawyer, and after being made a Baron took his seat in the House of Lords.

The case called in front of a Sheriff Hendry, who struck me as someone who took himself very seriously. He'd been shipped in to deal with the matter, as I didn't regularly appear in front of him as a defence solicitor. The fiscal depute was, if I recall correctly, Alistair Brown, who went on to become a sheriff somewhere. Whilst he was always keen to prosecute, unlike many he was by no means (at least not to my knowledge) a hypocrite, and always pleasant enough, even though I never lost a trial to him. In fact, if I'd beaten him one more time, I got to keep him.

Donald Macauley tendered the guilty plea on my behalf, together with the mitigation appropriate to the situation. He stated clearly that I had not been driving the car at Inspector McCrae but rather in his direction and reminded the court that I had not been driving at high speed. He further told of the considerable indignity I had been subjected to in prison, which you, dear reader, will no doubt recall.

At the close of Donald's plea in mitigation, the sheriff described what had happened as highly bizarre, but stated, 'I must deal with matters as they appear before me,' and I was fined £400 and disqualified from driving for twelve months. He then asked me, 'Do you require time to pay?'

'One week, my lord.'

'Very well.'

The sheriff clerk repeated the sentence, the time to pay and I stepped out of the dock, put on my court gown, as the sheriff clerk called the next case, 'PF against Mark Jones.'

I stepped forward, coming into the well of the court, much to the chagrin of the sheriff, and said, 'I appear with Mr Jones, my lord. He tenders a plea of not guilty.'

The late Donald Macauley was a gentleman, and refused to charge me a fee, but I delivered two cases of champagne to his house, which I'd bought from the once infamous Jimmy Boyle, who after leaving prison started buying and selling wine from abroad. My case was now over, and it was back to business as usual. But it was becoming crystal clear that things were getting way too hot for me in Edinburgh as far as the forces of the Crown were concerned.

29

Judge: 'Miss West, are you trying to show contempt for this court?'
Mae West: 'On the contrary, Your Honor, I was doing my best to conceal it.'
— Mae West

The District Court is basically a prank the Scottish legal system plays on the public, by summoning someone to what's called, rather paradoxically, the Justice of the Peace Court, as there's little peace, and even less justice.

These courts deal with minor crimes and offences, consequently a considerable number of cases involving people from different backgrounds are handled each week. Being convicted of any crime can have a calamitous effect on a person's life, relationships, career prospects, credit rating, plus cause a host of other problems, so to leave such matters in the hands of some cretin is beyond belief.

But here's the joke! In the district court, 'His or Her Honour' the magistrate, the person selected by the system as best suited to decide someone's guilt or innocence, knows absolutely nothing about the law. In this Topsy Turvy Land things are turned on their head. The judge is a layperson, while the clerk a lawyer. One almost expects the Mad Hatter to be the fiscal, and on some occasions could be forgiven for thinking he or she is.

Justices of the Peace are normally local councillors, or some equally worthy individual, convinced of his or her calling to pass judgement on their fellow man. Apart from an ability to consume a large liquid lunch, complete an expenses sheet (paid for by the public purse, filled by the very people being prosecuted), no other qualification is required for an appointment to the bench. Apart from one. This, however, is vital. While giving evidence, if the police state the moon is made of apple pie, or something of equal veracity, the Justices of the Peace are duty-bound to believe them and convict the accused, in the same fashion many sheriffs do in their courts.

Strict observation of this condition, together with the standard of selection of persons for this position, demonstrates clearly that the amount of care taken to safeguard against wrongful conviction is entirely and totally non-existent.

A client of mine, homeward bound after an evening outside of Glasgow, was travelling in a car which conked out yards short of the boundary of No Mean City. While others pushed, my client leapt into the driver's seat to jumpstart the vehicle. As he did so, a passing panda car pulled up and two cops who, apparently having nothing else to do on a Saturday night in the knife capital of Europe, alighted and decided to investigate.

It was a frosty February evening. A search of the car failed to find anything of an incriminatory nature and the cops were about to abandon hope of arresting someone and returning to the warmth of the station for tea and biscuits, when one woodentop spotted the tax disc on the windscreen was out of date. Being the owner of the vehicle, my client was duly charged with the relevant offence under the Road Traffic Act 1972.

Some months later, my client turned up at the office waving a complaint, citing a date for a pleading diet in the Justice of the Peace Court in Dumbarton. There are more heinous crimes than driving with an out-of-date tax disc. Unfortunately, that was the problem. My young brother, also a defence lawyer, who continues the fight against the forces of darkness, confirms that obtaining legal aid in most cases is more difficult and complicated these days; however, though things were a tad simpler during my time, even then, the chance of SLAB (Scottish Legal Aid Board) granting legal aid for a non-endorsable offence was so remote, the Hubble telescope couldn't have spotted it.

So it was, despite a full explanation of the extenuating circumstances, legal aid was denied. A second application employing some degree of poetic licence was also refused. Finally, I fired off a last-ditch attempt, basically a pack of porkies, with the view the end justified the means and phoned the fiscal's office in Dumbarton, advising I was unable to appear at trial and, rather than leave my client in the lurch, asked if they'd agree an adjournment to a new date until a decision on legal aid had been reached.

Normally this request would've been met with shrieks of hysterical laughter before being refused, but, as one of the cops was due to go on annual leave at the same time, the fiscal was happy to agree, and offered to make the joint motion in my absence the next day.

The following morning, two policemen arrived at my office and announced I'd been ordained. This had nothing to do with me taking holy orders. Before a person appears in court for trial they may be ordained, bailed, or banged up. Having experienced all these more than once, believe me, being ordained is by far the lesser of three evils.

On this occasion I was required to attend the district court in Dumbarton the next day to explain my non-appearance on the previous one. Taken aback, I told the cops about my call to the fiscal's office, the agreed joint motion to adjourn, only to have this fall on deaf ears. I also advised them that my client had been refused legal aid and the charity sign hanging outside belonged to the Saint Vincent de Paul Shop next door, and that I was running a business.

They in turn advised me that failure to appear would result in a warrant for my arrest and they'd be delighted to come back and drag me to Dumbarton in chains. And to think that some say the police don't offer a valuable public service!

I parked my car and headed inside. Despite having never visited this provincial outpost, I'd a pretty good idea what to expect and accordingly abandoned all hope of anything approaching a fair hearing.

Once inside, I introduced myself to the clerk of court with a cheery smile, advising him I'd a heavy workload in Glasgow that day, and would be obliged if this matter could be dealt with ASAP, only to find my fears confirmed. The clerk, a mouselike creature, obviously recovering from a recent personality bypass, pointed me to the public benches, in a manner that made it clear no preference was to be shown to solicitors who'd fallen foul of the law.

Ten minutes later the justice deigned to make an entrance, sweeping onto the bench in a majestic manner, lacking only a fanfare of trumpets to mark the occasion. He bowed to the clerk, who almost prostrated himself in return, and proceedings began. At least they did for everyone else. It was only after hearing every single case on the list that His Honour decided the time had come to deal with me.

Peering over a pair of pince-nez, doubtless purchased to appear as imposing as possible when passing judgement on some poor soul for littering, this pompous person proceeded to lecture me on the way to conduct oneself in court, as if he'd written the handbook himself. As it transpired, this joke of a justice was a primary school headmaster in real life, and he began to address me as if I were some six-year-old caught skiving school.

He was still droning on and on about the duties of an officer of the court when I enquired if he'd be much longer, as I had clients queuing up back in Glasgow. For some reason he reacted badly to this interruption, stating he was considering a conviction for contempt of court. I looked around, attempting to discover who he was referring to, but the public having left and the clerk smiling as obsequiously as ever, by process of elimination I took him to mean me.

On realising this, I enquired in what way I'd shown my contempt for the court. Staring at me over his pince-nez, the magistrate stated I should have attended his court when the case against my client first called. Realising he obviously didn't have a clue, I explained I'd agreed an adjournment in advance with the procurator fiscal's office. At this stage, His Majesty advised me that he, and only he, held the power to adjourn and by assuming he would grant the motion, I had usurped his authority. Usurped? Who did this guy think he was?

Trying desperately to keep it together, I informed His Pomposity that agreeing adjournments with the Crown were part and parcel of the everyday running of the Scottish courts, saving time and the expense of having witnesses turn up, merely to be sent away, only to be again advised by His Highness that he, and only he, decided what went down in Dumbarton District Court.

As it was becoming increasingly clear that what was very likely to go down was yours truly, I changed tack and explained my client had been refused legal aid, and, as I was not in receipt of funds, was not required to attend court, especially as the adjournment was not opposed, and began gathering my papers, preparatory to leaving. At this point, His Magnificence told me to stay where I was, and that as an officer of the court I indeed had a duty to attend, whether I was paid or not.

This was, of course, ludicrous. I invited His Honour to tell me if he was being paid today or merely sitting up there on the bench because he enjoyed the view. My remark resulted in the magistrate being momentarily struck dumb, allowing me the opportunity to point out that not appearing when there was no funding, and when an adjournment was agreed, was not contempt, and that if he had been a lawyer, he would know that.

Horrified at what he referred to as my 'insolence', in a tone he doubtless used when calling out, 'Settle down 3C and open your colouring books,' he stated:

'While I am a layman, as far as the law is concerned, my clerk is a qualified solicitor and perfectly capable of advising me of the relevant law in each case.'

There are times when enough is enough, and this was one of those times. I could see the contempt conviction was clearly on the cards; accordingly, I looked down at the clerk sat directly below his lord and master, before turning back to His Omnipotence, and telling him:

'I beg to differ, Your Honour. If the clerk were even half as capable as Your Honour claims, he wouldn't be wasting his time in Dumbarton District Court, advising magistrates like you, who clearly don't have a clue what they're doing.'

And that, dear reader, is how to get convicted for contempt of court in style.

30

'More things are wrought by prayer than this world dreams of.'
— Alfred Lord Tennyson

The gents' toilets could really have done with a lick of paint. Checking I'd locked the door, I knelt on the cubicle floor, crossed myself and started a prayer I hoped would travel past the peeling plaster on the ceiling.

'Lord, the Crown's so desperate to convict my client, they can taste it. "Let he who is without sin" doesn't cut much ice in this court. Please, help me get my client a walk. Amen.'

Crossing myself once again, I stood, dusting cigarette butts from my trousers and black gown. Tearing some tissue from a dispenser, I blew my nose, fished my money clip from my pocket, took out a tenner, rolled it into a tight cylinder and looked up at the ceiling.

'I know, I've said it so many times before, but I swear, I'm stopping this.'

I hit the handle. Flushing water smothered the sound as I stooped, snorting the white line that lay on top of the cistern. I blinked, my nasal membrane burning before Bolivia's best slipped into the bloodstream. Straightening, I shrugged my gown firmly onto my shoulders with a final sniff, checking my face in the cracked mirror above the sink.

My client, who will remain nameless, but known only too often as 'the accused', sat dwarfed between two security guards in the dock of the court. A skinny, massively made up nineteen-year-old, she wore the same micro skirt and white stilettos that'd drawn the vice squad's attention the night of her arrest. I caught her eye from my seat in the well of the court and pulled a 'look at you' face. Talk about dressing for the part? Poor kid. Her last punter had probably dropped her off about ten minutes ago.

I glanced over at the fiscal depute. She wore a tweed jacket, skirt and sensible brown brogues. The outdoorsy type, she was a great lover of nature, which was surprising when one considered what nature had done to her. She flicked through her file, her mission being to tick all the boxes, plug any gaps through which this poor wee Sugar Frostie might by some miracle escape. The macer called 'Court' and the sheriff, a fat man in his forties sporting a red face and white wig, entered the room; yet another failed advocate who had spent a spectacularly unsuccessful career at the bar before finally selling his soul to become a floating sheriff, although by the looks of him, he'd more than likely sink.

As I stood to bow, I spotted what looked like several holiday brochures under his arm, along with a notepad. We're all aware of what tends to float to the top, and Tubby was no exception, desperate to impress the powers that be and improve his chances of a permanent sheriffdom, somewhere, anywhere. If forced to remain at the bar and defend people, he could starve. Though that would take some considerable time.

Facing me sat fifteen solid citizens, each ready to perform their civic duty. Later, in his charge, the sheriff would explain reasonable doubt, hinting there was none whatsoever to trouble them in this case, coaxing them down the path to conviction. The fiscal drew the examination in chief to a close, performing a double act with her witness.

'So, to recap, detective constable, you observed the accused soliciting a client for sexual purposes.'

The witness nodded.

'She approached a parked car and got into the passenger seat. And when you attempted to arrest her, she struck at you with a knife, cutting your hand?'

'My right one, ma'am,' he answered, and held up his arm, so there could be no confusion about the fact he at least knew his right from his left.

'I understand this required you to attend the A&E for stitches?'

The witness nodded again. 'Yes, ma'am. Six in total.'

I whistled facetiously under my breath. The fiscal glanced sharply at me, but Billy Bunter on the bench heard nothing, his head bowed, doubtless browsing his brochure, 'Weekend Breaks in Barcelona', in his mind tasting tapas and sipping sangria in some backstreet bodega of the Catalonian capital.

'And this resulted in the accused being charged with assault to severe injury.'

'Correct, ma'am.'

The fiscal turned to the jury, ensuring they appreciated the savagery of this attack by a seven-stone girl on a seventeen stone policeman. Sensing a pause, the sheriff lifted his pen, pretended to make a note, while actually circling a price for seven sun-soaked days on a beach somewhere in the south of Spain.

'Did she make any reply to caution and charge?'

I was on my feet in a flash, pointing at the witness. 'Don't answer that!'

I turned to the sheriff. 'Nobody has said anything about my client being cautioned, my lord. Who's giving evidence here, the fiscal or the witness?'

The sheriff looked supremely bored as he turned to the detective constable.

'Was the accused cautioned?'

The witness nodded. He was getting good at that.

'Yes, my lord.'

The sheriff nodded back, and began once more to peruse his brochures, as if he'd solved the problem to everyone's satisfaction. I glared at the bench. Enough was enough.

'My lord is reading – I mean *leading*. We only know my client was cautioned because my lord decided to enter the forum and lead the witness.'

The sheriff's eyes rose over his half-moon specs.

'Merely clarifying the situation, Mr McIntyre.' He turned to the fiscal. 'Madame fiscal?'

The fiscal beamed. 'Obliged, my lord.'

She turned once more to the witness. 'Did the accused say anything in reply to caution, officer?'

The witness took out his notebook, purely for effect. He was word perfect. After all, a criminal injury compensation claim was on the cards.

'Yes, ma'am, she stated, "That bastard wanted the blowjob, why don't you charge him?"'

'Good question,' I said in a whisper that could've been heard halfway to New York. Two men on the jury glanced at one another and gave the glimmer of a smile.

'Did you say something, Mr McIntyre?' enquired the sheriff.

'It's not important, my lord. I think my client has clarified the situation.'

The sheriff drew me a look, which I studiously ignored. The fiscal ticked the last box on her sheet. 'No further questions, my lord.' And she sat, with a sweep of her barbed-wire skirt.

'Any cross-examination at all?' muttered the sheriff, I supposed at me, as he didn't bother to look up, doubtless mentally wading into the warm Mediterranean water.

I stood and began pacing in silence. Fifteen pairs of eyes followed me. Suddenly, I spun round, and spoke loudly to the witness.

'Get off, you fat bastard!'

The jury gasped in unison. The fiscal sprang to her sensibly shod feet, startling the sheriff. But before she could formulate an objection, I continued:

'Isn't that what my client said, when you grabbed her?' I asked, with as innocent a face as I could pull. Walter had taught me well.

I waited for his reply, as the fiscal sighed and sank back. The jury glanced at one another, a few started to giggle. The sheriff bit his lip, crimson, but impotent.

'Yes, but,' began the witness.

I cut him off. 'Because you were pulling her hair at the time!'

'I was arresting her for—'

'How could she know who you were?'

'We both showed her our warrant cards.'

'But at the time, my client was busy bent over and—'

'Mr McIntyre!' blurted Billy Bunter.

'—looking for her handbag, my lord.'

The sheriff didn't seem convinced that was to have been the conclusion to my question, but I continued, unabashed.

'Is it not a fact that, without any warning, you opened the passenger door, grabbed my client's hair, and as you pulled her out, she screamed at you and lashed out in panic?'

'She cut me with a knife,' he said.

I picked up a tiny penknife from the productions table. It had a tan coloured label attached, on which 'Number 1' had been written with a black magic-marker.

'This little toothpick? Label number one for the Crown?'

'Yes.'

'Hardly a machete, is it?'

'It's still a knife,' he replied, though rather weakly.

'Barely,' I said. 'Certainly not in the same league as the stuff cops carry . . .'

'Kindly refrain from referring to the officers as cops,' cut in the sheriff.

'. . . such as batons, tasers, CS gas, guns . . .'

'And kindly confine your cross-examination to asking questions!'

I smiled towards the bench. 'Certainly, my lord.' I turned to the witness. 'Isn't that right, officer?'

'Congratulations, Mr McIntyre,' said the sheriff. 'However, the witness needn't answer, as the point remains quite irrelevant.'

This was, of course, quite correct. Statistically speaking, the sheriff had to get something right at some stage; however, I continued to ignore Tubby, turned towards the jury and addressed the witness with my back to him, the way they do on American TV shows.

'Would you kindly tell the court what happened to the punter my client was with?'

'Mr McIntyre!' the sheriff cut in again, sighing heavily. 'I must insist you stop employing these colloquialisms. The jury may not know what a punter is in such circumstance.'

'I felt sure my lord would know from his experience . . .'

Someone on the jury suddenly giggled. A girl's voice, I thought.

'. . . of sitting on the bench,' I continued. 'As surely the term falls within judicial knowledge. Perhaps, as before, my lord could clarify the matter, as my lord is wont to do.'

The sheriff gritted his teeth.

'Rephrase the question.'

I bowed and turned back to address the witness.

'What happened to the person my client was with? Surely, he must have witnessed this alleged assault on you?'

'I can't say what he saw. As we were attempting to control the accused, the man drove off before we could obtain his details.'

'The fact is, you let him go, to keep things nice and simple, isn't that right?'

The fiscal rocketed to her feet. 'My lord . . .'

'Sustained!' shouted the sheriff. 'Mr McIntyre, this officer doubtless has other duties. Have you anything remotely relevant you wish to ask before I excuse him?'

'Forgive me, my lord, I was under the impression allowing a vital witness to leave the crime scene was rather relevant?'

The sheriff glared at me as I turned once more to the witness.

'You knew this mystery man could corroborate my client and let him go! Didn't you?'

The cop drew back in the witness box, doing his best to appear horrified, but before he could reply, I fired again.

'His evidence would not only scupper any conviction, but your compensation claim would have been up the creek too, correct?'

Fifteen faces stared at the vice squad officer, but by now he had perfected his horrified look.

'That's a lie!'

'You're an expert in that field officer, as your evidence has been a pack of them.'

The sheriff leapt to the rescue. 'That's quite enough!'

He turned to the jury. 'Ladies and gentlemen, I have to advise you, as a matter of law, there is no evidence to support what Mr McIntyre just stated as regards the person who left the scene.'

But the damage had been done. Walter's words came back to me once more. The sheriff may as well have dumped a lorry load of dung in the courtroom, and announced, 'As a matter of law, there is no smell.'

I beamed at the bench.

'No further questions, my lord.'

Strolling back to my seat, I caught the eye of a middle-aged lady in the front row of the jury. I winked, Walter style. She allowed herself a small smile. It'll come as no surprise when I tell you the second vice cop came up with an identical story, so I won't bother with the details.

The Crown closed their case, and it was now my turn to decide whether to have my client give evidence. One glance at the poor girl told me there was no point putting her in that box, when she was out of her own, having clearly shot up in the ladies' loo before the case kicked off. I turned to the bench.

'I lead no evidence, my lord.'

The closing speeches followed, with the Crown as usual completely counting on the cops being believed. Of course, nine times out of ten this works, where the sheriff or magistrate is the sole judge, but a jury trial is a totally different ball game. When my turn came, I pointed out to the good citizens that we only had the police witnesses' word for what happened, and no independent evidence whatsoever.

'Ladies and gentleman, the only independent witness in this case would have been the punter . . .' I glanced at the sheriff, then turned back to the jury. '. . . I should say, the person you'll recall the police allowed to leave the scene, very shortly after he'd paid my client to suck his penis.'

The jury glanced at one another, trying not to laugh, and I felt the sheriff's eyes burn into the back of my head, but I had their attention; now it was time to pluck at the heart strings. Walter's words rang in my ears. '*The last thing a jury ever listens to is the evidence.*'

'The cops, sorry, the *police*, told you my client's a heroin addict, who'd sell her body for a tenner bag, and they're right. But with her background, abandoned at birth, brought up in care, forced to survive on the streets, her chances of becoming prime minister were always slim.'

The jury smiled. The sheriff didn't.

'So it was, when a big burly guy grabbed her from behind, she thought she was being mugged, like the time before, and the time before that. It's an occupational hazard for these girls. Anyway, she was so far out her face, she didn't know if it was New Year, New York or New City Road.'

Then I hit them with what I liked to call 'The Three Ifs'.

'Ladies and gentlemen, *if* this was the High Court, and *if* this was not a charge of assault but murder, and *if* this was the year 1964, when capital punishment was still in force, are you so certain beyond, any reasonable doubt . . .'

I pointed at my client shivering in the dock –

'. . . of that poor girl's guilt, that you would send her to the gallows, to hang there by the neck until she was dead . . .'

I turned, pointing contemptuously to the two cops sitting at the back of the court.

'. . . on the evidence given by those two officers?'

I stared at the fifteen for a full five seconds, letting my words sink in. Then, my job done, I bowed respectfully and returned to my seat. The jury were led out to deliberate but were back within an hour.

The clerk of court stood and turned to face the fifteen men and women.

'Ladies and gentlemen, who speaks for you?'

The lady in the front row I'd winked at rose to her feet.

'I do.'

'Have you reached a verdict?'

'We have.'

'On the charge on the indictment, how do you find the accused?'

'We find the accused not guilty.'

'And is that verdict unanimous, or by a majority?'

'Unanimous.'

Bingo! I don't care what drink or drug anybody takes, bungee jumping, sky diving, riding a rocket into space: in my book, nothing comes close to the rush you get when a jury returns a not guilty verdict.

Ten minutes later found my client and me trotting down the court steps. Once outside, she turned to me.

'Thanks, James. I thought I was going to Cornton Vale.'

'Never say never. But not today.'

An awkward moment passed before she asked, 'Any danger I can tap a tenner?'

'Traditionally, the client bungs the lawyer,' I said.

'Just until tomorrow. I'll pay you back, honest. I'm gonnae get something to eat.'

We looked at one another: both of us knew what it was for, but neither of us said. I fished the tenner from my side pocket, unrolled it and handed it to her, in the sure and certain knowledge I'd never see it again. Her face brightened.

'You're a star. Catch you later.' And with that she pecked me on the cheek, turned and clattered across the street in her white stilettos, in search of one more bag of magic dust.

31

'Now this is the law of the jungle, as old and as true as the sky. And the
wolf that shall keep it will prosper, but the wolf that shall break it shall die.'
                                                              – Rudyard Kipling

Linlithgow Sheriff Court, and I was defending a client on a charge of
assault to severe injury. This was not a case of some innocent person
being assaulted, but rather a fight between two clients of mine, both
smack addicts, over a parcel of drugs, and one of them had slashed
the other. The police had arrived on the scene and charged one of
my clients, but after he got bailed both agreed there was no danger
of the guy who got cut sticking his mate in and identifying him at
court.

However, by the time the case came up many months after the
incident, I couldn't be sure if these two smackheads were still bosom
buddies or even recalled the deal they'd made, as both usually had
a hard enough time remembering what year it was. The client who
was the main prosecution witness had himself been in trouble during
the interim period, was banged up in prison, brought to court that
day by a couple of screws, and immediately placed in the Crown
witness room beside a bunch of cops. Clearly any conversation with
him to mark his card and assist his recollection of what had been
agreed between him and the client I was defending was now out of
the question.

Once the case kicked off, I had no option but to think on my
feet, or as it happened sitting down. Accordingly, when the main
Crown witness was called, and the preliminaries dealt with, the

vital moment came, and the fiscal said to the witness, 'I'd like you to take a look around the room and point out the person who slashed you.'

I couldn't take a chance on my client adhering to the criminal code. Accordingly, as the witness turned to look round, I started shifting my seat about in the well of the court, strategically positioning myself so I was sitting in as direct a line of vision as possible of the person giving evidence in the witness box, and the accused sitting in the dock.

I was wearing a black court gown, leaning back in my chair, elbows out, making myself as wide as possible, attempting to present the biggest obstacle I could, in order to obstruct the witness's view, and stop him from spotting and identifying my client. However, on looking round and seeing me sitting about five feet from the table, the fiscal tumbled to what I was up to and, turning to the bench, addressed the sheriff.

'My lord, Mr McIntyre has shifted his seat, so he is sitting in front of his client and blocking the witness's view, and I should be obliged if you'd order him to move.'

The sheriff looked at me, enquiringly.

'Well, Mr Mcintyre,' he said.

'Very, my lord. And you?' I smiled.

The sheriff sighed.

'The fiscal appears to think you're sitting in a position which prevents the witness from seeing your client.'

'My lord,' I replied, rising, 'I think the fiscal will find I'm allowed to sit where I wish, in the well of the court, without first asking her permission.'

'But he's blocking the witness's view,' the fiscal whined.

'Mr McIntyre?' The sheriff raised an eyebrow.

I nodded and moved my chair a couple of millimetres to the left.

'He's still blocking the view,' persisted the fiscal, petulantly.

'Mister McIntyre?' The sheriff's eyebrows rose farther up his forehead, almost reaching his wig. I sighed heavily, and moved my chair another fraction, this time to the right.

'He's just moved back to where he was,' moaned the fiscal.

At this point I rose to my feet with all the affected indignation I could muster.

'Really, my lord, things have indeed come to a pretty pass when the defence requires permission from the fiscal depute as to where they may or may not sit.'

At that point, I looked away from the sheriff and turned my gaze directly on the witness in the box, hoping that what was taking place in front of him might awaken some memory, spark some slight recollection of the deal he'd done about not identifying his mate. I continued, still staring at the witness, while addressing the bench.

'Perhaps, my lord, the fiscal would like to me to come over and sit on her lap. That way there'd be no chance of me blocking anybody's view, except for possibly the fiscal's.'

'That won't be necessary,' said the sheriff.

I nodded and sat back down.

The sheriff turned to the witness. 'Are you able to see everyone in the court?'

'Yes, Your Honour,' answered the witness, adhering to the long-standing tradition of clients addressing the sheriff by the wrong title.

'Very good.' He turned. 'Madam fiscal?'

The fiscal rose to her feet and asked the question again, this time at greater length.

'I'd like you to take a good long look around the court, and if you see the person who slashed you, point him out.'

I confess to feeling a tad nervous, but as I watched, any fear I felt faded away, for the witness began to take the good long look the fiscal had requested, by first staring at the sheriff for several seconds, then at the sheriff clerk, then slowly shifting his gaze and looking along both lines of the jury, then up and down the public benches, before he suddenly stopped and pointed.

'That's him there,' he said. 'Yes, that's him alright.'

However, unfortunately for the fiscal, this formal identification was to prove fruitless, as the person pointed out was a defence solicitor, who, while waiting for his own client's case to kick off, had taken a seat in the public benches to pass the time; plus, of course, to watch the master at work.

As a result of the accused not being identified, the case immediately collapsed, and my client left court a free man. Either the movements with my chair jogged the witness's memory, or he'd been sufficiently in touch with planet earth to recall his promise and keep the criminal code, and all ended well.

It never strikes the Crown that, while they are quite happy to prosecute someone for the possession of a tiny amount of a drug, they expect the same accused persons to play by their rules when they appear as witnesses in court.

Had this witness identified my client, and he been convicted as a result, the repercussions to the witness would have been immense in his world. I don't merely mean that revenge may have been taken, as they were hardly heavy hitters, but he'd be known as a grass, a midnight, a snitch, and would have found it difficult firstly to finish his time in prison unscathed, and secondly to score drugs on his release as he'd have been shunned by his peers.

The Crown, procurators fiscal and their deputes inhabit a different world than these people, live by different rules, yet expect others to do as they're told. Of course, as I've mentioned elsewhere, should a representative of the Crown fall foul of the law, a way will be found for him or her to at least avoid the full consequences. Accordingly, as far as I'm concerned, what's sauce for the goose is sauce for the gander, and all this nonsense about a defence lawyer being an officer of the court is exactly that, nonsense.

In my book, you're there for your client, and nobody else. Let's face it, there are plenty on the other side pulling more strokes than the Oxford rowing team, so the defence have got to even things up as best they can. I've been out of the defence game for a while now, but even when I was involved, there were more than a few defence lawyers who were far more concerned in sucking up to the sheriff than they were getting their client a result.

32

'A ferret-faced crook, with a cunning beyond his years.'
– Newspaper's description of Paul Ferris

'Got a knife on you?' asked Paul. Even back then, this struck me as a strange question considering we were sitting facing one another in a cell in Her Majesty's Prison Barlinnie. Nowadays in jail, the security checks are similar to those at airports. All sorts of scanners, metal detectors and machines are used to tell if you've touched any drugs recently, which for reasons best known to those who pass the laws at Westminster (in between falsifying expenses and getting half cut in the private members' bar) stops people visiting prisoners.

But, back in the eighties and the nineties, things were far more relaxed. I've known Paul for over thirty-five years. I first acted for him in an appeal against sentence when he was in Shotts prison serving three years. I was his solicitor and Donald Findlay his QC. There had been a recent riot at the jail, involving a great deal of destruction, and an officer was taken prisoner. Paul had acted as intermediary between prisoners and staff and succeeded in negotiating a deal. As a result, the prison officer previously held captive by several cons was released unharmed.

The governor of Shotts prison wrote a personal letter of commendation to the High Court, praising Paul's efforts; however, the appeal court took no notice of this and refused to reduce his sentence. I recall being very surprised at this, but Paul merely smiled and said he hadn't expected anything else.

'It's all politics, James. Just politics. They need to show who's in power.' Some years later Paul was charged with the murder of Arthur Thompson Junior, known as 'Fat Boy'. Paul and his friend Bobby Glover were both remanded in custody for seven days, during which time I received a phone call from Bobby from the untried hall in Barlinnie, asking me to come and see him. However, before I had a chance to do so, he was granted bail and murdered. After the then longest running criminal trial in Scottish history, Paul was acquitted of the murder of Arthur Thompson Junior by the unanimous verdict of the jury.

The incident related here took place in 1991, but before I began to write about it, I called Paul, himself a published author, whom I have collaborated with on other matters, to double check what happened back then. After hearing what he said, I realised his recollection was much clearer than mine; and he knew more about the background. So, I'll hand the matter over to Paul:

'I was in Barlinnie prison, serving a short sentence of three months due to driving a Sierra Cosworth that had been stolen and rung with new registration plates and tax disc. I received the vehicle as part payment of a debt I was owed. It turned out to be cloned, but I didn't know; how could anyone have known?

People in the business of cloning cars, or ringers, don't do it so that you know they've done it, as that would defeat the purpose in the first place. However, the judge decided that, despite all I said (which was completely true, I've no reason to lie now, I did at the time) there was no reasonable doubt, found me guilty, and I received a sentence of three months behind bars, for reset. Bit excessive don't you think, when a previously convicted paedophile got bail, seconds before I got sentenced. Justice? Ha!

So, I was in B Hall, middle landing, as a short-term prisoner. The opposite side of the landing housed some of the Paisley gangs who were on remand awaiting trial, which meant they had way more privileges than a convicted inmate. We were all kept apart, as were the Paisley gang members in B Hall and some of their opposition on remand in C Hall.

If you're ever in B Hall in Bar-L, which I hope you never are, when it rains outside, there is a form of one-hour exercise within the landing area – a bit like Midnight Express, only a Glasgow version. Convicted prisoners cannot mix with untried prisoners and as such, we all walk the same landing during inside exercise. One day my spyhole opened, and a voice said to me, 'Okay, wee man, how are you?'

I went to the cell door, looked to see who it was, and burst out laughing. It was my mate Addie's cousin, who told me to expect some canteen goods and asked if I wanted a bit of cannabis, but could I also do some of the untried prisoners a favour?

Who would refuse such an offer in these circumstances? I, like most convicted prisoners, was on less than £7 a week: meanwhile, the Paisley mob, being untried, were spending like sailors on leave at the canteen. So, I agreed, and we eventually formed a plan that the Paisley crew would leave items in the shower area for me, or, whenever they found my cell door open, they'd fire in and stick the canteen items under my bed if I was at work. By work, I mean going from my prison cell to sit in an induction area full of total madmen who wouldn't be getting any jobs at all.

In these days, untried prisoners, because they weren't convicted and so retained the rights of an innocent person until proven guilty, were allowed to have food sent in from outside, but this has all changed now due to drugs being smuggled into the prison by these means. Drugs are of course widely available inside and stopping the food deliveries merely meant finding other alternatives and depriving genuinely untried prisoners of this human right.

Anyway, back then the Paisley crew had take-away food sent into them from the local Chinese and Asian restaurants. I remember returning to my cell, and the smell of food hit me: no prison slops, this was real food. The screw who opened my cell door to hand in my share of the grub the untried Paisley boys had ordered stated he wanted some too. I nodded in agreement, and he closed the cell door. I opened the bags the screw had passed in, and what I saw next made me feel like a king! The bags contained chicken curries, madras, dopiaza, korma, rice, chips and a cardboard box full of crisps, Irn-Bru, chocolate, biscuits . . . There was no need for millionaire shortbread, I already felt like a millionaire! The deal was that we did this every second day, and it was magic.

I was due to be freed shortly – but then disaster struck. One of the untried Paisley crew stashed some drugs in my cell when I was out and the door was open. The guy'd had to get rid of it because they had been singled out for a search, as some smart-ass Sherlock Holmes screw got a whiff of cannabis from their cell, hence the need to stash it in mine.

I was made aware of what was going down in what's called a 'stiffy', which is a small note, folded and refolded, sealed with a cigarette paper, passed by one prisoner to another, till it reaches the person it's intended for, advising him of the position. On reading this, I looked under my bed and noticed a rather large mass of cling film, the size of a fist, and opened it. All I can add is that there was no heroin. But lots of cannabis, blues, other tablets and a bit of cocaine. I knew it was cocaine when I dabbed my finger and did the taste test and thought, 'Who the fuck wants to take that in jail?'

All this was done on the day right before my release date, and the reality was that there was no way I could get the parcel to the Paisley division. What the fuck was I going to do? Take it out of jail next day? No chance! I was pondering how I could possibly get this lot to the people it was intended for but had basically run out of ideas when my cell door opened and a screw told me I had a legal visit.

My lawyer at that stage was James McIntyre, who went on to be given the name 'Jimmy Two Guns'; a maverick in the legal profession, but enemy number one of the Crown.

Hearing he'd come to see me, I got ready, only to be informed by the prison staff that the visiting area was full and it was getting late in the day. However, James insisted on seeing me, and accordingly – and I've no idea how he talked them into this, but I can guess he started yelling about prisoners' rights – I ended up consulting with James in an empty cell on the ground floor in B Hall. I'd never known this to happen before, it was very unusual, but also very effective, and allowed me to formulate a plan to provide the Paisley crew with their parcel.

When I met James in the bottom flat cell, he told me he'd come to see me to get me out of my cell for a while and had kicked up a fuss when the agents' room was full, so ended up in B hall. The guy's more stubborn and aggressive than a Pitbull at times. As usual, we discussed many issues, we always did, we still do now we're both out, but there was one matter on the agenda I really wanted to put to him.

'Got a knife on you?' I asked. James nodded. It turns out he had two. (As his nickname suggests, he always likes at least two of everything!)

I told James the whole story, what I was going to do if he gave me one of the knives, and as I spoke, he sat there laughing his head off. Let me tell you, there's been no lawyer I've ever heard of, before or since, who would have gone along with my plan, but James was one of us. Whether he granted my request for the knife or not, I'll leave you to guess, but I'm sure it won't take you too long.

We concluded our chat as I was to be freed the next day and was escorted back to my prison cell. I waited just before lockup – 8.30 p.m. – and pressed my cell button so that the prison officer on duty on my landing would come to my door.

What follows is a matter of fact, there's no need to big up a story, it's true, and I couldn't care, nor will James, who we pissed off in the authorities; it was what it was.

I told the screw that there may be a security issue and wanted to speak with my Uncle Tam Ferris: this guy had the same surname, but in reality, was no relation at all, it was just a bit of prison banter.

My cell door was then opened, and I was taken down to the PO's (Principal Officer's) office. There were at least four prison officers, along with Uncle Tam. They asked me what the security issue was, so I explained that since I was going to be a free man the following morning, I was willing to surrender my personal weapon. I then produced a stainless steel lock-knife, opened it in front of a shocked audience, which suddenly froze on the spot, and I stuck the point straight into the desk, so that the knife quivered as I released my grip, and as I did so, suggested an amnesty. The look on the screws' faces was priceless.

The first question was, 'How many more blades are there?' I pretended to count to ten on my fingers, then shrugged and said, 'Several.'

Next question was, 'Can you get the rest of the weapons?' Of course, in reality there were no other knives even close to that quality or calibre – so bluff and counter bluff came into play.

I indicated that I would need to get some help from fellow inmates to surrender the fictitious weapons. Accordingly, I was then granted full access to all cells, which meant I could then pass on the Paisley parcel, and this worked out a treat.

Those in the know will know this – others may think 'bollocks'. It was as surreal as you can get and everyone was surprised how I got access to their cells and the screw walked away from a convicted inmate (me) to chat with the Paisley crew who were on remand – it should never have happened but this amnesty was very effective.

I gave to everyone who wanted what was theirs, then went back down the stairs and told Uncle Tam the lads would sort the rest of the weapons out, when in fact there were none.

There was a bit of a leaving party that night for me, as I'd done what had to be done under the circumstances, but without the help from James, things would never have worked out so smoothly. No credit to me and full credit to J2G for trusting me and before I knew it, I was in reception the next day – rough mind you – and that is one jail story that has never been told before.

33

'I had considered how the things that never happen are often as much realities to us, in their effects, as those that are accomplished.'

– *David Copperfield*, Charles Dickens

It was a Saturday night and some of my clients, all Celtic supporters, were enjoying a drink in the Nile bar, despite the place being recognised as one frequented by Rangers fans. To be clear, I acted for clients, many of them friends, from opposing sides of the old firm sectarian divide, and defended each to the best of my ability, so there was no question of favouritism on my part.

On this occasion, the client concerned was Frankie Donaldson, who the papers insist on referring to as 'Doughnuts', which implies someone of an impetuous nature, whereas the opposite is true. Frankie never made a move without planning it first with military precision. With him was James Skiverton, called, not surprisingly, Skivvie, and Alex McClure, known as Dady. Alex's brother Neil was fifteen months old when Alex was born, and, unable to pronounce baby, said 'Dady', and the name stuck.

After a while, they became aware of four men staring at them across the packed pub. Feeling the mounting tension, my clients thought it wise to avoid trouble and head to the Cotton Club, off Sauchiehall Street, a popular place during the eighties and nineties. Finishing their drinks, they left the bar, and were walking up West Nile Street when Dady suggested they take his car and collect Frankie's in the morning.

At that moment a voice behind enquired, 'What's the matter. Can you no afford the petrol?' This comment was accompanied by several sniggers.

Turning, Frankie realised the four guys from the bar had followed them out. He looked at the person posing the question.

'I'd shut my mouth, if I were you,' he said and turned back to Dady's car, which by now contained his friends.

However, this sage advice went unheeded, and the group advanced.

'Five-one, ya prick, ye,' said another of the four, referring to a recent Rangers win over Celtic, further provoking Frankie, a season-ticket holder at Parkhead. Skivvie and Dady, both as game as a pebble, made to get out the car to assist their friend, but Frankie waved them back.

'Forget these clowns!' And turning again to the group, he said, 'One more word, and your tea's oot!'

Should this book have attracted any reader from south of the border, not entirely au fait with the phrase 'your tea's oot', immortalised by the great Frankie Miller in Peter McDougall's film *Just a Boy's Game*, this doesn't imply the gong for dinner has just sounded, but rather that someone may shortly receive their comeuppance.

'Aye?' said guy number one. 'What're you gonnae—' But unfortunately before he could finish his question, events overtook him, as Frankie smashed his fist into the man's face, knocking him out cold. A second guy took a tentative step forward, only to be kicked in the privates, and the following uppercut left him on the pavement, alongside his associate.

At this point, two police officers in a passing panda car, noting the ongoing disturbance and Frankie's well-kent face, pulled over and leapt out. Discretion being the better part of valour, the two remaining antagonists took to their heels, Dady put the foot down and headed with Skivvie for the Cotton Club, while Frankie legged it up one of the lanes leading off the main street, leaving the fallen Rangers fans staring at the sky.

However, as fate had it, Frankie's escape route turned out to be a dead-end, and, cornered by the cops, who, recognising him and realising they had the prize, dragged him in cuffs to Stewart Street police office, where he was charged with a breach of the peace by fighting with persons unknown and released for citation.

I was in the office loo and had just torn a page from the glossy Law Society Journal, rolled it into a tube and was about to partake of a livener, when one of my secretaries, Michelle, shouted me to get a move on. I finished up quickly and headed through to find Frankie ensconced in my chair, chatting up Frances, another of my secretaries, a stunning girl with raven curls, former Irish dancing champion, whose mother, a devout Catholic and daily communicant, dropped in on her way back from Mass to clean my office and tidy the mess I'd made.

I shooed Frances back to reception and asked the bold boy what I could do for him. Frankie handed me a copy complaint he'd been served, apprising me, truthfully, of the events in West Nile Street that night.

At this juncture, it's important to state that, while it is perfectly permissible, and indeed often highly advisable, to lie to your wife, mother, the whole world, it is completely unacceptable to lie to your lawyer or priest. One deals with the court down here, the other the court above. In this instance, one glance at the charge confirmed all I needed to know. As per usual, the cops were at it.

In criminal defence, by far the hardest charge to be acquitted of is what's called a 'Two Cop Breach of the Peace', or indeed any case involving only your client and two police officers as witnesses. If such a case goes to trial, the court nearly always pretends to weigh the evidence of the accused against that of two police officers (sometimes there's very little pretence involved) with the result that ninety-nine times out of a hundred the accused is found guilty.

Frankie's case was set down for the district court, in St Andrew's Street, Glasgow. It always struck me as ironic this court was situated in a street named after Scotland's patron saint, apostle and martyr, when a flashing neon sign should have been hung over the entrance stating, 'Abandon Hope All Ye Who Enter Here!'

In these courts, as has been mentioned before, the clerk is a solicitor, while the lay magistrate knows as much about the law as a koala bear does about quantum physics. I had no idea what our defence was and decided all I could do was roll the dice and play it as it came.

On entering Court 7, after the call over, I clocked Frankie, Billy and James Monteith, Jacko, Dady, Skivvie, Toddy and a host of other clients, sitting at the back, waiting for the show to start. All that was lacking was someone selling popcorn.

Just then, the bar officer entered, calling, 'Court!'

Everyone stood as the justice entered. Everyone that is, except my clients who remained rooted to their seats, and, as there was no one else in the public benches, this lack of respect seemed more like a silent protest.

'Great start, guys,' I thought.

Frankie's trial was first up, and as the clerk called his case, he came forward to take his place at the front. I looked up at the bench, and suddenly noticed just who the justice was. When I say 'who', I mean 'what', as in what nationality. He was a Pakistani gentleman, immaculately turned out in a bespoke striped suit, blue shirt, yellow tie, matching the gold signet ring set with a red stone worn on his wedding finger. One glance told me the guy thought he'd arrived. Against all the odds, the abuse, racist references he'd doubtless put up with, obstacles he'd overcome, here he was, a councillor, someone of note, ready to decide the fate of a fellow human being. I beamed at him. He smiled back, nodding politely. The wheels in my mind began to turn.

Glasgow back then was a different place than now. It would be another year before Rangers manager Graeme Souness stunned the support by signing Mo Johnson, a former Celtic player and Catholic. Religious tensions ran high (they still do), Paradise flew the green, white and gold Irish tricolour, filled with fans singing rebel songs, while across the city at Ibrox the Union Jack fluttered in a breeze turned blue by the sound of the sash being sung.

As I stared at the justice, a particular song came to mind; one, in fact, I'd heard recently, at the Old Firm game referred to earlier, which I'd attended with Frankie, when Celtic lost 5–1. Admittedly, I'd heard a different, but equally racist, version at Parkhead too, but then, I was trying for three points here.

The clerk of court confirmed my client's name, things kicked off, and the fiscal called her first witness. Despite being heard by the lowest court in the land and the fact the case boiled down to a Saturday night rammy, the fiscal seemed to be taking matters very seriously. Doubtless the cops had advised her of my client's place in the pecking order of Glasgow's underworld, and she was very keen to convict a major player, even if it was for a minor offence.

Now sworn in, the fiscal led the first cop through his evidence, a work of fiction he and his colleague had collaborated on. Then came my chance to cross-examine.

'Constable, you've told His Honour,' I smiled to the bench, 'that on the evening in question, you were on duty with a colleague driving along West Nile Street, when you saw what appeared to be a fight in progress. Correct?'

'Correct.'

'So, as this fight was already in progress, you clearly didn't see how it started.'

A slight pause, then . . .

'No, not really.'

'By not really, you mean not at all. Correct?'

'I suppose not.'

'Yes, or no, constable?'

'No.'

'So, for all you know, my client may have been assaulted by these other men, before you and your colleague came on the scene?'

The cop hesitated again, glanced at the fiscal, then looked at me.

'I suppose it's possible,' he grumbled.

'Please, stop supposing, constable. For all you know, as you admit not seeing how things started, my client may have been the victim of a savage sectarian attack, is that right?'

'Maybe,' said the cop. 'But he was fighting too.'

'You also stated you alighted from your vehicle and detained Mr Donaldson, during which time the others involved fled the scene.'

'That's correct.'

'Clearly they were keen to avoid arrest?'

The witness hesitated a third time. I stared him down.

'These men didn't hang about to make a complaint of being assaulted, did they?'

'No,' he conceded, grudgingly.

'I mean it's not as if you just let them go, is it?'

'Absolutely not,' said the cop, apparently horrified at the suggestion.

'Then it seems very likely they were guilty of something, yes?'

'Perhaps,' he said, which was a refreshing change from, I suppose.

'Why else run from the police?'

The cop shrugged. The fiscal wriggled in her seat. I continued.

'Of course, it's common knowledge in Glasgow that the Nile Bar is a Rangers pub. In fact, it's nicknamed the Blue Nile.'

The fiscal started to rise . . .

'Isn't that right, constable?' I added, turning my evidence into a question.

The fiscal sat back down.

'It's been known to be frequented by Rangers fans.'

'Tell me, officer, at any point did you hear the men that ran away shout the following words at my client . . .'

At that point, I picked up a sheet of paper, apparently reading from it carefully. Of course, it was completely blank, and I was ad-libbing.

'Hey Donaldson!'

I looked towards the bench as I continued . . .

'Fuck you and your Paki pals, you Fenian bastard!'

The justice sat bolt upright and turned to the witness. The cop, stunned, didn't answer.

'Well, did you hear these men shouting that or not?' I asked.

'No, not at all,' replied the cop, struggling to understand what was going on.

'Do you know what someone means when they call a person a Tim, constable?'

'It is a derogatory expression for a Roman Catholic,' he replied.

'And is it your evidence to His Honour, you didn't hear these men chanting, "I'd rather be a darkie than a Tim"?' I asked, quoting the song I'd heard at Ibrox, a few weeks ago.

'I certainly didn't hear that, no.'

'But, of course, you admit you and your colleague missed the beginning of this fracas, so, though you didn't hear these words, these men may well have uttered them, yes?'

The cop looked lost. The fiscal leapt to her feet to assist him.

'If the police weren't there at that time, how could they possibly know what was said or shouted?'

'My point exactly. I'm much obliged to my friend.' I smiled at the fiscal and turned to the witness. 'So, you agree, constable, these words could have been said?'

'I . . . I suppose so.'

This time, the word 'suppose' suited me perfectly.

'Tell me, did you happen to notice a car with some Asian friends of Mr Donaldson drive off at any point?'

The cop's blank look returned, he glanced at the fiscal, who was clearly furious, but helpless to object to the question.

'No,' he said. 'I did not.'

'But again, as you've made clear to the court, you arrived late, therefore a car with some Asian friends of my client may well have driven off, for fear of being assaulted?'

The fiscal jumped up.

'Objection. That's not a question.'

'My friend must've missed the inflexion in my voice.' I smiled at His Honour. 'Let me rephrase that. What I meant was, it's entirely possible these Asian gentlemen, feeling extremely unsafe at the hostile attitude of those who attacked my client, had left before you arrived, isn't that right?'

By now, the fiscal was fuming, as her objection had allowed me to lead even more evidence. However, the justice, clearly concerned with the apparent danger the imaginary Asians I'd invented may have found themselves facing, was waiting for an answer, his pen poised over his pad. I turned back to the witness.

'Well, isn't that right, officer?'

'Well, yes . . . yes,' he spluttered, adding, 'I mean, anything's possible if . . .'

'Thank you, constable.' I beamed and bowed to the bench. 'No further question, Your Honour.'

The fiscal, her face like a horse in the buff, rose to re-examine, but the best she could do was get the cop to repeat he hadn't seen or heard any of the things I'd put to him, as he hadn't been there, and by so doing, succeeded in hammering home to His Honour what I'd said may have happened.

The second cop was called and the depute and I danced again. She confirmed what the cop saw and did, while in cross-examination I confirmed again, for the court's benefit, that though the cop hadn't witnessed what I said could have happened, it was entirely possible it could have before he and his colleague arrived.

At this point the fiscal formally closed the Crown case, and I rose, and bowed to the bench.

'Your Honour,' I said, 'I make the motion there is in fact no case to answer.'

Of course, this was utter nonsense. There was clearly a case to answer, but there was no harm in testing the water. For anyone not sure about the rules of evidence regarding criminal cases in Scotland, if two witnesses state Donald Duck is the President of America, while this isn't true, this would still mean there was corroborated evidence that one of Disney's most loved cartoon figures was the leader of the free world, no matter how unlikely, technically there would be a case to answer.

However, if only one witness stated the *Titanic* was an ocean liner that hit an iceberg, sinking with tragic loss of life, while true there would not be sufficient evidence in law to substantiate the fact.

In this case, two cops had given evidence to the effect Frankie committed a breach of the peace by fighting with persons unknown, so, true or not, there was a case to answer. But nothing ventured, nothing gained.

I remember once my old mentor, Walter Sutherland, returned from conducting a case before a lay magistrate in a district court in the Borders for a client, a farmer, who had been bang to rights, but who Walter had taken to trial before the magistrate. At the end of the case, Walter told the magistrate there was not enough evidence to convict his client, and if he was found guilty, Walter would immediately appeal the case to the High Court, with the result the magistrate acquitted the accused. I recall asking Walter at the time, 'Can you do that, Walter?'

'In Jedburgh you can, son,' replied the bold boy.

Okay, this wasn't Jedburgh, but it was the district court, with a lay magistrate and a fiscal on the verge of a breakdown, so I figured it was worth a shot and spurred on by these words, I'd chanced my arm and, bingo, it worked.

'I agree, there is no case to answer,' said the justice.

However, unfortunately, this wasn't the Borders, and this decision brought the fiscal rocketing to her feet, and despite the magistrate's ruling, the fiscal and the clerk together convinced him that, technically, he must refuse my motion, which he did, with reluctance.

The motion being refused, the fiscal eyed me with anticipation, desperate for me to put my client in the witness box, to back up that what I said may have happened had in fact happened, and ask him to produce his imaginary Asian friends, enquiring why he hadn't called them as defence witnesses, so she could rip him to pieces amid cries and accusations of perjury.

I rose and bowed solemnly at the justice, and said mistakenly, but deliberately . . .

'I lead no evidence, my lord. Or rather . . .' I corrected myself, 'Your Honour.'

This morsel of flattery was not thrown out in vain. The justice nodded regally as I regained my seat. The clerk rolled his eyes at me, as the fiscal, fizzing, rose to sum up and try to remove any reasonable doubt that had now arisen re my client's guilt. She banged on and on about the absence of any evidence of sectarian or racist abuse, claiming the court must look at the facts . . . But just then, rather clumsily, I knocked over a jug of water on the table and began patting the puddle dry with paper towels, causing an unfortunate distraction in the court that lasted throughout the whole length of the fiscal's closing address.

My turn to sum up arrived, but by then, from the justice's reaction to my earlier motion, I knew the seed had been sown in fertile ground and was bound to bloom. So, after lamenting the reality of racism, the need for mutual respect between religions and races, and painting my client as a modern-day hero, a citizen of the world, rushing to the defence of his fellow man, I invited the justice to acquit my client, and took my seat.

'Stand up,' said the clerk of court.

Frankie stood.

'I find you not guilty,' said the justice, to the applause, cheers and cries of: 'Nice one!' from clients watching in the public benches.

Before he left the bench, the justice bowed to both sides, but when he looked at me, gave a small smile. On my way out, the fiscal approached me saying she had a good mind to report me to the Law Society, for putting things to witnesses that hadn't happened. I smiled at her.

'Knock yourself out. But remember, firstly, you don't know if they happened or not; more importantly, I didn't say they did. I merely asked the police if they saw certain things take place. I could just as easily have asked if they'd seen the Pope and King Billy riding past their panda car on a bicycle made for two.'

As I left the building with my client and company, delighted justice had prevailed, even if I'd helped push it along the path, I wondered if by playing the race card I'd pulled the wool over the justice's eyes, or, like me, he thought it unfair one guy should be left to carry the can for a stramash outside a Glesca pub on a Saturday night. I recalled the smile he gave me as he left the bench and thought he certainly hadn't got where he was now, beaten all the odds by being taken for an idiot. Maybe he wasn't as wide as the Clyde, but the Ganges? Probably.

34

'Two things are infinite: the universe and human stupidity; and I'm not sure about the universe.'

– Albert Einstein

In any criminal prosecution the identification of the person charged with the commission of a crime is clearly crucial; accordingly, it's vital the case is conducted fairly. Despite the word 'dock' being used to describe the area where the accused sits, strictly speaking, no such place exists in a Scottish court.

Further, as the accused's future, relationships, employment prospects, etc. could all be adversely affected on conviction, it's clearly in the interests of justice that the person hearing the evidence and delivering the verdict has some semblance of an idea of what they're doing.

Unfortunately, as mentioned before, in my day, and I'm reliably informed the situation remains largely the same, many lay magistrates couldn't find their bum with both hands, never mind grasp the law applying to the cases brought before them; accordingly, desperate to convict, as with so many sheriffs, they simply believe the police: job done.

The worst type of sheriff to conduct a trial in front of isn't necessarily the most ill-tempered, nor the hardest sentencer, but rather some civil lawyer, or conveyancer, who wouldn't know his way round a criminal court if he had satellite navigation: one elevated to the shrieval bench as a reward for time served on some irrelevant Law Society committee, a Former Advocate Depute, a Fiscal Depute, or some sycophantic, unsuccessful defence solicitor, happy to throw such clients as he or she has to the wolves.

I was once one of four defence agents acting for four football casuals in a trial taking place at the old Falkirk Sheriff Court. Each client had been charged with a breach of the peace, having allegedly behaved in a disorderly manner, by shouting and swearing, and calling the police 'Gestapo bastards', which was then the standard phrase the cops claimed was uttered by anyone being arrested for this type of offence, thus ensuring they all got their story straight in the witness box.

When inventing what they were going to say the accused had said, one would've thought that the police may have mixed it up a little, varied the wording of the abuse allegedly uttered, but Scotland's finest nearly always stuck to the same old tried-and-tested script. After all, 'if it ain't broke, don't fix it', and they were going to be believed anyway.

The case called and all four clients filed into court and sat down in the dock in the order in which their names appeared on the complaint. The offence alleged had taken place at a football game many months prior, and presumably the police witnesses had arrested scores of other people at dozens of other matches, and elsewhere since.

Accordingly, unless these cops had been bitten by a radioactive spider, been exposed to the glare of gamma rays, or something similar, resulting in their gaining superhero-style powers, it was unlikely they'd be able to identify our clients after that length of time; that's if they told the truth, which was a huge 'if', and not one anybody really expected.

The police deal with many people during a stint on duty, and in nearly every case of this type, by the time the trial comes round, unless the accused is a repeat offender, and well known to the local constabulary, there's no danger the cops can truthfully identify the accused at court. These accused persons were from Edinburgh, attending a football match in Falkirk, and therefore completely unknown to the officers from that area who had arrested them many months before. As an old criminal defence lawyer of my acquaintance often advised the jury, 'The police have a very difficult job to do, and they do it very badly.'

However, long ago the cops came up with a solution to this conundrum. Undeterred by the dilemma which the passage of time presents, they enter the box, swear to tell the truth, then point to the person in the dock, and identify them as being the one responsible for the crime in question. This is a simple procedure, employed by the police and commonly called 'committing perjury'.

As I've mentioned previously, it's a little-known fact that the 'dock' is in fact an English term. Certainly, the layout of the Scottish courts is such that the accused sits at the front, directly facing the clerk, while above the clerk sits the magistrate, sheriff, judge, whoever's on the bench.

However, technically in a trial involving multiple accused, persons may elect which order they sit in. This very rarely happens, which is unfortunate, as when a witness is asked if they can identify the accused persons, it's a bit of a giveaway, since they're sitting in a row in the same order as they appear on the complaint. They'd be as well sticking them under a sign with a flashing neon light stating 'guilty person'.

Realising the police were about to do the same old dance, resulting in our clients being railroaded, found guilty and sentenced, I suggested to one of the accused's lawyers, Adrian Smith, that we move a motion to have the accused sit in a different order. Adrian agreed, as did Sarah Dougall and the other defence agent, whose name escapes me.

The sheriff in this case was a man, who I can only presume owed his elevation to the shrieval bench as a reward for perhaps having been some pen pusher, or past president of the Law Society, or something equally irrelevant to the life of a court lawyer, as it can't have been because he'd the least clue as to what he was doing.

The man entered the courtroom with the same expression of wonderment which doubtless appeared on Columbus' face when he set foot in the Americas for the first time.

The case called, and I stood to move the motion each of us had agreed upon.

'My lord, I move that the accused persons be permitted to sit in positions different to the ones in which they are presently placed.'

Adrian, Sarah and the other defence agent rose, aligned themselves with my motion and retook their seats. The sheriff looked baffled, rapidly removing his glasses, to kill time and try to work out what was happening; then, after glancing at the fiscal, asked me, 'And why do you want the accused persons to change position?'

'Because at present, my lord, our clients are sitting in the same order as they appear on the summary complaint.'

'And?' enquired the sheriff. The man on the bench was not being facetious, he simply hadn't a scooby doo what I was on about.

'Well, my lord, the cops – rather the police witnesses in this case also have a copy of the complaint, and therefore know the order in which each of the accused is seated, which could adversely affect identification.'

'In what way?' asked the sheriff, apparently still clueless in regards to the point being made.

'Because,' I began, embarrassed to be stating what seemed the incredibly obvious. 'The police witnesses may identify the accused from their order on the complaint, rather than rely on their own memories.'

The fiscal, now alerted to the motion, and alarmed at the fact that if it were to be granted and a departure from the normal course of events allowed, there was an imminent danger of justice being done, immediately got to her feet.

'The Crown strongly resents the implication made by my friend in his remark about the police and opposes the motion. It is standard practice for the accused to sit in the order on the complaint; accordingly, there's no reason to depart from the normal procedure. Furthermore, the motion is pointless as it would make no difference to the police identification of the accused.'

The fiscal's last sentence gave me an in.

'Since my friend believes the accused swapping seats will make no difference, there can be no prejudice to the Crown case, and therefore our motion is clearly in the interests of justice.'

The sheriff allowed my words a second or two to sink in, then slowly his lips began to move . . .

'Motion denied.'

He beamed at the Crown, like a big baby seeking approval for pooping in his potty.

I stood, affecting a heavy sigh.

'In that case, my lord, as a result of certain advice I shall be giving my client at the close of today's proceeding, I may be instructed to take the matter further. Accordingly, I'd ask my lord's clerk to note that . . .'

And I looked at the clerk of court, who was already picking up a pen, and continued.

'. . . while formally opposing the motion, the fiscal depute specifically advised the court that the Crown case would not be adversely affected were the motion to be granted; that being so, one wonders why it was objected to in the first place . . .'

To my left, I could feel the fiscal fizzing. I glanced up at the sheriff. He was all ears, and that wasn't just because they were humungous. I turned back to the clerk.

'. . . yet, despite no valid reason being given for opposing said motion, made in the interests of justice, the court has denied said motion.'

I sat down, satisfied I'd pronounced the word 'motion' a sufficient number of times to get my point into the sheriff's head. Sure enough, a moment later, he beckoned to his clerk, who stood and turned towards him. As the sheriff was sitting behind the bench, their faces were level for a moment. The clerk muttered something quickly, the sheriff nodded, and the clerk turned and resumed his seat. The sheriff looked over his rimless spectacles.

'I'm going to rise for a few moments, as there is a matter I wish to discuss with my clerk.'

Accordingly, the bar officer called 'court'. We all stood. The sheriff rose, bowed briefly and, nodding to his clerk, beat a retreat to chambers.

Ten minutes later the sheriff was back. The bar officer called 'court' again, we did the bowing bit again, and got down to business. The sheriff cleared this throat.

'I've, eh, taken some time to, eh, reconsider the defence motion, and after some thought, come to the conclusion that, on this occasion, it could possibly be argued, at least to some extent, that it is in the interests of justice and accordingly the defence motion is granted.'

The old boy, clearly worried we'd appeal, had had a word with his clerk, who'd recommended he grant our motion. After all, it was no skin off his nose who sat where. The depute drew the defence a look as if one of us had stolen her dolly.

The motion now granted, we set about shifting our clients, so instead of sitting in positions 1, 2, 3 and 4 they now took positions 2, 1, 4 and 3. I'll spare the reader the details of all that took place next: suffice to say four police witnesses followed one another into the witness box, and when asked to identify which of the accused had acted in the manner libelled on the complaint, every officer successfully picked out the wrong person on each occasion.

Finally, at the conclusion of this farce, the Crown closed their case. But, despite the complete lack of identification, the fiscal did not move to withdraw the complaint. Clearly, she'd realised, like the rest of us, that the sheriff hadn't a clue what he was doing and decided to wing it. Justice, as in the case of many fiscals, was the furthest thing from her mind.

As solicitor for the first accused, I was in the act of rising to my feet to submit there was no case to answer, when suddenly a voice rang out from the bench.

'I find each accused guilty as libelled.'

Taken aback, I turned to the other agents, who were likewise lost as to why the sheriff would deliver his verdict at this stage: nor were we alone, as the fiscal, the clerk and indeed our clients all seemed equally confused. I stood.

'Forgive me, but is my lord not rather premature? I was about to submit, due to the non-identification of my client by any Crown witness, there is no case to answer.'

I turned to Adrian Smith and my colleagues as I continued. 'Plus, I understand my colleagues all intended making similar submissions.'

The other three nodded vigorously in agreement, and stood to advise the court they had intended making a submission on behalf of their clients. The clerk, clearly embarrassed, stood and, turning to the sheriff, addressed him in an inaudible undertone. After a few seconds, the clerk resumed his seat and the sheriff announced:

'Very well, Mr McIntyre, I'm prepared to hear your submissions.'

I got to my feet again.

'My lord, my submission is in short compass. As none of the Crown witnesses were able to identify my client as the person acting in the way described on the complaint, there can be no case to answer, and he must be acquitted.' I sat down, ready to be finished with this farce.

Adrian Smith rose next, made an identical submission, followed by Sarah and the other agent, who also requested the court to acquit. At this stage it was the fiscal's turn to try to convince the sheriff he should consider there was sufficient corroborated evidence to convict each accused. Normally, the fiscal would have had more chance of convincing the court that, in the event of a foggy Christmas Eve, there was sufficient evidence Rudolph the Red-Nosed Reindeer guided Santa's sleigh.

However, there was no need for the fiscal to move, as before she could clamber to her feet and try to come up with some reason why the case should continue for another nano-second, a voice sounded from the bench . . .

'I find each of the accused guilty as libelled.'

Once more, silence reigned in court. Everyone looked at everyone else, and all looked embarrassed – apart from the sheriff, who seemed to think the matter done and dusted. I was forced to get to my feet again.

'My lord, you haven't heard the Crown's position as regards defence submissions.'

The sheriff's face fell.

'Ah!' he said, and turned to the Crown, questioningly, 'Madam fiscal?'

The fiscal rose, and said simply, 'In my submission there is a case to answer, my lord,' and sat down, fully aware that she was lying her backside off but needn't elaborate further for the sake of Old Elephant Ears, who was clearly desperate to convict.

The fiscal's bottom had no sooner touched the seat than we heard again . . .

'In that case, I find each of the accused guilty as libelled.'

There was an audible groan from the clerk, as I stood up once more.

'My lord, the defence haven't had an opportunity to intimate whether we intend to lead any evidence.'

The sheriff's face fell even further.

'Whoops. I've done it again,' he said, predating Britney Spears by several years.

I forced a smile. 'It would appear so, my lord.'

'Do you, in fact, intend to lead any evidence?' asked he of the huge ears.

'I certainly don't now, my lord.'

Adrian, Sarah and the other defence agent all stood and intimated they would not be leading any evidence either.

The reader would be entirely forgiven for assuming, as would any sane person, that, by this time, it had to have dawned on the balloon on the bench, having completely cocked things up so far, that it was best to find all the accused not guilty and catch the next train back to Cloud Cuckoo Land. But no! Instead, the Brain of Britain announced, 'In that case, I find each of the accused guilty as libelled.'

By now, the clerk of court was on the point of collapse, the fiscal-depute had dodged behind a stack of files on the table, while I and the other defence agents were looking about us, half expecting Jeremy Beadle to burst into the courtroom crying, 'You've been framed' (and not by the cops for a change).

Yet again I got to my feet.

'My lord, with respect, you haven't heard closing speeches from either the fiscal, myself or my friends.'

'Very well, proceed,' sighed the sheriff.

So, proceed we did.

The fiscal got up, advised the court to find each of the accused guilty, and without another word, quickly sat down. But, as her bum hit the seat and before anyone from the defence side could move, once more, Big Ears on the bench pronounced . . .

'I find each of the accused guilty as libelled.'

This latest pronouncement left the clerk pulling his hair out by the roots. I rose.

'My lord, with all due respect –' My tone making it all too obvious I considered no respect whatsoever was due to this numbskull, who saw his entire raison d'être as being to convict all four accused, '– this is the fifth time you've convicted my client, and the other accused, and on this occasion without bothering to hear from either me on behalf of my client, or any of my friends on behalf of theirs, as to why you should acquit. Suffice to say, not one of the Crown witnesses has identified any of the accused, and therefore as there is not a scrap of evidence they committed any offence, I invite my lord to acquit my client.'

As it was impossible to state the matter any more clearly, I sat down.

Adrian Smith, Sarah and the other defence agent followed, inviting the court to acquit their clients due to the complete lack of evidence against them.

The sheriff nodded and without waiting announced for the sixth time . . .

'I find each of the accused guilty as libelled.'

By now, having little hair left to pull out, I thought that the clerk of court was going to grab a letter opener from the table and commit seppuku on the spot. Enough was enough. I rose once more. I hadn't had so much exercise in years.

'My lord, in view of the court's decision to find my client guilty, despite the fact no witness identified him as committing any crime, I intend to tender him certain advice, and I feel sure my colleagues will act likewise, which will lead to this matter being taken elsewhere. May I suggest my lord adjourns for a few moments to consider matters fully, before finally deciding on a verdict.'

The clerk turned and glared at the bench before nodding pointedly at the door. The sheriff took the hint.

'Very well, I'll rise for five minutes,' he said, and headed back to chambers, the clerk hard on his heels.

Shortly after, the sheriff returned, we went through the bowing malarkey again and took our seats. As we did so, I caught the clerk's attention and he gave me a knowing look, before rolling both eyes heavenward. The sheriff cleared his throat.

'I've given the case considerable thought and concluded a reasonable doubt does exist as regards the evidence in this case. Accordingly, I find each of the accused not guilty.'

It took all the self-control I could muster to stop myself jumping up and shouting, 'Evidence? What evidence? What single solitary scrap of incriminating evidence was there against any of the accused you were clearly desperate to convict, and did convict, six times? You had your head stuck so far up the fiscal's bum it's a wonder she couldn't smell your Brylcreem.'

But I didn't. We'd won. And I'd quite enough convictions for contempt of court to last me a while.

35

'You pays your money and you takes your chances.'

– Old proverb

Even in my day, SLAB (Scottish Legal Aid Board) made the firm of Scrooge and Marley seem like the Salvation Army. I'm advised that the hourly rates for criminal defence lawyers have remained static since 1995, and waiting times, mileage, the cost of travelling to the different courts scattered around Scotland, have all been scrapped, kicking into touch the concept of 'delectus personae', so denying a client's right to choose who they wish to conduct their defence, unless they can afford to pay, or the lawyer decides not to bother feeding his family, and acts for a fraction of the fee the defence deserves.

The argument from the pen pushers at SLAB (who know as much about defending criminal clients as the Pope does about polygamy) is that all defence agents are of equal ability. Of course, the idea is ludicrous, as anyone who's been charged and defended by some conveyancer who happened to be on duty that day will doubtless be aware.

This ridiculous concept also comes into play when a client requires the services of a member of the Faculty of Advocates and is known as the 'Taxi Rank'. In the same way as someone standing in a taxi rank can catch the first cab that comes along and find it equally capable of conveying them to their destination, so the availability of a particular counsel is considered of no account, as their abilities are deemed to be equal. This logic is clearly flawed. There are some excellent defence counsel, Donald Findlay, Gordon Jackson, Edgar

Prais, Neil Murray, and others, who over the years have produced results in cases where the Crown considered a conviction certain, but at the other extreme there are some real duffers.

Back in the early nineties I was instructed to conduct the defence in numerous jury trials each year and sometimes, the cases would overlap. The trouble was, if you gave the file to a solicitor from another firm, you'd never see the client again, such was and doubtless remains the cut-throat nature of those involved in criminal defence. This meant I required to instruct junior counsel to handle the case if I was double booked.

Indeed, a great deal of pinching went on, when defence lawyers persuaded other solicitors' criminal clients to sign mandates, transferring their outstanding cases, and therefore the legal aid, to their own firm. I was very guilty of this myself, and in fact at one Bar Association dinner, I was called up to the top table and presented with a bottle of aftershave named 'Mandate' for being the solicitor who had managed to sign up more clients from other firms than anyone else.

Anyway, on one occasion having two indictments calling for trial simultaneously, the first in Edinburgh Sheriff Court main building, which at the time was at the top of the Mound and is now the High Court of Justiciary, and the other calling in the Sheriff Court Annex, on the ground floor of Argyle House, which is in the shadow of Edinburgh Castle. Though always keen to take on the forces of the Crown, I hadn't, nor have yet, acquired the ability to bilocate, and so appear in two places at the same time.

Accordingly, having no wish to try for a hat-trick as far as accusations for contempt of court were concerned, I asked my assistant to arrange for a suitable junior counsel to appear for the defence in one of my other client's cases. The next day I was in Parliament House, talking to a friend of mine, when I spotted my assistant approaching me from the Advocates Hall. For anyone who doesn't know the Advocates Hall, it is (as the name suggests) a hall situated next to the Advocates Library, and was originally an area where, in years long gone by, judges would sit and hear counsels' pleadings on behalf of their clients.

These days, senior and junior counsel walk up the length of the hall, then turn together and walk back, all the time talking to one another. Ostensibly, the reason for this is that, as they are walking, the incredibly important matters being discussed between them cannot be easily overheard by anyone else.

Of course, they could be talking about anything, and when you see a lone advocate walking up and down, hands clasped behind his back, head bowed apparently deep in thought, the chances are he has absolutely nothing else to do, and rather than being busy deliberating on some particular point of law, is desperately trying to figure out how he's going to pay his mortgage, afford his kids' private school fees, or even feed himself. Still, it looks good.

Anyway, my assistant came up and told me that she had just spoken with a junior counsel, but as she was handing him the papers for the trials, he asked her if our client had any defence witnesses to corroborate his innocence. I told her she had to be kidding. She assured me she wasn't. In Scots law, as the reader will doubtless be aware, an accused person is innocent until proven guilty, does not require to lead any evidence to prove anything, and certainly does not need to corroborate his own testimony, should they ever decide to give it.

Unable to quite believe what my assistant had just told me, on spotting the advocate standing at the door to the library, I approached him.

'Excuse me, but I believe my assistant has just handed you a set of papers for a forthcoming sheriff and jury trial.'

'That's right,' he replied, recognising me. 'I have the papers here,' and he held them up.

'And I'm told you asked her if my client had any evidence corroborating his innocence?'

'Yes, that's quite correct,' he smiled.

'Thank you,' I said and, taking the papers from him, left counsel with his mouth wide open. That same afternoon, back in the office, I got a phone call from the advocates' clerk, Douglas Neave, asking why I had taken the papers from one of his counsel after having instructed him in a case. I explained to him that clearly the guy hadn't a clue what he was doing; accordingly, I'd withdrawn the instructions, and we no longer required his services. There was a pause, then Douglas sighed.

'Very well, but of course, counsel will still be sending you a fee for the consultation.'

'He's very welcome to send a fee, Douglas,' I said. 'Of course, I won't be paying it.'

The junior counsel in this case didn't realise that, as mentioned before, an accused does not require to give evidence at all, not to prove or corroborate anything. Of course, with credentials such as those, this very same counsel took silk, becoming a QC, then Lord Advocate, and now sits on the bench as a High Court judge. The defence rests.

36

'If I had a world of my own, everything would be nonsense.'
— Alice's Adventures in Wonderland, Lewis Carroll

Sheriff William T. Hook was as mad as a box of frogs, but a unique and quite unforgettable character. I first appeared in front of him, as an accused, when I was a teenager and took shelter one winter's night in Linlithgow Canoe Club with some pals of mine, which the boys in blue, of course, deemed to be a break-in. During the years that followed, I appeared for the defence in front of the learned sheriff on many, many occasions, one of which was a jury trial that took place in the Assembly Rooms on the Mound, in Edinburgh.

My client on this occasion was the cousin of former Celtic player and coach Neill Mochan. Mr Mochan was facing two charges: one of assault on a civilian, someone who, after a short deliberation, the jury had no problem disbelieving, as they'd all been steaming at the time (the accused and the witness, not the jury), and acquitted my client; however, he had also been charged with assaulting the two cops who arrested him.

While giving his evidence, Mr Mochan had admitted on oath (never a good idea) to having drunk eight pints of heavy, over the course of the whole day, hardly a superhuman feat for a man his age. During my address to the jury, I advised those fifteen solid citizens there was no reason to prefer the evidence of the cops over my client, urging them to acquit him of this second charge. The case was heard in front of the legendary Sheriff Hook, who thanked me politely for my closing speech, and proceeded to address the jury, during which time he advised them:

'Ladies and gentlemen, Mr McIntyre is perfectly correct, you are required to balance the evidence before you decide which parts of it you accept and which you reject; however, you may think that, on the one hand, we have two, young, sober serving police officers going about their duty, both with perfect recall, and on the other Mr McIntyre's client, who, by his own admission, had drunk a gallon of beer.'

There are no prizes for guessing what the verdict was.

Sheriff Hook was one of a kind: some would claim a loose cannon, others call him quite simply insane. Certainly, anything could happen if he was on the bench. His wife, the owner of a travel company, was a multi-millionaire, meaning the sheriff's salary was mere pocket money.

Accordingly, Sheriff Hook was rolling in it, and didn't require to toe the line laid down by the Crown and followed religiously by most incumbents of the shrieval bench.

On one occasion I was appearing for a client of mine, Jimmy Inkster, a delightful, friendly guy, a drug addict who died during the aids epidemic ravaging Edinburgh in the eighties. Jimmy had been lifted more times than Joan Rivers' face and had a rap sheet thicker than the Oxford dictionary.

One day, Jimmy was passing Old Saint Paul's Church in Jeffrey Street, a very high Episcopal Church, the services filled with all the 'bells and smells' normally associated with Mass at a Catholic Church. However, he wasn't there for any religious reason. Noticing the outside door was ajar, he crept inside, and seeing nobody about, stole an acoustic guitar before beating a retreat. Unfortunately, he was captured in a boozer in Rose Street, trying to punt the stolen Gibson for a tenner to score a bag of smack.

Next morning in the cells, Jimmy was coming down faster than a punctured parachute and, coupled with the fact the cops told him Hook was on the bench, was certain he'd be hit with a sixer (six months). I appeared with Jimmy, pled him guilty and put forward everything I could think of by way of mitigation, including his two weeks in the Boy

Scouts, trying desperately to keep him clear of 'The Stardie', as Jimmy called the jail, a term used by Travelling people, from whom Jimmy proudly claimed descent, however distant.

I knew Sheriff Hook was himself an Episcopalian, and, coupled with Jimmy's atrocious record, accordingly entertained no very high hopes of a non-custodial sentence for my client. The fiscal in court on this occasion was a large stick insect of a man, who, had he belonged to that era, could have had his portrait painted by L. S. Lowry. He sported a military-style moustache, plus he possessed a pair of particularly large ears. Careerwise, I neither know nor care how far he succeeded in his climbing of the Crown's greasy pole.

This fiscal depute had appeared in the same court as me, before Sheriff Martin Mitchell, AKA Santa Claus, a lovely man, who'd regularly announce on Fridays that it was bargain basement day. If a client copped anything remotely resembling a guilty plea, the sheriff would hand out what were considered by other sheriffs to be ludicrously small sentences but were in fact extremely fair. Unlike so many on the bench, the man had a heart.

On the occasion referred to, I'd been acting on behalf of a soldier who had pleaded guilty to a minor assault and was keen his conviction did not count against him in his army career. Accordingly, during my plea in mitigation, I did everything in my power to make this young man's offence seem as trivial as possible, and he more saint than sinner. Whether Sheriff Mitchell swallowed a word of the story I was inventing as I went along remains a matter of conjecture (he was lenient, but by no means a mug). However, being the big hearted man he was, realising the difficulties this conviction could present to the young private's prospects, after duly warning him with regard to his future conduct, he granted him an absolute discharge, so that the no conviction would appear on the soldier's record, and he would leave court without a stain on his character.

The bench had spoken, and one would have thought that that would be that. Alas, no. The fact is that Ichabod Crane for the Crown happened to hold some ridiculously high rank in some equally ridiculous regiment of 'Weekend Warriors' (as Sir William Connolly, comedian, so aptly describes the Territorial Army) and rising to his feet announced, in the circumstances of the case he felt it incumbent upon him to personally write to the soldier's regiment in order to draw the matter to their attention. This incident speaks volumes about the man. He'd all the compassion of a block of concrete.

Anyway, back to my client Jimmy, who stood sweating in the dock as a stern-faced Sheriff Hook turned to stare at him.

'James Inkster.'

'Stand up,' said the sheriff clerk.

Jimmy stood. Sheriff Hook continued to stare straight at Jimmy for several seconds before beginning . . .

'You have pleaded guilty to theft of an acoustic guitar, which you found in an Episcopal Church. I have rarely heard of an incident more lamentable, one demonstrating a clear lack of respect for the religious convictions of others, and the sacredness of the surroundings.'

I tensed for the inevitable tsunami, Jimmy's knees knocked, while Ichabod's moustache bristled in anticipation. However, Hook turned his hawklike gaze upon the fiscal.

'I refer of course to the fact that an acoustic guitar was ever to be found in an Episcopal Church in the first place. There is to my knowledge an excellent organ on the premises, perfectly capable of providing suitable music, without the need for a folk group, or some such tomfoolery.'

The sheriff turned his icy blue eyes back to Jimmy.

'You'll be fined the sum of £40. Time to pay?'

I advised the court that my client was unemployed, in receipt of benefits, but offered to pay at the rate of £5 per fortnight.

'It shall be so ordered,' and Hook smiled that mad smile of his, like Shere Khan in Kipling's *Jungle Book*, before turning to the clerk.

'I'll rise for a few minutes.'

The bar officer called 'court'. We all stood and bowed as Sheriff Hook headed for his chambers, leaving Jimmy and I silently crossing ourselves in gratitude.

37

'The gem cannot be polished without friction, nor man perfected without trials.'

– Seneca

My client Willie, whose surname, for reasons that will become obvious, we'll call Debeers, after the diamond company, hailed from the Calton in Glasgow; the area where the infamous gang "the Tongs" once ruled the streets. I understand the name arose after some local boys attended the matinee in the Scotia cinema in Dennistoun, to watch a Charlie Chan movie, entitled *The Terror of the Tongs*. On the way out, Oweny McIntee (I had the honour of meeting the man personally, in Baird's bar at the Barrowland in Glasgow), accompanied by Tam and Bunty McGarvie and others, suddenly shouted, 'Tongs ya bass,' and the name of arguably the most famous Glasgow gang was born.

Anyway, my client had carved out a successful career stealing diamonds. Travelling to Geneva, Amsterdam and elsewhere on forged passports, he would dress immaculately; bespoke suit, hand-made shoes, gold half-moon spectacles, carrying a leather attaché case. His fingers were manicured to perfection, apart from the nail on his right pinkie, which he grew to about half an inch in length.

On arrival in Switzerland, he would check into an hotel under a snide name, and over the next couple of days head to the area of the city where diamond merchants plied their wares. On arrival at a shop, he'd ask to see a selection of loose stones from first one tray, then another, then another. After closely examining these, he'd make the excuse of thinking things over and leave, only to repeat the same performance in several jewellers.

Blessed with a photographic memory, my client also knew a great deal about precious stones: the cut, colour, clarity and carat. After a couple of days browsing, he'd head to a backstreet shop where he was on confidential terms with the owner, and have copies made from paste to the exact size, shape and colour of a couple of the stones he'd viewed.

Next morning, he'd check out of his hotel, head to a bar, leave his overnight bag behind the counter and after picking up the paste copies, return to the jewellers of the previous day. The fact he'd come back, his immaculate appearance and charming personality all combined to put the jewellers at their ease. My client would hide the fake diamond in one hand and ask to view the stones he'd seen on the first tray. After looking them over, he'd ask for the second tray, and as the jeweller turned, he'd hook his pinkie nail under a diamond, flip it in the air, catch it in his mouth and put the paste stone in its place on the pad.

Job done, my client could now relax, and after a lengthy perusal of the second tray he'd sigh and claim such was the quality of the stones he was spoiled for choice. He'd tell the jeweller, though it was meant to be a surprise, he'd have to bring his fiancée in to choose herself, as it was for her engagement ring, and he'd hate to get it wrong, 'You know what women are like.' He'd then leave, promising to return with his bride-to-be.

After visiting each of the shops he'd visited before, my client would collect his bag from the bar, catch a taxi to the airport, swap his suit for jeans and a shirt in the gents' toilet, and fly back home to No Mean City.

He once explained to me that unless they have suspicions, jewellers don't check stones when dealing with customers, merely glance over the tray with an expert eye, counting to satisfy themselves there are no spaces, so no stones are missing. But you must look the part, be able to walk the walk and be sure you can talk the talk before pulling off this kind of stunt.

By the time the CCTV is examined, he told me, he'd be safe back in Bonnie Scotland, and, after a little laxative, the stones retrieved, washed, polished, fenced, sold for a third of the bat, and it was champagne and Charlie time again.

On a day trip to Edinburgh with a friend, whose name doesn't deserve to appear in the same sentence, Willie, a man of culture, discernment, and eclectic taste, was visiting the National Art Gallery at the foot of the Mound, probably casing the joint for good measure, while his friend went off to meet a mate who'd been banged up in Edinburgh Prison and recently released.

Unbeknownst to Willie, the friend and his mate had gone on a shoplifting spree and, spotting a store detective, realising it was on top, speedily parted company. When Willie's friend came to collect him at the foot of the Mound, the car boot was stuffed with swag.

Unfortunately, two store detectives had followed this idiot from Princes Street, and approached the car, shouting at them to stop, with the result the mate made a mad dash for it, leaving a bewildered Willie lumbered with the loot.

I appeared with him when he appeared from custody on Monday morning before the sheriff. Despite my best efforts, he got sentenced to three months, known colloquially as 'a carpet', but he turned to me with a shrug and said, 'You win some, you lose some,' before trotting down the stairs to the cells.

His philosophical view surprised me: however, on reflection, I suppose, if you had to lose one, this was the one to lose. A sentence of three months (six weeks with good behaviour) for something he didn't do was a lot less than any sentence he'd have got in Geneva if he'd been caught for the things he'd done there, where his crimes had been of a completely different carat.

38

'Yesterday upon the stair,
I met a man who wasn't there,
He wasn't there again today
I wish, I wish he'd go away . . .'

– 'Antigonish', by William Hughes Mearns

It was a frosty February night in Edinburgh when a friend and favourite tailor of mine left an exclusive men's clothing shop in George Street. Crossing to his parked car, he got in and headed for home. I say, 'favourite tailor' as he formed part of a highly trained team of professionals which supplied my suits for court, and much of my leisure wear (though, like the cops, as a defence agent, you're never off duty). Due to take his girlfriend out to dinner at Rogano's restaurant, once an excellent eatery, in Glasgow, he was running late and, eager to avoid an ear bashing, put the foot down.

So it was, while shooting along Slateford Road, making for the M8, he was pulled over by the traffic police for speeding. Asked to provide his name, driver's licence and insurance documents, he advised the cops he was William Monteith, gave his address in Govanhill, Glasgow, but stated, because of the number of car break-ins and thefts, criminals stealing people's identities, he didn't keep personal documentation in his car.

Accordingly, the cop presented him with what was back then a Home Office Road Traffic form, known as a HORT1, requiring him to produce his licence and insurance within fourteen days, charged him with speeding and let him go. Taking the ticket, my client smiled politely and drove off, careful to keep within the speed limit.

Some months later, William Monteith called at my office in the Bridgegate, Glasgow, and handed me his copy complaint for speeding, now coupled with two additional charges of driving without insurance or a licence, as the HORT1 requesting the production of same had not been complied with.

Of course, there was a very good reason for the non-production of the aforementioned papers. The person the police gave the HORT1 to wasn't William Monteith.

It turned out that, when the traffic cops stopped the car in question, one of William Monteith's crew, Jacko, was driving. Jacko was a cheery guy, who always had a smile on his face, and unfortunately that evening he also had a haul of gents' suits in the boot of the vehicle: a new line in menswear which had only hit the shops that morning, most of which had been successfully hoisted by him and his associates that same afternoon.

On being stopped and having no licence, no insurance, no nothing, Jacko had given his name as William Monteith. Now, the copy complaint had been served to the real William Monteith, known as Billy or Buffalo Bill, who understandably wasn't over the moon about matters. However, as the boss and brains of the outfit, he couldn't complain too much if, finding himself in a tight spot, Jacko stuck his name up to stop getting his collar felt, and simultaneously save several grands worth of quality clobber.

Finding myself in the highly unusual position of having an innocent client, I had one of my secretaries send off a letter to Edinburgh Sheriff Court, pleading 'not guilty' to the charges on the complaint and a date for trial was set for later that year.

I say one of my secretaries, as I had four, all great girls. Lynsey McGovern, the daughter of my dear friend and best man, Joe, head of the infamous family of that name in the north of the city; Michelle Giannotti, daughter of my very good friend Frank, sadly no longer with us, formerly married to young Bernard Queen from Castlemilk; Frances Donnelly, a black-haired, black-eyed beauty, whose ancestors hailed from the Emerald Isle, and an Irish Dancing Champion;

and Susie Greechan, a charming girl, from Moodiesburn, outside Glasgow, a terrific secretary, who I could always count on to open the office on time, and she could equally count on me being late.

A week or so before trial, Billy dropped by my office to discuss our plan of action. Of course, in a perfect world, there'd be no problem. Billy would appear at court, and, as he hadn't been driving that day, the cops would state he wasn't the driver and that would be that.

In an eighteen-month period, approximately five hundred and fifty days, how many people would the traffic cops deal with? How many different faces would they see; male, female, old, young? In that timescale, how many incidents would they have been called to, speeders stopped, plus people without road tax, jumping red lights, driving with bald tyres, parking offenders, drunk drivers, drivers with no licence, no insurance, no permission to drive the vehicle?

Does anybody, honestly, really believe the police genuinely remember what someone they stopped for speeding over eighteen months ago looks like? I was once done with speeding three times in three years, but do you think I could remember the faces of the cops who charged me? Even though these were three relatively memorable occasions for me, they would have been utterly forgettable to the three separate lots of officers involved, but there's no danger I could ever have identified the cops who charged me.

Yet the law demands cops go to court, climb into the witness box, raise their right hands, and swear by almighty God they can remember the offender and the offence from all that time ago. The idea is clearly ludicrous. Basically, the rule followed by the police is lie, lie till your pants are on fire. If they didn't, the system would collapse, as it is built on lies, depends on lies, feeds on lies, and bears little resemblance to the whole truth and rarely anything remotely like the truth.

'What'll we do?' Billy asked me. 'The Rotten Mob (a Glasgow term of endearment used to describe members of the police force) will dig me out, swear I was driving, and I'll have a fine and a ban rammed up me, thanks to Jacko!'

I looked at Billy's troubled countenance.

'Turn up sharp at Edinburgh Sheriff on the trial date,' I told him, 'and make sure you bring Jacko.'

Billy looked at me, clearly puzzled.

'Jacko! But . . .'

'Do I teach you how to acquire suits?' I asked.

'No,' he conceded with a shrug, adding, I thought unnecessarily, 'you'd stick out like a veal chop at a vegan wedding.'

'Just bring Jacko,' I reiterated.

'Look, I know he got me into this mess, but I'm not sticking him in. I'm no midnight and . . .'

'Billy,' I again interjected, 'just turn up on time, bring Jacko, and leave him outside in your car, okay?'

'But why?'

'Just do it.'

Billy sighed, nodded, and left.

Edinburgh Sheriff Court, back in the eighties, was constructed of granite and marble, and looked rather like a large Victorian lavatory, though it had seen a lot more shit.

So it was, on the morning of the case, Billy and I left Jacko perusing a daily paper in the back of Billy's car, parked out of sight, round the side of the sheriff court and headed indoors. Billy's case was set down to be heard before Sheriff Martin Mitchell, who I've previously said was often referred to as Santa Claus. While this had something to do with his size, it had more to do with the fact he was an extremely fair man, and incredibly soft sentencer.

Though prone to the odd fit of rage and known on occasion to tear off his wig and throw it across the court at me, indicating he took issue with my line of cross-examination, he had a heart bigger than a whale's belly, and, in my opinion, should have been cloned for the benefit of future defence agents and the justice system in general.

The fiscal depute on the day was Margaret Kernahan, an attractive, battle-hardened professional in her mid-fifties, married to a man who I think was, or had been, or would become, I can't really recall nor care, Moderator of the Church of Scotland. Back in the day, the defence and prosecution shared the same basic facilities: room, lockers, unisex toilet and wash basin.

Margaret Kernahan would sweep into the agents' room wearing a contrasting combination of a black court gown and black fishnet stockings, and taking a seat beside a fellow fiscal come up with all sorts of banal comments, a favourite being, 'People are so kind, aren't they?' I confess to never having a clue who the nice people she referred to were, unless it was some obsequious cop who'd held the door open for her, or some other agent of the Crown: certainly not any accused she yearned to see swing from the yard arm, given half a chance.

Margaret had the habit of leaning across the table in court, patting the back of my hand in a patronising fashion, and advising me in a whisper that could be heard in New Zealand, certainly by the bench, she hoped I was 'going to behave myself today'. They say hope springs eternal, but believe me, Maggie's still waiting.

In court each morning, before anything really kicks off, there's what's known as the 'call over,' when each of the cases set down for trial is called out, to ascertain if the accused person is present and now pleading guilty or has the temerity to go to trial and dispute the Crown evidence. During this time no witnesses are present, they stay in the appropriate waiting rooms allotted to the defence and prosecution.

So it was, in due course, the clerk called William Monteith. Billy came forward, and I rose to advise the sheriff my client was adhering to his previously tendered plea of not guilty. The clerk announced 'trial later', but as I gathered my papers together, Margaret Kernahan held up my client's complaint and, adopting a quizzical look for the benefit of the bench, sighed and said sarcastically:

'I presume your client is completely innocent, as usual, James?'

'Of course,' I answered truthfully.

'Seriously, what possible defence can he have to speeding and not producing his licence and insurance?'

'Stick around, Margaret, and you'll doubtless find out.'

'I won't have long to wait,' she said. 'You're first up.'

The game was afoot. I turned to Billy, told him to take a seat at the back of the court, and left.

The two cops who'd stopped Jacko that evening all those many months ago were waiting in the Crown witness room, drinking coffee from plastic cups, courtesy of the Women's Institute. I entered and asked if I could have a word. They agreed, and I advised them that this seemed a very straightforward case. My client had clearly been speeding, failed to produce his documents, and it all boiled down to a matter of identification. Both cops agreed again. Being sparing with the truth, I told them I didn't know exactly when the trial would start, and as it looked like being a busy court today, they could be hanging about till the cows came home before the case kicked off.

I suggested, to speed things up for all concerned, the cops take a quick look at my client, tell me if it was the same guy they caught driving that night. If so, he was the guilty party, end of story.

The cops gladly agreed again, and I left the room for ten minutes, nipped outside to Billy's car and told Jacko to come with me. I returned to the corridor outside the Crown witness room with Jacko in tow. Entering, I asked the two police witnesses to step into the corridor for a moment which they did, then I asked, 'Is this the guy who was speeding that night, and you gave the HORT1 to?'

As previously mentioned, despite the incident having taken place well over a year ago, all cops have been blessed with total recall, and both officers immediately assured me this was indeed the man they had stopped, which of course, it was. I turned a grim face to Jacko.

'Looks like you're bang to rights, mate,' I said. 'They can identify you, so, I'm afraid that's that.'

I thanked the officers for cutting matters short, told them I'd talk to the fiscal and have the case called quickly, so they could get back on duty. Doubtless they had doughnuts to consume, coffee to drink while parked up in some lay-by watching the cars pass, looking forward to the future and their ludicrously large pension; however, I missed that bit out.

Once in the corridor, Jacko turned to me, 'Now what do I do?' he asked. So, I told him.

Ten minutes later saw the clerk of court calling the case.

Billy promptly came forward, took his seat in the dock, I confirmed my client's plea of not guilty, and the fiscal called her first witness. Cop number one came into court, entered the witness box and, after being sworn in by the sheriff, the fiscal rose to examine him.

'Officer, I think on the twenty-fifth of March of last year, around six o'clock in the evening, you and your colleague had cause to stop a car in Slateford Road, Edinburgh, is that correct?' said Margaret, leading evidence shamelessly, as was ever her wont.

'That's correct, ma'am.'

'Kindly tell the sheriff, do you see the driver of that vehicle here in court today?'

This, of course, would have been rather difficult to do, as the driver was at that moment sitting on a train that was hurtling back to Queen Street, Glasgow.

'Yes, ma'am,' began the cop, turning, 'that's . . .'

He stopped suddenly as he caught sight of Billy in the dock.

'Is something wrong, officer?'

The cop looked confused, embarrassed, and glanced across the court at me, before turning back to the fiscal.

'That's, eh, that's not the man we stopped, ma'am.'

'What?' exclaimed Margaret, unable to believe that perhaps this one particular policeman had not been blessed with the total recall referred to previously.

'But your statement here –' She waved the document in the air, ' – says you stopped a man who gave the name William Monteith.'

'Objection, leading,' I said, rising. 'Perhaps the fiscal would like to supply all the evidence in the case.'

'Sustained,' said the sheriff.

Margaret drew me a cold look, and turned back to the traffic cop.

'You're sure this isn't the driver of the car?' she asked again, hoping the cop was suddenly going to change his mind, and say, 'What am I talking about? Of course, he is.' But having just a few minutes ago identified Jacko to me, this was impossible, however much he longed to do so.

'Positive, ma'am.'

A long pause followed, during which Margaret stared at the statement in her hand. Finally, she sighed at the cop. 'Very well, you may go,' she said, in the tone of a primary school teacher dismissing a particularly disappointing pupil.

The cop glared at me as he left. I made a mental note never to speed again on the Slateford Road. A rule I was to break a few years later though, and how!

'As there can be no corroboration, I lead no more evidence,' said Margaret, looking at me suspiciously.

'Stand up, Mr Monteith,' said the sheriff.

Billy stood.

'I find you not guilty, you're free to go,' said Sheriff Mitchell, and he and his bar officer hurried off the bench, back to chambers.

I nodded to Billy, who took the hint and headed for the pub across the road. As I got my file together, the fiscal looked across at me. 'I can't believe that police officer failed to identify.'

'Why wouldn't they, Margaret?' I said. 'You were correct. My client was completely innocent.'

39

"Is there anybody there?" said the Traveller, knocking on the moonlit door.'
— 'The Listeners' by Walter de La Mare

It was a crisp winter morning in 1991 and I was heading up the Mound to the old Edinburgh Sheriff Court, situated directly across the street from Deacon Brodies Tavern. So close was the proximity of the two, my mentor, Wattie Sutherland, regularly confused them, with the result he'd spend entire days at the public bar not the criminal one.

Christmas was just round the corner, a time no client wants banged up. Not that many clients ever fancy going to jail, except perhaps some poor jaikie in need of a room and three squares a day, bless them. But for career criminals, the lead up to Christmas is a busy season. The shops are bursting, customers bustle about buying gifts, burning plastic, splashing cash. Shelves are loaded with stock, comprising all sorts of goodies, and the shoplifters are out in force, fulfilling orders people had put down on their list for Santa.

My client that day is probably still in business, so I'll call him Robin, as in Robin Hood, rather than robbin' bastard, as many of the items he appropriated on his highly successful shoplifting sprees were made available to those unable to afford the ludicrous prices charged by the High Street stores. Okay, so my client's motives weren't completely altruistic, but a great deal of so-called designer gear is made in sweatshops in Asia, arrives illegally at the port in Naples, from where the Camorra clans distribute the goods throughout Western Europe and the UK, where they're sold at vastly inflated prices, resulting in massive profits for companies. These, in my opinion, are the real crooks. Robin had been working hard visiting several boutiques and high-end high-street stores, and his list was almost complete. After all, everybody loves a bargain, and these often come from 'Hookie Street'. Unfortunately, as he was finishing up for the day, Robin got either too cocky or careless, but two store detectives clocked him, with the result the cops were called and he was caught, bang to rights with several bags of expensive items, which led him to spend a weekend lie-down in St Leonard's police station.

I managed to get my client bail when he appeared from custody, but the court set a very early date for trial, meaning a conviction would see him locked up over the festive season, which was very far from what my client wanted for Christmas.

For those not entirely au fait with Scots law, the fact he'd been captured with a load of allegedly stolen gear, while going a long way towards it, still wouldn't be enough to secure a conviction for theft. Before this can happen, there must be evidence of ownership and loss.

Very often, defence agents were asked to agree to labels in lieu of the stolen items being lodged, to save witnesses coming to court and the items requiring to be produced. However, when asked, I declined to agree to the labels, attempting to put every possible obstacle in the Crown's path. After all, the fiscals already had the police and sheriff on their side, and my client only had me.

The trial date rolled round. The shop assistants from the boutiques my client had been charged with rattling were cited to court. These witnesses were kept in a Crown witness room, just round the corner from the one where the trial was to be heard. The cops who arrested Robin were kept in a separate room, further down the corridor.

The police witnesses had written in their notebooks that my client had confessed to stealing the goods, which was, of course, complete nonsense, but despite that they'd be telling this to the court in evidence, and, in all probability, the sheriff would pretend to believe them.

I recall having a pint after court in Glasgow one afternoon with a mate of mine, a Queen's Counsel, in the Old Burnt Barns beside the Barras known as Lynch's, after the proprietor, John Lynch, a dear friend of mine who, like the counsel in question, is sadly no longer with us. The QC was a thoroughly decent guy, and at that time was acting as a temporary sheriff in Glasgow. I'd just lost a trial in front of a sheriff, a rather nasty individual, known mainly for his massive ego, and equally massive ears (I seem to keep appearing before sheriffs with big ears) which stuck out, almost at right angles, similar to that of Plug's in 'the Beano'. These elephantine appendages apparently served no practical purpose (certainly he never seemed to hear a word the defence said) other than perhaps prevent him from sticking his head too far up the procurator fiscal's backside.

After I summed up, the sheriff spent a nanosecond considering matters before claiming he believed the cops' evidence (a fairy story Hans Christian Anderson would have been proud of) convicted my client and sent him to Bar-L for three months.

Not pleased at losing, especially when my client, guilty or not, on the evidence should have walked, I pointed out to my friend that the cops clearly told a pack of lies under oath, even a complete imbecile had to realise that, and, though my client was as guilty as Crippen, the Crown could not possibly have proved it without the perjured evidence of the Police.

My friend took a sip of his G&T, placed his glass back on the bar mat and met me with his gentle smile.

'James, dear boy, the police have to lie their backsides off, else nobody would ever be convicted.' He went on to state the average beat policeman was as observant as an oyster who'd overdosed. I confess, though entirely correct, I was taken aback at this frank assertion; though, to be fair, this counsel always fought tooth and nail for his client, and the Faculty of Advocates is a much poorer place without him.

The sheriff on the bench that day was a very harsh sentencer; a man with a slit of a smile, like a machete mark on a melon, and a facial expression of something between chronic constipation and a volcano on the very brink of erupting.

Apparently, he was an exceptionally clever man; indeed, he must have been psychic, as he was able to decide an accused's guilt before hearing the evidence. They say a fine line exists between genius and insanity. I never saw any sign of the former but am assured by fellow lawyers he believed a horse regularly sat beside him on the bench, and some defence agents made neighing noises, resulting in him glancing to one side, to take his equine associate's advice, from the horse's mouth as it were.

Upon learning who was to hear my client's trial, all hope of any acquittal vanished faster than the morning mist, and I realised I had to think about getting the case out of his court. Accordingly, I approached the fiscal, assumed my best boyish smile, and asked if she'd have any objection to an adjournment of the trial, as it was possible my client had an alibi witness (well, anything's possible) and I required further time to prepare.

The depute pretended to pay attention, then stated all her witnesses were present, I'd had ample time to prepare, and it'd be a cold day in the Congo before she'd agree to my motion. She told me she'd a continued trial which would last till lunch, after which my client's case would start, and enquired why I didn't plead guilty and save time and trouble. Rapidly crossing myself at her ridiculous suggestion, I retreated from this devil woman and headed for the agents' room.

Walking away from Court 5, I was aware of the fact the fiscal opposing my motion meant the sheriff would without doubt refuse it, resulting in my client going to jail, not passing go, and me not collecting £200, as his bum and my bung would be out the window.

Most criminal cases, when I was practising, were paid for by SLAB, which kept a vice-like grip on the purse strings, paying a pittance no self-respecting plumber would get out of bed for, so an iron lung (bung) was the order of the day when dealing with the professionals of the underworld.

Entering the agents' room, an area which back then we shared with the fiscal deputes, I saw Walter Sutherland, sitting in his shirt sleeves, smoking, doing *The Sun* crossword.

'Alright, Wattie?' I enquired.

He grunted, eyes still glued to his paper. I slumped into a seat, still wracking my brains for some way out for Robin. At this rate, I'd be paying exorbitant retail prices for designer gear in future. Just then, a bar officer entered, informing the fiscal depute, Agnes Nizer, that the sheriff was due on the bench to start her first trial.

Bar officers, often retired cops, are responsible for reporting to the fiscal as to witness attendances, plus bringing sheriffs on and off the bench, in case they lose their way from their chambers to the courtroom, a distance that can at times exceed ten yards or so. The depute nodded, stubbed her ciggie out in the yellow-and-red Tennent's lager ashtray Walter had acquired from Deacon Brodies, checked her make-up in a small mirror, applied a smear of scarlet to the already bright slash across her lips, and slipped into her gown.

A handsome woman in her forties with short dark hair, Agnes didn't suffer fools, or anyone, gladly. As she swept out, her gown brushed against Walter's blue blazer with gold buttons, which hung on the back of his chair, unknowingly knocking it to the ground.

At that moment, the bold boy was busy looking at a photo on page three of *The Sun* newspaper, displaying the undoubted charms of a buxom young lady named Brenda, whose idea of fighting for feminism involved displaying her naked boobs to the public, thus making it abundantly clear how free and equal she was. A caption below this woman warrior claimed she was currently a student, concerned about global warming, which may have explained her lack of attire. As I lifted Walter's blazer to hang it back up, I saw the bar officer following Agnes out. Suddenly, a thought struck me.

Catching up with the fiscal, seconds before court kicked off again, I told her I'd reconsidered and confirmed she could recall my client's case before her continued trial started. Delighted I was apparently about to tender a guilty plea, she agreed. The bar officer brought the sheriff back on, we all bowed, and I began to address the bench. But much to the fiscal's chagrin, instead of pleading guilty, I merely renewed my motion to adjourn the case in the strongest possible terms, pleading further time to prepare, the absence of a vital alibi witness, right to a fair trial, the presumption of innocence, and other matters, routinely thought irrelevant in the Scottish criminal courts.

The fiscal sprang to her feet to object, but the sheriff waved her down, clearly viewing this as another pathetic attempt on my part to postpone matters, stating he'd already ruled on the matter, and there would be absolutely no question of any adjournment for anyone, for any reason whatsoever. End of story.

Apparently defeated, I shrugged and advised the sheriff that, since my motion had been refused yet again, I hoped the court would adopt a similar attitude towards the Crown, should they make a similar motion. The sheriff gave me a 'how very dare you' glare, ripped into me, describing my remark as rude in the extreme (I wasn't even trying) stating that I was a hair's breadth from being held in contempt of court, that he resented the suggestion he'd treat the Crown any differently than he did the defence, declared he was entirely impartial and my client's trial would be heard after lunch whatever happened. I gathered my papers, bowed, and got out of Dodge, fast.

On my return to the agents' room, I noted Walter wasn't there, and was advised he'd headed 'across the road'. 'Across the road' was a term defence lawyers normally used when referring to the Court of Appeal, across the High Street, in Parliament Square. In a similar way, the House of Commons refers to the House of Lords as 'That Other Place'. You wonder why they just don't call each by their names, but I guess it's all to add to the mystique, this insider lingo, drawing a distinction between themselves and the great unwashed.

However, in Walter's case, the term 'across the road' meant Deacon Brodies public house, at the top of the Mound, where he'd regularly repair to refresh himself with several large rums and pep. I took my client aside and held a quick, quiet, confidential consultation. Robin listened, took what I said on board, and we left the court together.

We found Walter in the bar, blazer over the back of his chair, finishing his crossword and a rum and pep. While Robin bought a round, I told the bold boy of my dilemma. Walter's many years at the criminal bar had made him fireproof. He got away with saying and doing things no other lawyer would dare. An old campaigner and a living legend, he held a low opinion of sheriffs and fiscals alike, adopting a highly unorthodox approach to defending clients. I knew he was the man to talk to, take advice from and ask a favour of.

Two o'clock found me back in Court 5, the sheriff on the bench, my client in the dock, and the clerk calling his case. Robin confirmed his name, the Crown kicked off their case, and the bar officer was sent to fetch the first civilian witness, who'd speak to the alleged theft from one of the shops. Minutes later the bar officer returned and announced loudly, 'No reply, my lord.'

The fiscal looked puzzled, but assuming the witness must've nipped to the loo, called the second on the Crown list. The bar officer left, returning moments later, and again announced, 'No reply, my lord.'

By now, the fiscal was looking flustered, but sent the bar officer for the third witness. I began tapping the tips of my fingers on the tabletop, checking my watch in as theatrical a manner as possible, none of which went unnoticed by the bench. Shortly after the bar officer returned, announcing for the third time, 'No reply, my lord. In fact, there is nobody in the Crown witness room.'

The Depute let out a croaking sound and, forgetting to bow to the bench, hurried out, apparently to satisfy herself of the situation, leaving the sheriff and me to await her return. I checked my watch again, sighed deeply and, shaking my head at this shocking delay, once more began to drum my fingers on the table. The fiscal returned a few minutes later.

'Are you ready to proceed, Madam Depute?' asked the sheriff.

The fiscal forced a smile.

'Actually, my lord, there appears to have been some sort of mix-up. The witnesses were present earlier, but unfortunately, they all seem to have left.'

I rolled my eyes and sighed again. The sheriff glared at me before turning back to the fiscal.

'And?' he asked.

The fiscal swallowed hard.

'In these circumstances, I find myself having to move the court for an adjournment.'

The sheriff's jaws snapped shut, like a Venus fly trap. He inhaled deeply through his nose, exhaling slowly before turning to me once more. I smiled back up at him, cherub-like. We both knew it was game, set and match. He turned again to the fiscal, his frustration now fully directed at the Crown.

'I made matters perfectly clear this morning. There will be no adjournment, and, as you are in no position to lead evidence . . .' He turned to my client. 'Stand up. I find you not guilty,' he said, with all the relish of someone drinking a cup of cold sick. Then, rising, he glared at the fiscal.

'My chambers, if you please.' And he stormed off the bench without waiting for his bar officer.

I said goodbye to a delighted Robin, pocketed the bung he'd given me and headed off to the agents' room. Walter was studying the racing section of his paper.

'Well?' he asked, not looking up.

'Not guilty,' I replied, pulling out a twenty and placing it on the table beside him.

Walter didn't reply, simply picked up the twenty and put a tick beside a horse's name.

No one found out what happened to the civilian witnesses. One theory is that shortly before the court broke for lunch, someone sporting Walter's blue blazer with the gold buttons, very similar to a bar officer's, knowing an adjournment was no longer on the cards, briefly entered the witness room, announced the trial had been adjourned, causing the Crown witnesses to leave and the case to collapse. But then, that's pure conjecture and there's no proof that's what actually happened.

40

'Le bon Dieu est dans le détail.' ('The good God is in the detail.')
                                                    – Gustave Flaubert

Usually, when someone appears in the Scottish criminal courts on summary complaint, charged with an offence, or is sent a citation by post, according to the Criminal Procedure (Scotland) Act 1995, they may 'appear personally, and if he does, he must state his plea personally, or be represented. He can also respond in writing to the complaint, and tender a plea of guilty, or not guilty.'

It would appear from the wording of the act women never commit offences, as only 'he' is repeatedly referred to, while 'she' is never mentioned. Certainly, my wife has never been in the wrong. I know this is true, as she's told me so herself on many an occasion.

However, there are times when a simple plea of not guilty isn't enough. This occurs when a client is charged in what's known in law as a 'Special Capacity'. This may apply to a person said to be on bail, or the licensee of a hotel, restaurant, public house, owner of a piece of land, or a dog, the captain of a ship, or even a prostitute, anyone who is deemed to be in a special capacity at the time the offence is alleged to have been committed. In these cases, the act dictates, 'If an accused person is charged in a special capacity, in terms of Section 255, he or she must challenge that special capacity before a plea is recorded.'

Such was the situation a client of mine found himself in. I'll call the gentleman in question Paddy, and he was the licensee and owner of a bar in Glasgow's East End. The pub was typical of the area, a good solid working man's bar, serving whisky, vodka, Guinness, heavy, and where lager and lime was classed as a cocktail.

One day a couple of men called into the pub and proceeded to order a round of drinks. Paddy was happy to serve them, but unbeknownst to him, these guys were officers from the Weights and Measures Department of Her Majesty's Customs and Excise. When they left, they took with them several samples of spirits. After testing, it transpired the vodka Paddy was serving had been tampered with and, though claiming to be Russian, had more water in it than the Volga, while the Irish whiskey was so weak, one would have to down two dozen bottles before breaking into a rousing rendition of 'Danny Boy'.

I called into Paddy's pub for a pick-me-up after court one morning, when he appeared from the cellar and presented me with a copy complaint which had been served on him that day, stating he was the owner of the bar and accusing him of selling substandard booze.

'Have you a receipt for any of the spirits you served?' I asked, expecting a no.

He didn't disappoint.

'They all sort of fell off the back of a lorry,' he said, rather unoriginally.

'Going by the amount of water in them, it was off the back of a boat,' I said, and lifted my pint glass, eyeing it suspiciously.

'What do you take me for?' Paddy said, looking hurt. 'That stuff was strictly for Teuchters.'

In the rest of Scotland, the word 'teuchters' refers to those hardy men who hail from the Highlands; however, in Glasgow the term applies to anyone beyond the city boundaries. Indeed, many locals believe you need a passport to get by Glasgow Cross.

I finished my drink, which was on the house, and headed to my office where I read Paddy's complaint. The boy was certainly in soapy bubble. A plea of guilty would result in him losing his licence, his livelihood, and the closing down of a favourite watering hole of mine. On the other hand, a not guilty plea would result in a trial with a defence weaker than the spirits Paddy'd been serving.

I took a copy of the Criminal Procedure (Scotland) Act down from a shelf, blew off the dust and turned to section 255, praying for inspiration. After a few moments, an idea struck me. It wasn't a slam dunk, but well worth a pop.

On the date of Paddy's pleading diet, I turned up at court on his behalf and the clerk called the case. I rose and smiled at the sheriff.

'I appear in this matter, my lord, my client pleads not guilty to all charges.'

'Madam fiscal?' enquired the sheriff.

'I move for trial, my lord,' responded the depute automatically, without looking up.

'Very well; trial,' said the man in the wig.

The clerk set a date some months ahead, I bowed to the bench, and glanced over at the fiscal, still busy with her pile of files. I turned to the clerk and before leaving, casually handed him a sealed envelope, seemingly as an afterthought.

'What's this?' he asked.

'My client's not guilty plea.'

'You've just tendered it.'

'I know, I was going to post it, but . . .' I smiled confidentially. 'He's a good client, so thought I'd appear in person. Belt and braces, y'know?'

The clerk shrugged a big 'whatever', stuck the envelope in the file and called the next case.

Six months later, Paddy and I turned up for his trial. The clerk called the case, and the fiscal led her first witness. This expert in weights and measures banged on for an eternity on the quantities of ethanol, potassium and every other ingredient that goes into the making of Irish whiskey and Russian vodka, concluding by advising the court that the samples of spirits taken from Paddy's pub had been drastically watered down, and in the case of the whiskey, food colouring had been added. The fiscal took her seat with a satisfied smile. The sheriff turned to me.

'Cross-examination, Mr McIntyre?'

'No questions, my lord.'

The fiscal looked puzzled, but I pretended not to notice, picked up my pen and began to write furiously in my notepad. Somewhat perplexed, she called her second witness. This guy proved as tedious as the first. The fiscal took him painstakingly though his evidence, crossed every T and dotted every I as he corroborated his colleague's findings and drew the same damning conclusion. The fiscal sat. The sheriff turned to me once more.

'Mr McIntyre?'

'No questions, my lord.' Again I grabbed my pen and started scribbling in my notepad. My frantic antics had the effect of having the fiscal flick through her file, checking she'd ticked every box, left no loophole, no gap in the Crown evidence, through which I could squeeze my client. Eventually, satisfied, she turned to the sheriff.

'That concludes the Crown case, my lord.'

Looking down at me, the sheriff enquired, 'Mr McIntyre?'

'I lead no evidence, my lord. However, I have a motion that there is no case for my client to answer in this instance.'

The sheriff looked surprised and the fiscal stunned. I continued.

'As the court will be aware, the complaint states my client is the licensee and owner of the public house in question.'

'Yes,' said the sheriff.

'The thing is, no evidence has been led to establish this fact, which is, of course, crucial to the Crown case.'

The fiscal and sheriff exchanged a glance, before both turned to me, a look approaching pity on their faces. The fiscal, apparently feeling almost embarrassed for me, got to her feet.

'My lord, the libel of the complaint in this case contains a special capacity, and accordingly, under Section 255 of the relevant act, the Crown need not lead any evidence to establish an accused's capacity, unless of course a challenge to said capacity has been previously taken, before a plea was tendered.'

The sheriff turned to me, smiling. 'Well, Mr McIntyre, what have you to say to that?'

I beamed back at the bench. 'My lord, my friend is quite correct. Which is exactly why I challenged the special capacity in this case at the pleading diet.'

'What?' exclaimed the fiscal, picking up her papers. 'I have no note of that.' She fumbled through her file before again turning to the bench. 'None whatsoever!'

'With respect, my lord,' I said, 'what the fiscal at the pleading diet noted, or didn't note, is neither here nor there. As my friend knows the act so well, she's doubtless aware that it clearly states it is the court which must be advised of any objection, and if my lord's clerk would be kind enough to check, doubtless she can confirm the appropriate challenge was taken at the proper time.'

The sheriff nodded to his clerk, who rummaged rapidly through the file in front of her and, after a few seconds, came across the sealed envelope I'd handed the previous clerk at the pleading diet. She opened the letter and scanned it quickly.

'There is a letter from Mr McIntyre amongst the papers, my lord, dated the day of the pleading diet,' said the clerk, handing it up to the sheriff, who scanned it before reading it aloud verbatim.

'We write on behalf of, etc., etc., etc., and hereby challenge the special capacity alleged and libelled on the complaint, and thereafter tender a plea of not guilty to each charge.' The sheriff looked over at the fiscal. 'Well, Madam Fiscal?'

Well was about the last thing she was. The fiscal's face and the Crown case were both falling faster than a fat boy on a seesaw. Turning to the bench, the fiscal clutched at one last straw.

'I'd move the court for an adjournment, to allow me to produce the necessary witnesses to prove this man is the owner and licensee.'

'My lord,' I said, affecting understanding, 'while sympathetic to my friend's plight, perhaps she's forgotten that she closed the Crown case, therefore cannot reopen it, and as I have led no evidence, considering the objection previously taken, it'd be impossible to . . .'

'Yes, yes, yes,' said the sheriff, waving me down, aware the Crown were well and truly up the creek. 'The accused will stand.'

The sheriff looked at my client. 'In view of the Crown's failure to present the required evidence in this case, I find you not guilty on all charges.'

I winked at the fiscal and left.

Forty minutes later found me in the office, a fat envelope in my pocket expressing Paddy's gratitude, plus a crate of genuine Irish whiskey on my desk. By Glasgow standards, I may have been a teuchter, but in my case, Paddy had made an exception.

41

'Speech is silver. Silence is golden.'

– King Solomon

'Don't cry,' I said, handing my client a hanky from a box on the desk. 'I hear they've done away with capital punishment for this kind of crime.'

My attempt to lighten the mood landed on deaf ears. Debbie didn't smile but dabbed at her eyes with the tissue.

'It's so difficult, James. I work every hour Heaven sends; but, after I've paid the child minder, and the other bills, there's not a lot left over.'

She smeared more mascara across her already streaked face.

'Why did you let them in without a warrant?'

'I didn't.' She shook her head and sank back in her seat. 'To be honest, I don't know what I was doing, everything was getting on top of me. As soon as they started talking to me, I broke down on the doorstep and admitted I didn't have a licence. I don't even get a chance to watch the bloody thing, but it keeps the boys quiet for a few minutes at tea time.'

By now the reader has doubtless realised my client had recently been charged with not possessing a television licence. This was way back in the day, when there was some semblance of an excuse for charging a fee for viewing, unlike today, when they should be paying people to watch the programmes, apart from *River City*, by far the best soap on the box in the twenty-first century.

Of course, back then, the Crown couldn't have cared less if Debbie'd been bringing up her boys while living in a cardboard box

199

on fifty pence per week, nor would it now. She didn't have a TV licence and both they and the Beeb demanded their pound of flesh.

Some months after attending my office, Debbie's case was called in the district court. Readers will recall my previous references to this particular forum, and so be aware of the level of esteem in which I hold it and those who sit in judgement there.

The Crown case was in short compass, comprising two witnesses, whose job was to go around gathering evidence by snooping on people, to catch folk watching telly with no licence for the box. The first witness stated he and his colleague attended at the address in question, and on enquiring whether my client held a current television licence, the accused immediately admitted to not possessing one, and was accordingly charged with the relevant offence. The fiscal, having finished, returned to her seat.

'Mr McIntyre?' the magistrate enquired.

'No questions, Your Honour.'

The magistrate nodded, with a rather patronising 'What could you possibly have asked?' sort of smile, as the fiscal called her second witness, who corroborated the first.

'Mr McIntyre?' the magistrate enquired again.

'No questions, Your Honour.'

Apparently, people were keen on throwing me looks, as the fiscal tossed me a 'That was a total waste of time' one, then without bothering to rise, said, 'That completes the Crown case, Your Honour.'

'Mr McIntyre?' enquired the magistrate for the third time.

I stood.

'Your Honour, I have a motion to make, namely that there is no case to answer, as at this stage, even if Your Honour accepts the Crown evidence at its height, there is insufficient to convict my client.'

The fiscal threw me a second look. I was getting good at catching them. This one said, 'Are you insane?' She stood and addressed the court.

'Your Honour, I'd ask you to refuse the defence motion. The court has heard corroborated evidence that the accused confessed she was not in possession of a television licence at the time of the inspectors' visit.'

I stood once more. 'Your Honour, I fear my friend has put the cart before the horse. The court has indeed heard corroborated evidence that my client was not in possession of a television licence, but, of course, the court has heard no evidence whatsoever that she ever possessed a television in the first place.'

Ta-dah!

Needless to say, my client was acquitted, quite rightly so. And now, the weather . . .

42

'Beware the Ides of March.'

— *Julius Caesar*, William Shakespeare

Okay, so what follows actually happened in February, but that's close enough. First, let's go back four months.

I'd known Evelyn since we were at school. She'd been a close friend and classmate of the elder of my two younger sisters, Margaret, and I'd always fancied her. (Evelyn that is, not my sister, I'm no hillbilly.) Truth be told, I think she had a bit of a thing for me too.

After leaving school, Evelyn worked in Edinburgh for a while, before moving down to the Big Smoke; she got married, divorced, moved to Spain, met a guy, had two kids, split up and headed back home with her two sons, aged eighteen months and three years.

So it was, in November 1992, of all the gin joints in all the world, she walked into a boozer in Linlithgow where I was having a drink, and, spotting her and her mum come in, I made my way over to reintroduce myself.

Unfortunately, halfway across the room, I managed to fall over a fire extinguisher, which wasn't easy, considering it was attached to a wall. But my antics made Evelyn laugh, set off a spark, reigniting the old flame (enough already!) that had once existed.

However, Evelyn's mother, Jean, wasn't quite as overjoyed at our meeting again after all these years. At least that's what I took from her telling her daughter, 'Of all the people I wish you hadn't run into now you're home, it's James McIntyre.'

Seems pretty clear, but who knows, maybe I'm oversensitive.

There isn't enough room, nor I'm sure interest from anyone reading this, to go into depth about matters: suffice to say I was married at the time, the father of a beautiful baby girl, and a terrible husband. Believe me, I don't say this lightly, nor am I proud of it, in fact, I'm profoundly ashamed. However, I'm immensely grateful that now both Evelyn and my ex-wife, Alicia, are best pals, and even plot, I mean holiday together.

But back then I'd been bitten, and such was my desperation to go out with Evelyn, I tried every trick in the book, lying to such an extent my pants were in urgent need of the fire extinguisher I'd tripped over back in the bar.

However, Evelyn made it clear from the get-go she wasn't into married men. I said I didn't blame her. I wasn't into married men either. She didn't crack a smile; however, after making all sorts of promises, I eventually managed to persuade her (I've had easier times with a jury), as she was looking for some way to support her sons, to come and work for me.

Following the attempted murder charge, despite the charge being dropped, Edinburgh had become a bit too hot for me, and I'd opened a new firm called McIntyre & Co in the Briggait, just off the Saltmarket, in Glasgow. Evelyn began working there in November 1992. So it was that one snowy evening at the end of the following January we all jumped into a hired car and headed to Inverness, where a client of mine was appearing in the High Court known as 'the Castle'.

The further north we drove, the heavier the snow fell, until we found ourselves in the middle of a blizzard. The traffic was end-to-end, the going slow and, not being blessed with an over-abundance of patience, I pulled out, passed several cars and ended up behind a very large, slow-moving lorry. Despite Evelyn continually telling me to calm down, I decided to pass this vehicle too, pulled out, overtook and suddenly the windscreen turned white.

'Well done, Einstein,' said Evelyn, 'You've just overtaken the snowplough.'

I required, rather sheepishly, to draw into the hard shoulder and allow the snow plough to pass, plus all the cars I'd previously overtaken took the opportunity to do likewise, leaving us once more at the back of the line of traffic. Eventually, we reached Inverness safely, and I booked us into a family room at a local hotel.

However, next day at court, the Crown offered my client a deal, which involved copping a plea to a reduced charge; so, rather than go to trial, he threw his hands up, sentence was deferred, and the case was done and dusted by lunchtime. However, by then, the snow, which had not stopped falling since we arrived the night before, had formed drifts that had rendered all the roads to and from Inverness impassable, requiring us to stay in the hotel for another four days till the snow had cleared.

It so happened some advocates who also had cases calling at 'the Castle' were staying in the same hotel, and we had a ball. Holed up for four days, we ran up a bill of just under £1,000 on the legal aid, which wasn't bad going for 1993. However, all good things come to an end, and on 4 February, once the snow cleared, we had to call a halt to the hilarity and head back to work.

On our return to Glasgow, I was driving the car back to the hire company and approaching the Kingston Bridge when suddenly the vehicle lurched heavily to one side. Though not an expert mechanic, even I realised one of the front wheels had fallen off, and I remember the old song 'Three Wheels on my Wagon' coming to mind.

Whether or not the pressure put on the tyres by forcing them to plough through snowdrifts had brought this about, I don't know, but Evelyn, the boys and I had to abandon the car and catch a taxi to the office.

That day, round about lunchtime, three men suddenly burst through the door. One of them ran straight at me and started punching my face. I had no idea what it was all about, but immediately grabbed the guy round the neck, and began returning the punches.

I still had my assailant's head trapped under my arm, when he suddenly pulled out a knife with a serrated edge, and before I could do anything jammed the point of the blade into my leg, just above the left knee, and pulled upwards, slicing my thigh in half.

As I turned to get away, he swung the knife at me twice, slicing into my left shoulder blade and lower back, leaving long, deep cuts, though I only felt the impact of the weapon and no pain at the time.

Seconds later, the men bolted out of the office. I staggered to the door, just in time to see a car carrying all three men speed away, before I slid down onto the pavement, blood pouring from various parts of my body, forming a pool on the ground where I sat.

My wounded left leg lay wide open, like a piece of raw beef in the butcher's window. I could see the thin, shiny silver membrane, as the cut was clean through to the white bone. Evelyn rushed out of the office after me, dropped to my side and grabbing my thigh in her two hands, held both halves together as tightly as possible, trying to staunch the flow of blood. I remember her kneeling next to me, her hair falling forward, and her sweeping it aside, causing red streaks across her face and lips.

It's strange the things you recall, but this was the early nineties. People thought you could catch AIDS from a toilet seat and so avoided contact with other people's blood like the plague. Literally. Yet here was Evelyn, with my blood in her hair, on her hands, arms, neck, face, in her mouth, with no thought for herself, holding me together till help arrived.

I remember a woman coming out of the Old Ship Bank Pub, next to my office, putting a cigarette in my mouth and lighting it, and as I was sat in a bloody puddle, smoking, a man started to cross the street towards us. I hadn't a clue who or what he was, but Evelyn guessed he was an undercover cop. She was correct, and he was soon joined by a uniformed one. Quick as a flash, Evelyn dipped my inside suit pocket, pulled something out, and stuck it under her blouse. The uniformed cop clocked this but wasn't sure what she'd done and asked her.

'I was taking these out of his pocket,' she said, holding up my rosary beads. This was true, but those weren't all she took. I'm sure, dear reader, you'll understand if I don't state here what else she took. Let's just say if I'd been caught . . . But, thanks to Evelyn, I wasn't.

Suddenly, blue lights flashing, sirens blaring, an ambulance screeched to a halt beside us, and two paramedics jumped out. These boys were brilliant, took over from Evelyn, quickly assessed the damage, got me onto a stretcher, into the back of the ambulance and headed up the High Street, lights flashing and sirens sounding once more.

43

'Whoever appeals to the law against his fellow man is either a fool or a coward. Whoever cannot take care of himself without police protection is both.'

– The Code of Omertà

I arrived at Glasgow Royal Infirmary's A&E, where nurses appeared like angels, clamping shut my gaping wounds and painting me from top to toe in iodine, to prevent infection. Suddenly, the curtains surrounding my bed were swept to one side as two cops from the serious crime squad appeared, alongside the nurses attending to my injuries.

'So, what happened here?' said one of the officers, nodding down at my heavily bandaged left leg, while the nurses, unconcerned by the sudden intrusion, continued to attend to my injuries.

'I tripped,' I said.

'We want to know who it was who did this,' said his colleague.

'I want to win the lottery. Let's see who gets lucky first.'

'For the last time. Who did this?' asked number one again.

'Could you close the curtains on your way out?' I said. 'It's getting kind of chilly in here.'

Silence reigned for a few long seconds. Then cop number two leaned towards me.

'Anything happens to him, McIntyre, we'll come looking for you.'

'Good. I'll be here for a while, but thanks for your concern.'

A final glare, and both cops left.

Clearly, the cops knew perfectly well who'd attacked me. As did I. But did they really expect me to give them a name? If they did, it was high time the serious crime squad got serious. At the risk of blowing my own bugle, I've never believed in telling tales, especially if one is to any extent involved in that world. However, not everyone's so tight-lipped.

Joseph Beltrami was a well-known Glasgow lawyer. Back in the day, when dinosaurs roamed the earth, before DNA, CCTV, etc., he got a guy called Walter Scott Ellis off with shooting a taxi driver, at that time a hanging offence. Apparently, whoever had committed the crime had worn a brown suit, so that narrowed the list of suspects down to only a few thousand or so, and it took the jury all of forty-five minutes to acquit the accused.

Having a brother who was a photographer with a daily newspaper, Beltrami received a great deal of publicity and so got the name back in the day as being the go-to lawyer for the underworld. However, Big Joe was well in with the boys in blue, the Crown and the establishment.

Somebody allegedly punched him in the face one day when he was walking in the Bridgegate, the same street in which I was stabbed. Big Joe's response was to immediately report the incident to the cops. Mine had been the exact opposite. As the title to this chapter infers, you've got to find your own code and live by it. Anything else is mere hypocrisy.

I was once approached by a client who hailed from Sierra Leone, the land of my birth. He was a huge man, and he and some others from that same idyllic corner of the African continent were currently in Scotland apparently committing all sorts of frauds on the banks. What these crimes were and how they were carried out, he never got into, but apparently, he had a pal who thought they were bound to get a pull from the police at some stage and was keen to retain my services in case such an eventuality should arise.

I agreed to act for them, and he gave me a sum of money up front: half from him and half from his friend; however, he wanted to add a condition, which was that I would give him a receipt, but then kick back his half to him, without telling his pal. Basically, not happy with defrauding the banks, he wanted to bump his mate too.

I had a different – in my opinion far better – idea, which was simply to trouser the lot.

Some days went by, and Mr Sierra Leone got in touch looking for his half of the dosh, which he'd done nothing to earn.

'Neither had you,' I hear someone say. True, but I was being retained for possible legal services, but for only half the fee his friend thought I was being paid.

Accordingly, I refused to part with a penny, and the big guy started getting heavy about it. He demanded to meet me in a bar and told me to bring the money with me. Instead, I chose the Spring Inn, in Springburn, a pub I knew well, frequented by members of a family I was and remain very friendly with, and after a phone call, I made my way there.

The big guy turned up, and when he came into the bar, he took a seat and demanded the dough. I thought it was a poor show, doing his pal out of his own cash, but to be honest, the ethics of the situation wasn't uppermost in my mind when I refused to hand over half the money, as contrary to the popular saying, less is more; in this case, less was a lot less.

He started to get angry, and assumed that because he was about a foot taller and a yard broader than me, I was going to give in. He was mistaken. I told him I was happy to act for him and his pal, but the retainer was being retained, and pointed out various persons scattered about the pub: two standing at the bar, one at the puggy machine and three others at a table across from us. Each time I pointed, the people waved over, giving me a knowing smile.

Fraudsters, because of what they do for a living, tend to be very good at reading the situation, telling by the looks they receive, the body language of others, the atmosphere around them, how well things are going, and this guy caught on very quickly, got to his feet and left.

About a week or so later, I happened to be getting into the lift in Glasgow Sheriff Court, to go up to the agents' room, when suddenly I was joined by Joe Beltrami, who stood alongside, towering over me, as he was a big man. He stared straight in front, and without turning his head, said something like, 'I'm acting for those clients from Africa now.'

I was taken by surprise at this sudden statement, which, as there were only two of us in the lift, was either directed at me, or else the door he was facing. I turned to him and said, 'You're welcome to them.'

However, he then went on to tell me that I had money belonging to these people, and that they wished it returned immediately. I told him that was none of his business, to which he replied, 'You never know what they could do to someone's wife or family, they're very dangerous people.'

I confess, I could hardly believe my ears. The Big Salami was actually trying to threaten me. The lift stopped, and the door slid open.

'I know a few dangerous people myself, so tell your new pals I'm asking for them,' I said, and after adding a little more than I'd like to say here, walked out of the lift. I heard no more about the matter.

Beltrami also told one of the tabloids some total bollocks about solicitors getting too close to their clients. This from the man who got ringside seats and VIP treatment for himself and his wife, from Godfather Arthur Thompson, for the Muhammad Ali–Joe Bugner bout in Las Vegas in 1973, claiming he developed a 'relationship of trust with his clients'.

Big Joe had a partner, Willie Dunn, who I got to know quite well, and when he fell on hard times, Willie came to work with me. Unfortunately, not long after that he left this life. No doubt many defence agents will have tales to tell about Willie, a legend of a lawyer, so I'll leave it up to them: all I know is I found him to be a great guy, big drinker, even bigger character, and in a different league to the Big Salami.

While I was in hospital the jungle drums had been busy, word had got out about what had gone down, and two clients, both good friends of mine, Billy Montgomery and his younger brother, James, were already by my bedside. What we discussed at that time doesn't matter. What does matter is they were there. I lay on the bed, swathed in bandages, when suddenly I felt myself passing out.

My friends alerted the medical staff, and someone gave me a shot of something which brought me back around. As I came to, I heard a voice.

'Don't worry. Your blood pressure dropped, but we've got it back up again.' I looked up and saw a young man in a white coat. 'I'm going to be your anaesthetist,' he smiled. 'We're about to take you into theatre.'

My two friends took this as a sign they should take their leave, which they did, after I thanked them warmly for coming, and moments later someone wheeled me away. The last thing I recall was looking up into the eyes of this smiling anaesthetist and thinking to myself, 'You look really, really young . . .'

44

'It was a blonde. A blonde to make a bishop kick a hole in a stained-glass window.'

— *Farewell, My Lovely* by Raymond Chandler

Something was grabbing my right bicep, squeezing it over and over again. My mouth was opened gently, something cold, wet, and lovely was placed inside and began to melt slowly. This, along with the intermittent pumping motion, caused me to open my eyes. I looked about, slowly taking in my surroundings. A blood pressure machine was attached to my arm, and slowly the realisation of what had happened, where I was, came back to me.

Footsteps approached. I looked up. This time the eyes that met mine didn't belong to the young smiling anaesthetist, but to an older man. He turned out to be the senior consultant anaesthetist for the Glasgow Royal Infirmary.

'You gave us all quite a fright last night, young man,' he said. At the time I hadn't a clue what 'quite a fright' meant, but later discovered that during the operation to stitch me back together I'd taken an allergic reaction. My face and throat had swollen up, with the result the surgeons required to ram tubes and stick other stuff down my throat (forgive me for sounding so technical) to keep me breathing, and zap me, to get my heart beating.

Nobody knows what caused this reaction, but I'm grateful to the medical team, and thank God for being there for me.

After I'd recovered, I was due to attend Glasgow Royal Infirmary for tests; however, on the day of the appointment, I was defending one of the McGovern family in Glasgow district court. The case ran on, my client was found not guilty, but I got to the infirmary too late and was informed the doctor had left, wouldn't be back, and was off to New York, so to this day I still don't know what caused the reaction.

In intensive care, I was trying to talk to the anaesthetist when another figure appeared beside my bed: it was my father. He looked down at me and gently took my hand. Strange, I was thirty-seven years old, all the man I'd ever be, yet he made me feel safe, and I knew everything was going to be alright. However, I've been blessed with two parents, and moments later I heard a voice from the other side of my bed.

'Who's the blonde?'

Startled, I turned to see my mother standing there. I didn't realise that since I'd been stabbed, the story had hit the headlines, and the tabloids stated my life had been saved by a 'Mystery Blonde'. I've no doubt my mother was absolutely delighted with the saving part, it was the bit about the blonde she wasn't quite so happy about.

At this time, I was married to my first wife, and understandably my mother wasn't pleased I had another woman in my life, especially when I had previous for that sort of thing.

I started to explain but recall my Dad, always the peacemaker, suggesting this was neither the time nor place, and my mother relenting. On reflection, my mum's response to what she had read was perhaps just a way of keeping her mind off what had happened. But that didn't mean she wasn't going to get to the bottom of the blonde business: big time!

During my time in the Royal, Joe McGovern, Tommy McGovern, Frankie Donaldson, the Montgomery brothers, and other friends/clients, including the mystery blonde, all visited me, bringing the obligatory cards and grapes. My operation resulted in the stab wounds in my shoulder and back being stitched and my thigh, which had been sliced in half from the top to my knee, had been stapled together. However, as the nerves were cut through, even today, I have very little feeling in the upper part of my left leg, which is why at times I use a walking stick, though that can come in handy on occasion; but that's a whole other story.

A couple of days later, the cops got in touch again: this time to tell me that the person who'd stabbed me had armed himself with a gun. This begged the question why they bothered to ask who my assailant was in the first place, when clearly they'd known his identity from the beginning. This was merely an attempt to frighten me into giving them the information they wanted to make an arrest. However, to be on the safe side, I called someone in the know, who confirmed the guy in question had got hold of a gun but assured me this was solely because he expected retaliation. Either way, I told the police nothing.

After a few days, as my wounds began to heal, I was able to hobble slowly to the toilet and back, and decided it was time to make a move. Don't get me wrong, the nursing staff where fantastic, but I got the distinct feeling from some doctors doing their daily rounds that patients who weren't willing to cooperate with the police weren't quite so high on their list of priorities. Okay, maybe it was all in my mind, I don't know, what I do know is I wanted out of there ASAP.

I made a phone call and, next day, still dressed in my pyjamas, assisted by my friend James, managed to slip out of the ward and make it down the backstairs of the hospital to a car where Evelyn was waiting, and we headed home.

At that time, Evelyn was staying in Linlithgow High Street; however, my idea of quietly leaving hospital, without being discharged, putting thirty miles between me and Glasgow, then slipping unseen into her flat, while sounding good quickly proved to be a non-starter.

The second after I got out of the car and stuck the crutches under my arms, reporters from the *Daily Record* and *The Sun* newspapers were over me like a cheap suit. I was in no condition to do a hundred-yard dash to Evelyn's flat, nor wished them to know the address. There was nothing for it but to do a deal.

I'd been in the newspapers before. Nine times out of ten the picture the press print makes you look like Daffy Duck, and the quote they print is simply made up. So, we arrived at an agreement where I posed for a few photos, gave them a line about not knowing the who or the why about what happened, and they'd leave me in peace. I did my bit, they did theirs, and it was all done and dusted.

I still wasn't sure about staying in the flat until I'd heard back from various people in the west about the way the wind was blowing, so I took Evelyn and the boys to the Barnton Hotel in Edinburgh for a few nights.

While in hospital, several friends who visited me had urged me to take revenge as soon as possible. Of course, the idea was tempting, and would be to anyone, especially if in the position to respond appropriately. It was the first thing that occurred to the police when they warned they'd come looking for me should anything else happen and had also immediately crossed the sick mind of the person who stabbed me, resulting in him arming himself against the likelihood.

In my opinion that's exactly the course the cops wanted me to follow. They'd known the identity of the person responsible from the get-go, so any revenge taken could confirm, even corroborate matters, having clearly come from me, leaving myself wide open to being fitted up.

I asked myself, what would having a comeback accomplish, apart from, as I've already stated, providing the police with proof positive of who'd been involved and leaving myself liable to prosecution. The Chinese philosopher Confucius is accredited with saying, *'Before you embark on a journey of revenge, first dig two graves'*, and in his letter to the Romans, 12:19 Saint Paul states *'Vengeance is mine says the Lord, I will repay.'*

Had it been a member of my family who had been harmed, my decision may well have been different, but it wasn't them it was me, so it was my choice. Someone reading this may consider I was afraid to go down that route. They're wrong. People can believe what they like, but before drawing a conclusion (not that I give a toss what they decide) has anything I've written so far suggested I'm some sort of shrinking violet, someone short of friends from that world, or the type to run to the cops looking for protection?

A friend of mine, a successful bank robber, who helped support me during my convalescence, said to me, *'The best revenge is to live well.'* This man was no coward, no stranger to violence and the outcomes of violence. I took his advice and try to continue to, though it's difficult at times.

45

'Any lawyer worth his salt will tell the suspect in no uncertain terms to make no statement to the police under any circumstances.'

– Robert Jackson, Attorney General of the USA (1940)

It was 1994, and Tommy McGovern, younger brother of my friend and future best man, Joe, was wanted for murder, namely the shooting of a member of another infamous family. That family, who shall remain nameless, to their great credit stayed tight-lipped on the subject, not from fear but true to the code by which they'd chosen to live, feeling no need to involve the authorities, preferring rather to handle matters personally.

Tommy had disappeared for a few days. Meanwhile, the police ransacked his home, looking for incriminatory evidence. Amongst the items taken away were two books on firearms, both referring to revolvers, so both irrelevant, as the weapon used was a 0.22 semi-automatic. It's a wonder the cops didn't arrest everyone working in the National Library, as it contains an entire section on firearms.

During this time, while in Tony McGovern's car, I and some of Tommy's brothers were stopped and the car was searched in their hunt for Tommy. The police love to play cops and robbers, and it turned out, as we'd told them, Tommy wasn't in the boot, or the glove compartment. Two weeks later, though, he was arrested at his home and taken to Maryhill police station. I headed over as quickly as possible, because in those days, on a surprising number of occasions, when a client was in custody and a lawyer wasn't present at the interview, immediately the tape and video were turned off, the client often apparently felt an overwhelming desire to make a clean breast of things, even confessing to crimes they hadn't committed.

In my presence, Tommy was formally cautioned and charged with murder, but made no reply. Next morning, he appeared from custody at Glasgow Sheriff Court, where I tendered no plea or declaration on his behalf, the case was continued for further enquiries, and he was banged up in Barlinnie Prison for seven days.

Later that week, the Crown contacted my office to advise an identification parade would be held the following day at Maryhill police station. I duly attended at the appointed time and Tommy was brought in cuffs from Barlinnie. Back then, parades were held using stand-ins, people who were meant to bear a resemblance to the accused person. The fact is, the folk who were used were often winos, or those looking to earn a few quid for their services, whose sole similarity to the suspect was confined to the fact they had a pulse.

For any who've never been to an old-fashioned ID parade, I'll briefly describe what used to happened, having taken part as both solicitor and accused. As depicted in the film *The Usual Suspects*, everyone took their places in a row against a wall, with numbers above their heads, behind a partition fitted with a one-way glass screen. This arrangement allowed witnesses to view the line-up, whilst preventing themselves from being seen, so ensuring an accused person remained unaware of who had picked them out and who had not. So, it caused me no small surprise when the police led in a witness dressed from top to toe in overalls, wearing a ski mask, looking to all intents and purposes like a bank robber.

On my questioning why the witness was dressed in this fashion, the police advised this precaution was deemed necessary as, due to my close relationship with the McGoverns, it was considered likely I would relay relevant information about the witness's identity to Tommy's family and proceedings may be put into place, causing the person to withdraw his evidence.

Clearly the cops' remark cut me to the quick, but I consoled myself with the fact Glasgow's finest had overlooked the fact the person's name would soon appear on the list of witnesses, rendering the carry-on with the ski mask completely pointless.

The parade took place, and the officer conducting the farce asked the witness to point out the person he stated he'd seen firing a gun at someone in the street on the night in question. The witness walked up and down, up and down, as if deliberating carefully, then stopped in front of my client, pointed his finger, stating, 'That's him there. Number 7.'

'Number 7, what is your name,' asked the officer in charge.

'Thomas McGovern,' came the reply.

Tommy was immediately returned to jail.

A few days later, I appeared at Tommy's full committal hearing. At that time, unlike now, there was no bail for the crime of murder; in any event, Tommy's surname made it uncertain he'd get bail for dropping litter, and he was remanded in custody for trial.

Speaking about bail, people often think, after watching American cop shows on TV, that this involves lodging money for someone's release. In Scotland, money bail has long been done away with. In certain circumstances people may be asked to find 'caution' (pronounced 'kayshun') for their good behaviour, but in general, if an accused is to be released on bail, he or she must agree to certain conditions. The standard conditions are:

A) Not to abscond, but to attend court at the appointed day and time.

B) Not to offend while on bail.

C) Not to interfere with witnesses.

Sometimes, other special conditions may be added to suit a specific case, such as cooperating with social services, avoiding a location or person, handing over one's passport until after trial, etc. The conditions of bail are read out in court by the sheriff, and the accused must agree to them to be released. However, like everything else, what's meant to happen can differ greatly from what really takes place.

I once acted for a highly intoxicated woman with obvious mental health issues, before a female sheriff who appeared from custody (the woman that is, not the sheriff) charged with assault. Unfortunately, the courts have little time for those who suffer from mental problems and keen to move them on as quickly as possible, prefer to spend their time praising the police, which is why the hearing went as follows.

Sheriff: 'You must turn up at court at every appointed diet. Do you understand?'

Woman: 'Whit, come back here? Aye, that'll be bloody right!'

Sheriff: 'You must not offend while on bail, do you understand?'

Woman: 'What're you saying, hen? I cannae hear you!'

Sheriff: 'Finally, you must not interfere with any witnesses, or otherwise obstruct the course of justice, do you agree to the conditions?'

Woman: 'No danger! That bitch is getting it the minute I'm out of here!'

'Bail granted,' said the sheriff. And the accused was allowed to leave.

This sheriff wore her hair in a lopsided beehive style, a sort of salute to the leaning Tower of Pisa, imbibed bucketfuls of booze, and, having a heart of concrete, sentenced people to prison in a voice contrived to sound like Maggie Thatcher.

The fact that in Tommy's case this supposed ID witness wore a ski mask made no difference whatsoever, as far as disguising his identity was concerned. Word would still have got back to the family as to who was underneath it. In any event, when it came down to whoever had committed the crime under investigation, both sides knew the guy in the ski-mask hadn't a clue.

What transpires after the police have decided on a suspect, and what the defence do about matters, may involve the truth, or not, as the countless numbers of wrongful convictions and the many more that haven't been investigated attest to. From the off, it's basically a battle between the Crown and the Defence, and the truth is a casualty of war.

This witness's positive ID struck the defence as strange for several reasons. I was advised the witness knew Tommy, posing the questions why in that case would he pick him out in the first place, why take so long, and was he obeying orders, playing a part, pretending to take his time, all the while told who to choose?

I was advised this so-called independent witness had a vast number of previous convictions, so thick they could've been published in paperback. Plus, apparently the person possessed the ability to bilocate, as despite being nowhere near the scene of the crime he proved able to provide an eyewitness account and point to my client as the perpetrator.

This development obviously required a sit-down, and I met with several parties, including senior members of the McGovernment, the name attributed to the family due to their control of the area, at my friend's house in Springburn. At that meeting it was raised that a source who worked as a turnkey in a local police station had confirmed to them this witness had been offered a deal by the Crown. I don't know if this was true or not.

The deal, it was claimed, was that all this witness's outstanding cases would be dropped, he'd be given a new identity, passport, fresh start, the works, providing he testified in court to seeing my client pull the trigger that night.

Hearing this, someone present, furious that this person was apparently prepared to perjure himself to convict Tommy, suggested taking the witness out, and not for dinner and drinks. There was a murmur of approval and my friend turned to look at me.

'What do you think, Jazza?'

I remember looking at him, then round the room, trying to take things in. What did I think? This was the witness's life on the line, someone who'd apparently agreed to perjure himself to escape justice by putting someone else in prison for life. Whether Tommy was guilty or innocent was beside the point, this guy's evidence would be perjury. Number six of the ten commandments states: 'Thou shalt not kill.' However, number nine states: 'Thou shalt not bear false witness against thy neighbour.' Clearly, number nine is missing in the police copy of the Bible.

'There's no doubt it would remove one problem,' I said.

A nod of assent from the others.

'On the other hand, it could complicate matters and leave even more problems.'

'In what way?' asked my friend.

'We know the guy's a liar, but still, we know where we stand. If the guy goes missing, it'll look very iffy; what's more, the cops could get even more creative to fill in the gap.'

I shrugged at the assembled troops. I knew the police wouldn't just sit back and swallow the fact they'd another body on their books. From what we'd heard about the man in the mask, the mob were already hard at it and if that guy got so much as a dirty look, never mind ending up in a skip somewhere, the other side were going to get even more inventive than usual with their evidence.

'You're saying, we don't touch the guy, even though he's lying his arse off and trying to put Tommy away?'

'I'm saying, it could backfire, big time. The Crown need corroboration, they can't count on just one witness, and we'll be attacking his character anyway.'

'If we do that, won't they attack Tommy's character when he gives evidence?' Everyone present was fairly au fait with court procedure.

'Tommy won't be going anywhere near the witness box if I've anything to do with it,' I answered.

'You know best, Jazz,' said my friend, and put a hand on my shoulder.

I nodded. But did I? A great deal of preparation was carried out by myself and my office, which we needn't go into, but included precognosing over a hundred and fifty witnesses, planning the defence, plus numerous consultations with Donald Findlay QC, who the family wished me to instruct to represent Tommy at the High Court.

Donald Findlay, despite being a rabid Rangers supporter, is in my opinion the finest defence counsel in the country, one I'd heartily recommend to anyone in serious trouble.

Eventually, after a year, which involved the Crown obtaining a lengthy extension of the time an untried prisoner could be lawfully held in custody, my client's case was called at Glasgow High Court.

The trial was heard before the Lord Justice Clerk, the most senior criminal judge in the Scottish judicial hierarchy, and prosecuted by the Solicitor General, the second most senior prosecutor. Murders in Glasgow are hardly rare, but clearly, this one was getting top priority.

The case kicked off, routine ballistic and forensic evidence was led, cop after cop, Crown witness after Crown witness took the stand, to little avail. I won't bore the reader with a blow-by-blow account of all that transpired. At the conclusion of the Crown case, it boiled down to the matter of corroborating the account of the man in the mask, and the Crown counted on the evidence of one wee woman who had seemingly seen the incident from the window of a block of flats, overlooking the crime scene. After she gave her initial testimony regarding the shooting she'd seen take place, the Solicitor General asked the vital question:

'Do you see the man who fired the gun in court today, and if so, please point him out.'

There was a deafening silence as the witness looked all around the room and back again, before shaking her head.

'No. He's not here.'

Suddenly, she turned and looked straight at Tommy in the dock. The Solicitor General stared at the witness, expectantly.

'Yes?' he asked.

The woman raised her hand and jabbed a forefinger in the direction of my client, sitting between two police officers, and stated:

'Whoever it was, it wasn't him. The man I saw was much taller, and he'd dark hair.'

And with those words, the Crown case dissolved faster than an aspirin in acid. My client had red hair and stood about 5 feet 7 in height. The Solicitor General, with evident reluctance, turned to the judge.

'My lord, in all the circumstances, I have no alternative other than to withdraw the indictment and ask the court to return a formal verdict of acquittal.'

The Lord Justice Clerk, clearly not a happy chappie, had no choice, and told Tommy to stand up. Tommy stood.

'In view of the Crown's withdrawal of the indictment, I find you not guilty,' said His Lordship.

A great cheer went up from Tommy's family and friends filling the gallery. During this commotion, Donald Findlay rose, and apologised to the court for the outburst; however, I know he didn't mean a word of it. Like everything in law, it was all to do with appearances and little to do with the truth. None of those who proposed 'taking care' of the witness are with us now. If I'd agreed with the idea, things would have taken a very different turn. Did I really believe it to be a bad idea, that it may backfire, or ruled it out because a man's life was at stake, even one willing to commit perjury to convict another? This raises the question, would I have given the same advice if the accused had been my brother or sister? I'd like to think so, but still have avoided giving myself an answer.

46

'The true hypocrite is the one who ceases to perceive his deception, the one who lies with sincerity.'

– André Gide

Back in the nineties, there was a junior fiscal working in Linlithgow Sheriff Court, who, in my opinion, bore an uncanny resemblance to Buzz Lightyear, but without that cartoon character's pleasant personality.

Once, before getting his wings, Buzz was in a bar in Edinburgh, and, despite it being way past drinking-up time, refused to finish off his beer. The barman, after being patient for as long as possible, eventually picked up the pint perfectly legally, and requested he leave. But Buzz's reaction was to run outside, flag down a passing panda car, flash his Fiscal ID, demand the cops arrest the barman and charge him with theft of his drink. Believe it or not, the two woodentops did what he asked, and the poor publican was hauled before the district court. However, at trial, the barman's evidence was believed, resulting in him being acquitted, completely exonerated, and Buzz left looking like a right rocket.

After this, Buzz took off from the capital and landed in Linlithgow to become one of procurator fiscal Hugh Annan's protégés. Full disclosure, Hugh Annan isn't on my Christmas card list. He's always struck me as the sort of person my dad would have called well-balanced, because he'd a chip on both shoulders.

On one occasion, which one escapes me, (there were so many in the good old, bad old days) I'd been charged under the Bail Act for not turning up at court for trial at Linlithgow Sheriff for some road traffic offences which I'll talk about later. My defence to the Bail Act charge was that when I'd contacted the PF's office, I'd been given the wrong date by Buzz, hence my non-appearance.

Of course, the Crown wouldn't accept that, and the alleged Bail Act contravention went to trial before the road traffic one did, meaning the bold Buzz was the main witness against me. Sheriff Jonathan Mitchell, an advocate, was on the bench, and my good friend George More was acting for me. Carlsberg don't make defence solicitors, but if they did, they'd probably make George More. He's quite simply one of the top criminal defence agents ever to walk the planet. The man's way up there with Walter Sutherland and me!

Anyway, the case kicked off and basically, Buzz gave his evidence, I gave mine, George was brilliant, as usual. Buzz wasn't believed, as usual, and I was found not guilty.

I returned to my office in Glasgow. The following day I met some friends for a few drinks after work, and as a result arrived home very late for dinner. I'm a big fan of all things Italian, Evelyn was making my favourite food, Osso Buco, and I wasn't missing it this time. Technically, I didn't miss it last time either, or rather, it didn't miss me. On that occasion I'd also gone for a drink after work, to Thomson's Bar in Springburn, with Joe McGovern, and some friends. The quick drink wasn't quite as quick as I'd promised, and on arriving home, Evelyn announced dinner was ruined, picked up the large dish containing the meal she'd lovingly prepared, and hurled the lot at me.

I tried dodging to one side, but some of the contents caught the sleeve of my suit, while the rest shot over my shoulder landing in the kitchen sink. I sniffed my sleeve. It smelled fantastic. I lifted my arm and licked it. Tasted even better. Without further ado, I grabbed a spoon and scoffed the lot straight out of the yellow basin.

Evelyn screwed up her face.

'You're disgusting,' she yelled at me. But, deep down, I knew that she knew, I couldn't have paid a greater compliment to her cooking.

Anyway, back to the motorway. I was making good time, but, as I left the M8, I was pulled over by a traffic car containing two cops, who, having consumed all their coffee and doughnuts for the day, were clearly at something of a loose end.

They examined my vehicle closer than a border patrol at Crossmaglen, decided three of the tyres looked a little worn and asked for my licence and insurance documents. I told the cops I didn't have those items to hand, and they issued me with a HORT1, basically a form requiring a person to attend a police station within seven days and produce the relevant driving documents. I took the ticket, stuck it in the glove box and promptly forgot about it.

Some weeks later I received a copy complaint, claiming I'd been driving without a licence or insurance, and the tread on three of the tyres fell below the required minimum. Back then, I was a busy young lawyer, shooting about the country, down south in Dumfries, up north in Shetland, and many courts in between. I made a mental note of the pleading diet, stuck the complaint in a desk drawer and forgot all about it, with the result a warrant was issued for my arrest due to my failure to appear. I called and arranged to answer the warrant a few days later. This involved handing myself in to the cops at crazy o'clock in the morning, then appearing in court, but, when my case called, despite the fact I'd phoned and appeared voluntarily, the procurator fiscal had ordered the fiscal depute that day to move the court to remand me in custody for four weeks.

However, Sheriff Fleming was on the bench that day and aware the road traffic contraventions I was accused of, even on conviction, didn't carry a custodial sentence, and coupled with the fact he was a fair man, granted me bail and set dates for intermediate and trial diets

My readers may not be aware that intermediate diets are fixed for about two weeks prior to trial, to ascertain everything is ready for the big day. Intermediate diets are a brilliant idea and like so many brilliant ideas, very rarely work.

I turned up at court, again with my solicitor, George More. As a matter of interest, George never charged me a penny for appearing, although I once gave him an old penny, dated 1944, as he was born on D-Day that year. When my case called, George produced a letter I'd given him, from my insurance company, stating I was insured to drive the car. However, I was bang to rights on the bald tyre charges. But Buzz wasn't satisfied with this and moved the court to adjourn the matter for seven days, for him to check the letter, so desperate was he to convict me of the more serious charge, which could result in a ban.

One week later we were back in court, and Buzz was flying high. He happily informed the court he'd contacted my insurance company, who had advised him they could find no record of me being insured with them. I couldn't understand this, but that's what the letter said, so George and I told Buzz I'd plead guilty to driving without insurance if he agreed to drop the bald tyre charges, which were only barely under the limit anyway.

Buzz nearly bit our hands off, so delighted was he to agree a deal which he dearly hoped would see me disqualified from driving. Accordingly, I pleaded guilty to no insurance, the other charges were dropped, but, as I didn't bring my driving licence to court, the case was adjourned for a further seven days for me to produce it.

Another week passed, George and I appeared again, but in the interim period, my insurance company had written to George to advise they had re-checked their records, discovered an error on their part, and confirmed I was insured to drive my car on the date in question.

Accordingly, when we came back to court, the plea of guilty to no insurance could no longer stand, so was withdrawn, meaning Buzz was forced to accept my not guilty plea to that charge, and as all the charges involving the tyres had already been dropped, I walked out of court acquitted of the lot. Of course, Mr Lightyear was furious, as seeing people suffer for their sins, however minor, was food and drink to this dyed-in-the-wool hypocrite.

Apparently, later in 2005, Buzz, by then a senior prosecutor, attended at the former Police Headquarters, Pitt Street, Glasgow, to talk to the cops about controlling and cutting down prostitution in the city's red-light areas. However, later a couple of beat cops investigating a noise coming from a close in the city centre came across the bold Buzz being given a blowjob by some girl on the game.

On seeing the police, Buzz tried to flee but tripped over his trousers, which were round his ankles, and his struggle with the officers resulted in charges of indecency and resisting arrest. However, unlike my bald tyre case, Buzz's didn't go to court, as the Crown took the decision that prosecuting one of their own was not in the public interest.

Really? Shouldn't the public, especially prostitutes, be advised that one of the people who prosecute them for a living, who preach about cracking down on them and their profession, is breaking the very laws he is prosecuting them for?

Anyway, the charges were dropped. Apparently, it was claimed Buzz'd been suffering from post-traumatic stress disorder, after being in The Gulf with the Territorial Army; a weekend warrior, as Billy Connolly called them. I'll let the reader decide whether they think the Lord Advocate would have found it in the public interest to let a defence lawyer walk away from these charges, with or without the excuse of PTSD.

However, Mr Lightyear's rank hypocrisy didn't end there. In December 2012 after a tip-off and obtaining a search warrant, the cops searched Buzz's family home, including a garden shed, with a plaque on the door that stated, 'Dad's Den', from which they seized two laptops and an external hard drive. These were analysed, and according to the press, the police apparently discovered that the computers contained thousands of indecent images, mostly involving children from as young as three to four-teen years of age, adopting what were described as erotic poses. He confessed he took or allowed these disgusting photographs to be taken or made, in contravention of the Civic Government (Scotland) Act of 1982. In mitigation, the court was once more advised he'd previously claimed to suffer from post-traumatic stress disorder (as mentioned when previously charged) after serving with the Territorial Army in Iraq. Why this should cause him to take or possess filthy photos of toddlers isn't immediately apparent. However, the sheriff, claiming to recall a recent appeal court decision, and sentencing guidelines, allowed the accused to continue with the treatment he was already undergoing, claiming that it would be best not to impose a custodial sentence, and that counselling would ensure minimum risk to the public.

Call me cynical, dear reader, but wouldn't the best way to 'ensure minimum risk to the public' have been to bang Buzz up behind bars? But, of course that wasn't on the cards, as, in my opinion, the Crown was looking after their own again, and he was handed a community service order and told to keep seeing a shrink. Apparently, possessing two pistols without the relevant licence deserves three years' imprisonment, while possessing thousands and thousands of disgusting images of young children doesn't merit a single day inside.

47

'No good deed goes unpunished.'

– Oscar Wilde

'I'll pull over here, Pat,' I said, and parked in the bus stop. My assistant and I had just left Edinburgh Sheriff Court, and, on our way back to Glasgow, I wanted him to nip into a shop and pick up something I'd ordered. As I waited, a double decker drew up and, annoyed at my parking there, the driver, despite the fact he or she was unable to see me due to being on the other side of the bus, decided to teach me a lesson by blocking my car in whilst the passengers alighted.

However, being blocked in didn't bother me in the slightest. Pat hadn't returned, so I wasn't going anywhere. After the passengers got off, the bus driver, satisfied I'd learned my lesson, prepared to pull away, but when the brake was released, due to the street's steep incline, the bus lurched forward, and being so close to my car, nudged the wing. At that moment, Pat returned, and the driver, realising what had happened, panicked and took off as if Jenson Button was behind the wheel.

Pat and I laughed as we watched the bus roar round the corner into Princes Street, as if the hounds of hell were at its wheels. I got out, checked the wing, saw a tiny wee mark but no real damage, and we headed back to No Mean City without another thought.

Months later, I got a call from the cops who wanted a word with me at Linlithgow police station. I went along, wondering what was up, to be told it was about a collision with a bus in South Frederick

Street, Edinburgh. I assumed some solid citizen witnessed what happened, and concerned my car was damaged by the bus, reported it to a passing policeman. Accordingly, I told the cops that the bus driver, whilst trying to make a point, hadn't meant to be malicious, and as there was no real damage done I didn't want him getting into any trouble with his work, so I neither reported it, nor wanted anything done about the matter.

The cops smiled at one another and advised me there was a problem. The Crown's version of events (never to be confused with the truth) was the bus driver had called in the matter.

'You've got things the wrong way round,' sneered one cop. 'We're charging you with driving into the bus and leaving the scene of the accident.' And they proceeded to caution and charge me. I made no reply, not just out of habit, but rather because I was speechless.

Shortly after this, Tommy McGovern called and asked me to go with him to collect some belongings of his that the cops still had from the High Court trial. I picked Tommy up and drove him down to Baird Street police station to retrieve various items of clothing, books and other stuff taken from his house at the time it was searched.

While at the station, the duty sergeant advised me another client of mine had been arrested and was in custody there. I decided to see him, and Tommy asked to use my car meantime, to take his things home, saying he'd pick me up in twenty minutes. I agreed and headed to the cells.

True to his word, Tommy came back shortly after. However, as I walked to my car, two cops came up behind me, stated they'd checked the police computer, Tommy was a disqualified driver, and claimed that, as his lawyer I should know that, so I was guilty of allowing him to drive my car without a licence or insurance. Tommy and I were charged on the spot under the relevant sections of the Road Traffic Act 1972, made no reply, and were released for citation.

I'd been preoccupied with the fact that one of my clients was in the cells, but in any event didn't know Tommy was disqualified, as I hadn't appeared for him in that case. Of course, Tommy couldn't have given a toss and just took off. The two cops, aware of Tommy's ban, knowing he was uninsured, unconcerned about what could happen to some innocent person if there was a crash, didn't mark my card but let Tommy drive away, so that they could charge us both when he came back.

I wasn't unduly concerned, as Tommy arrived safe and told me he'd throw his hands up and plead, provided the prosecution dropped the charge against me, thus saving the time and expense of a trial. We were to appear some weeks later, on a Friday, when I happened to be defending a client in the same court.

I'd just dealt with my client when our case called. Tommy was, as usual, fashionably late (in fact he didn't turn up at all) and, still wearing my gown, I entered the dock, to adhere to my plea of not guilty for myself. As I did so, two police officers entered the court and arrested me in front of the bench, claiming there was an outstanding warrant in connection with my car colliding with a double-decker bus, that I'd failed to appear at Edinburgh for trial, and took me away, much to the satisfaction of the stipendiary magistrate.

I tried to explain this was the first I'd heard of the matter since being charged months ago, but par for the course, my plea landed on plastic ears. Despite being a minor road traffic matter, and apart from the fact I was innocent, the charge I faced was being treated by the Crown as important enough to put me on Interpol's ten-most-wanted list.

Handcuffed, to add to the humiliation, I was dragged downstairs to a holding room, to await transport to London Road police station. Once there I was advised officers from Lothian and Borders would come to collect and escort me to Edinburgh later that evening.

Readers will be delighted to know the taxes they pay from their hard-earned wages, rather than being squandered fighting serious crime, instead fund overtime jaunts for cops in the most trivial of cases, in this instance, to pick me up and drive me across country for a non-imprisonable offence, which they knew I hadn't committed.

Whilst in the holding room, I used my mobile to call the office and cancel my appointments for the afternoon, as I was in custody. Evelyn answered, sighing audibly . . .

'Not again! What for now?'

'A non-appearance warrant, and tell Lindsey' – my friend, Joe McGovern's daughter, my secretary, '– I wouldn't have been there to arrest, if her uncle Tommy had turned up.'

On reflection, there was more chance of Tommy Cooper turning up.

'Get hold of the fiscal's office in Edinburgh, and find out what the score is,' I said and hung up to save the mobile's battery.

True to form, the fiscal's office claimed they could do nothing about the matter. I contacted my brother, William, also a criminal lawyer, but fight as he might, and he did so valiantly, he could get nowhere. As a last resort, my phone battery failing fast, I called a friend of mine, a senior QC who I regularly instructed in High Court cases, thinking I'd use a sledgehammer to crack a rather minuscule nut.

The QC in turn contacted Crown Office and spoke directly to the then Lord Advocate, with whom he was on friendly terms. However, the most senior prosecutor in Scotland stated (for some unaccountable reason) he wasn't willing to withdraw the warrant, even for a non-imprisonable offence, nor allow me to appear under my own steam.

I confess it came as rather a surprise that the Lord Advocate took this very hard line when told of my dilemma. In the past, while a young advocate trying to earn a crust, our firm had instructed this same gentleman, considering him to be a very competent clever individual. While at university, I had avoided sitting the accountancy and taxation exams necessary for me to qualify as a solicitor. Accordingly, while working as an apprentice, I was also attending Edinburgh University for lectures in these subjects a few times a week and had been receiving private tuition from an accountant friend in Edinburgh.

One evening, after a tutorial, I was on my way to Waverley Station to catch a train when I decided to grab a cup of coffee and had no sooner taken a seat than this same advocate turned up at my table, drunk as a skunk, and virtually collapsed into a chair facing me.

To this day I've no idea why he was there, or where he'd been, but feel certain it wasn't a temperance meeting. I bought him a couple of cups of black coffee, missed my train buying him a third, attempting to sober him up, before offering to call him a cab.

However, he refused my offer, stating if his wife didn't see his car in the drive the next morning, he'd be in hot water, as she'd know he was drunk. I told him she'd know that when she woke to find the house reeking of alcohol, and if he got behind the wheel, he or someone else may not see the next morning, and he'd end up in more hot water than the angriest wife could rain down on him. However, nothing I said made any difference, he was driving home, that was that. He slurred his thanks and staggered off in search of his vehicle. He went on to become Lord Advocate, and in due course a senator of the College of Justice, sitting in judgement on his fellow man, but thankfully he and his car made it home without further incident, or at least, none the public know about.

So it was, when my QC called the Lord Advocate, I thought he may, for old time's sake, have shown a modicum of mercy to a fellow alleged road traffic offender set to spend the next four days in a cell, for a far less serious offence than the one he'd intended to commit. However, he refused to interfere. Perhaps, due to his inebriated condition during our meeting in Waverley station, he didn't recall the assistance I'd rendered him, certainly he didn't return the favour.

Accordingly, I required to remain in custody over the weekend, Sunday being Father's Day, until the following Tuesday, Monday being a bank holiday. Happy Father's Day to me!

48

I was lying in a cell in London Road police station when a couple of cops arrived to escort me to Edinburgh that evening. From there, I was driven across country to the south-side of the capital and stuck in another cell in St Leonard's Street. As the door slammed behind me, I noticed a cigarette lighter had been used to write 'Hibees' and 'King Billy', on the wall, and underneath was the outline of an ArmaLite rifle. Clearly the cell's previous occupant had been suffering from a split personality.

On further investigation, I spotted some small spatters of blood on the floor. At this time, it was considered possible to catch AIDS from a black pudding supper, so taking no risks I pressed the bell on the wall. Eventually, the metal slat in the cell door slid open, and a turnkey asked what I wanted. I told him going home was at the top of my list, but if that wasn't on the cards, new accommodation would have to do. He mumbled something about rooms with an ensuite and pool view being hard to come by this late on a Friday, but eventually agreed to move me to another cell.

I spent that evening, the next day and night, alternately staring at the walls and sleeping, wrapped in a blanket apparently knitted from barbed wire. The day after this was Father's Day. To my joy, Evelyn, my long-suffering girlfriend, now my wife (and not so long-suffering) turned up at the station. The police wouldn't let me see her, that would have been far too humane, but she'd brought cards from the kids, magazines, newspapers, bars of chocolate and an assortment of crisps:

a welcome change from the mysterious microwaved substances served in polystyrene cartons I'd been fed for the last forty-eight hours.

I read for a while, ate some crisps, then, remembering it was Sunday, pressed the button on the wall again. After what seemed a fortnight, the turnkey managed to travel the entire twenty feet to my cell, and slide the slat open again.

'Yes?' he asked, wearily.

'I want to go to Mass.'

A long pause then . . .

'You what?'

'I want to go to Mass.'

An even longer pause.

'You mean you want to go to church?'

'Unless you've taken holy orders, or have a priest handy, yes.'

I could almost hear the wheels in his head turning.

'But . . . but . . . you can't.'

'So, you're refusing me my human rights, are you?'

Silence.

'Well?'

He stared at me through the slat for a long moment, then . . .

'Wait there,' he said, rather unnecessarily I thought, slid the slat shut and I heard his footsteps retreat.

Fifteen minutes or so passed. I was perusing one of the newspapers Evelyn brought me, whilst tucking into a bar of Turkish delight, when the slat slid open once more, and a different face appeared, that of a uniformed cop.

'Yes?' said the man in blue.

I approached the door.

'I want to go to Mass.'

'You want what?'

'Didn't the turnkey tell you?'

'I thought he was having me on.'

'That would involve a sense of humour.'

'But you can't go to Mass, you're . . . You're a prisoner.'

'An untried prisoner. Who enjoys all the rights of a free man, including those concerning his religion. Or are you refusing them?'

A pause.

'Well?'

He stared at me a moment.

'Wait there?'

Where did these people think I was going? Another half an hour or so passed. Suddenly the slat slid open and yet another face appeared.

'What's all this nonsense?'

I approached the door again. From the pips on the newcomer's shoulder, I realised my request had resulted in a response from someone considerably higher up the chain of command.

'It may be nonsense to you, inspector, but in my book, it's not a laughing matter.'

'You're not seriously suggesting I send officers to escort you from here to church?'

'Why not? You sent them all the way to Glasgow to escort me back here.'

A pause. I was getting tired of pauses.

'Look, St Margaret's Church and St Leonard's police station are in the same street . . .'

'Forget it, you're going nowhere.'

'I'm untried, presumed to be innocent, and your refusal to let me attend Mass places me in a state of mortal sin.'

Of course, my claim was complete nonsense. Being banged up, and so in a situation outwith my control, I couldn't be held to be guilty of any failure to attend to my religious duties; still, it was worth a shot.

'You'll just have to add that sin to the list,' he said with an unpleasant smile. 'Course, if you like, I could always send the serious crime squad down to hear your confession.'

'I'd prefer to make my own confession to a priest,' I replied, 'rather than have it made up for me by your mob.'

For a moment, the inspector looked almost hurt, then he slammed the slat shut. I called out . . .

'I take it that's a no then?!'

Retreating footsteps were the only reply, and I was left languishing in my cell, unwashed, unshaved and unshriven; but with a plentiful supply of chocolate, Father's Day cards and, much more importantly, the love of my family.

49

'The innocent is the person who explains nothing.'

– Albert Camus

Sunday and Monday dragged past, the time broken only by the turnkey (who, due to me kicking off about missing Mass, seemed convinced I was a religious crackpot) coming to hand me more microwaved mush in polystyrene containers at periodic intervals.

Eventually, Tuesday turned up, bringing with it the van to take me to another cell, in Edinburgh Sheriff Court and a visit from my younger brother William, also a criminal lawyer. I'd managed to call him on my mobile from the district court, four days ago, before I'd been banged up. To say William and I are different is the understatement of the millennium: we share the same parents, belief in God, sense of humour, rugged good looks, but that's where it ends. While we're very close, our natures couldn't be further apart.

Willie took a seat behind the glass partition separating us, looked me over, and shook his head.

'Some people suit stubble. George Clooney for instance. You? Not so much.'

'They're not too hot on personal hygiene around here,' I informed him, feeling the five days' growth on my face.

William lifted a polystyrene cup to his lips, took a sip and placed it back down on his side of the partition. He caught me watching him.

'I bought you coffee too, but they wouldn't let me bring it down here,' he said.

'You parted with cash?' I exclaimed. 'What time is the Red Arrows fly-by?'

My brother let out a bored sigh, as he produced a pad and pen from his briefcase.

'So, what's your defence this time?' I noted his emphasis on the word 'this'.

'I didn't do it.'

'Seriously, James.'

'I'm telling you. I am an innocent man!'

Willie sighed again, unconvinced by my Billy Joel routine, and put away his pen.

'Fair enough. They're calling your case shortly. You can tell me your fairy story later.'

'It's true. I'm innocent.'

'You said.'

'I didn't bang my car into any bus. He bumped into me.'

Willie was still far from convinced, so I decided to drop the subject for the moment.

'Who's on the bench?' I asked.

'Lothian.'

'Lucky white heather.'

My brother nodded. 'Just as well the Crown's not opposing bail.'

'Am I supposed to be grateful? I've been banged up for five days for doing sweet Fanny Adams!'

'Apart from failing to appear at court.'

'I didn't receive the complaint.'

William rolled his eyes.

'Honestly!' I said.

William gave me the look I'd seen so many times over the years; like the one he gave me one bonfire night when we were boys, and I denied strapping a banger to one of his beloved action men and blowing it to bits. Or when our ball sailed over the wall and landed among our neighbour's award-winning roses. I'd swear to keep watch, while Willie jumped into the grumpy old git's garden, and as his feet touched forbidden ground, I'd yell, 'Mr McKenzie,

238

there's a strange boy wrecking your flower bed!' (The number of times my brother fell for this was truly astronomical.)

'Alright.' I shrugged. 'Maybe I mislaid it. I've been busy.'

'Really?' said William. 'Because I'd nothing better to do this morning than traipse across the country to bail you out. Again!' he added, I thought a tad unnecessarily. His tone confirmed my decision not to insist on my innocence at this stage and I remained silent.

My kid brother smiled. 'Good. Keep it shut. Let me do the talking.' And with that, he headed back upstairs.

An hour or so later, a cop came to my cell, let me out, and led me to the custody court and straight into the dock. Sheriff Lothian was a large, toadlike individual who, when not beating up his wife, was to be found squatting on the shrieval bench. I was brought before this domestic abuser after being banged up for five days in the cells, so wasn't in the best of moods. As I entered the dock the clerk of court called out:

'Call the case, PF against James McIntyre.' He looked at me. 'Are you James McIntyre?'

'That's correct.'

My brother stood. 'My lord, my name's McIntyre, and I appear for Mr McIntyre who pleads not guilty.'

The sheriff glanced up from his papers at me. 'Is that right?'

'That's correct,' I answered.

The toad turned to my brother. 'What's the defence in this case?'

My brother walked over to the dock. 'He wants to know your defence,' he said.

'I'm not deaf, Willie.'

'So, what do I tell him?'

At that moment, the effect of being dragged in cuffs from Glasgow, banged up for five days, including Father's Day, for a non-imprisonable offence I hadn't committed, and fed food tasting of molten plastic, took its toll. I said to Willie, in a loud voice:

'If he wants to know my defence, tell him to turn up at the trial and he'll find out!'

Willie closed his eyes, and turned back to the table, but before he could speak, the sheriff cut in.

'Apparently, the accused is being uncooperative. The case will recall at the end of the roll. Take him downstairs.'

William thanked me with a glare, not happy he had to wait until the case called again. So, I was locked up until everyone else in custody had been hauled up in front of the old fart.

Unless you're a sheriff, magistrate, judge, policeman, or work for the Crown in one way or another, if there's so much as a whiff of a suggestion of a domestic disturbance, the position is that the pendulum has swung to a ridiculous extreme, and political correctness, vote winning and virtue signalling has seen common sense thrown out of the window.

Happy to lock other people up, when not on the bench, this lump of lard's private life left a lot to be desired. Of course, the police and procurator fiscal's office were all well aware Lothian was a wife beater, but he was never made to account for his crimes. On one occasion, while indulging in a violent, drunken episode of domestic abuse, the cops dragged him from his house and charged him, but the Crown decided, despite the evidence (even the press knew and were poised to print) this serial abuser should be released and not prosecuted.

However, the Blob was finally brought to brook during a lightening raid on a massage parlour, where the learned sheriff was seemingly found tied to a table, being beaten vigorously by a busty dominatrix in a basque. Of course, despite his fall from grace, his handing out rigorous sentences while spending his salary on hookers, the ranks closed and this hippopotamus of a hypocrite was allowed to retire with his full pension. It always puzzles me why he paid to be thrashed: so many folk would have done it for free.

50

'Liar, liar, pants on fire.'

— Adapted from William Blake's poem 'The Liar'

The road traffic trial date rolled round, and I duly turned up at court, where I met my brother.

'Come with me,' said William, as we entered the court cafe. 'I'll buy you a cup of coffee.'

'You'll buy?' I felt his forehead for any signs of fever.

'That was funny the first five hundred times. Now shut up and get us a seat!' A few minutes later, he was back with two cups of something warm and wet that had once passed for coffee.

'Remember when you appeared from custody, Sheriff Lothian asked what your defence was?' asked William, taking a seat across from me.

'I told him to turn up at the trial and he'd find out, and he sent me back downstairs.'

'Couldn't help yourself, could you?'

I was about to answer his rhetorical question, when my brother butted in.

'Anyway, now I know,' he said.

'Know what?'

'Your defence.'

'You mean, that I'm innocent?'

'Incredible as it seems, yes.'

'Trouble is, being innocent doesn't cut it when you're up against the cops,' I said.

'No. But I've had a glance at the fiscal's papers in your case.'

'Does he know that?'

'She. And don't be ridiculous. I was reading over her shoulder. Anyway, listen . . .'

An hour or so later the case called before Sheriff Sandy McIwain, a past president of the Law Society. He was no doubt an amazing husband, parent, grandparent, conveyancer, but I never heard of him acting for a client in a criminal court, and his elevation to the bench apparently, like so many past Law Society presidents, procurators fiscal and failed advocates, was doubtless a reward for playing the establishment's game, with no concern for the plight of the punters who appeared before him.

The case kicked off. Crown witness number one, the bus driver, small, morbidly obese and sweating profusely, entered the box, took the oath and the fiscal began her examination, holding in her hand the sole Crown production, a car registration document.

The bus driver accused me, the driver of the maroon BMW 3 series, of bumping into his bus, then leaving the scene, and provided the car's registration number. When asked if he could identify the driver, he turned, and without hesitation pointed to me. At this point the depute sat down, and my brother stood to cross-examine the witness.

'Is your evidence about the car in question, its colour, make, model, the identification of the driver, as you recall it was that day?'

'Yes,' said, the driver, starting to sweat.

'Were you not seated in the driver's cabin of the bus?'

'Yes.'

'And weren't passengers getting off at the stop between you and my client's car?'

'Yes.' The bus driver produced a hanky and proceeded to dab his brow.

'Clearly my client's car would be well below your eye-level on the double decker?'

'Yes,' said the driver, mopping his neck as if swabbing the deck of a fishing trawler.

'Kindly tell the court how, sitting in your cabin, on the far side of the bus, above eye level of other vehicles, with passengers alighting between you and the car in question, you could see the driver, never mind identify him in court over a year later?'

'I ... I just can, that's all,' he stuttered, squeezing his soaking hanky in his hand.

'Has anybody told you what to say today, or influenced your evidence in any way?'

'No ... no,' he replied, applying his hanky fervently, but now uselessly.

'And you realise your evidence is on oath?'

'Yes ... yes.' The driver was now swimming in sweat in the witness box.

'Nothing further.' William smiled to the sheriff and sat.

'I don't think we need keep this witness,' said the sheriff, realising the man was on the verge of collapse.

The sheriff thanked the driver for performing his public duty, which in this case involved committing perjury on behalf of the Crown, and the fiscal called the first police witness.

The cop took the stand, stated the bus driver reported my maroon-coloured BMW as being the car that collided with his vehicle and left the scene, with me behind the steering wheel on that date, at that time and location, and confirmed the registration. My brother glanced over at me. I shook my head, and we both chose not to cross-examine the witness but let him happily go with the flow.

The Crown then led the second cop, whose evidence, surprise, surprise, proved identical to his colleague's. But this time, as the fiscal regained her seat, my brother glanced at me. I nodded, he smiled, and rose to address the witness.

'Officer, you weren't at the scene of this incident, were you?'

'No sir, we merely cautioned and charged your client.'

'So, who advised you of the details of the incident?'

'The bus driver.'

'You're saying that the bus driver, alone and unassisted, provided you with the colour of the car, the make, model, registration, etc., as he had noted all this information down at the time?'

'That's correct, sir.'

William nodded thoughtfully, then quick as a flash, leaned over and snatched the Crown production lying on the table in front of the fiscal depute.

'The difficulty is, constable,' William said, looking at the production as he spoke. 'The vehicle documentation lodged by the Crown states the car in question was indeed a BMW; however, it was not maroon in colour but white, not a 3 series, but rather a 7 series, and manufactured in a different year, with a different registration number.'

The cop turned as white as my car had been that day and glanced round desperately at the first police witness, who'd chosen a seat in court to comfortably spectate my downfall. However, due to this unforeseen turn of events, the witness only caught sight of his colleague's back, as now the proverbial was hitting the fan, his pal was beating a retreat to the door.

'The registration documents must be from another case,' he volunteered.

'No, this refers to my client's case, merely a different car.'

The cop swallowed and tried again.

'Maybe . . . his firm had two BMWs, a maroon and a white one . . .' He was clutching wildly at straws.

'My brother's firm did indeed have two BMWs.'

The cop relaxed a fraction.

'But never at the same time,' concluded William, with a smile.

The cop tensed again and drew the depute a terrified look.

'You see,' my brother continued, 'when the white BMW 7 series was being driven by the accused that day, the maroon BMW 3 series you've referred to, whose details you claim were given to you by the bus driver, wasn't purchased till ten months after this alleged incident. This means it was a physical impossibility for the bus driver to have seen, known about, or noted down the details you and your colleague have sworn on oath he gave you.'

This cop's face was by now changing back from white to a deep shade of red, as William continued his cross-examination.

'The question is, how could this bus driver possibly know that ten months further down the line, my brother's firm would decide to get rid of the white 7 series BMW, and buy a maroon 3 series BMW? Did you happen to notice a crystal ball lying about when you took his statement?'

The sheriff shot my brother a look, which William ignored. By now the cop was lost, staring into the distance, doubtless imagining his pension winging its way out the window.

'I take it, constable, you're not suggesting that, rather than a BMW, this car was a DeLorean, as in the film *Back to the Future*, capable of travelling forwards in time, where it could conveniently bump into the bus in question?'

'No, no,' stammered the police witness.

'Then the only way the bus driver could know about the colour or kind of car in question, is if you and your colleague assumed the car my client had when you charged him many months later was the same one he'd been driving that day, and provided the bus driver with those details, perverted the course of justice, suborned perjury and lied on oath in court today. Correct?'

By now the cop's eyes were rolling like the tumblers on a one-armed bandit.

'Further, as far as identification of my client is concerned, the driver couldn't possibly see him from his cabin, so you simply told the driver to point out the man in the dock!'

The fiscal shot to her feet.

'Objection! The defence is giving evidence,' she said.

'At least mine is true,' said William and turned to the sheriff.

'If my lord would grant me a brief adjournment, I can have my client's office fax through the finance document for the car in question in a matter of minutes, which will establish conclusively that he did not own the maroon BMW at the time of this incident.'

But the sheriff knew exactly what that would lead to: proof positive of perjury, the perversion of justice by each witness, collaboration between the cops and the bus driver, plus the loss of pension for the police and imprisonment for all.

Make no mistake, sheriffs are quite content to sit on the bench, listen to lies from legions of cops, take copious notes of the Crown evidence, even pretend to jot down the odd word of the defence case, before announcing they'll retire to deliberate on matters. These deliberations can take place in court, with the sheriff on the bench, which tends to happen if it's near teeing-off time, or his train home is due. However, if the clerk has hinted a further trial could start in his court after the present one is finished, the sheriff must waste time or be landed with more work, and so will deem it necessary to retire to his chambers, to go over the evidence in detail before delivering his verdict. On this occasion there was no time for deliberation; rather, immediate action was required.

'There's obviously been some mix-up, wouldn't you say, Madam Fiscal?' said the sheriff, apparently calmly, but accompanying his question with a wide eyed, laser-like stare that screamed, 'Get on your feet, you moron, and move to drop this case, before the cops and the driver all end up in the clink!'

He needn't have worried. This unexpected evidential departure from the previously prepared script caused even the fiscal to wish she could be immediately beamed up to the Starship Enterprise. The truth was out. Hard, indisputable, documented evidence, proving beyond any doubt, that both police witnesses and the bus driver had committed pre-planned perjury and perverted the course of justice, was only a phone call away. Clearly this had to be stopped at any cost.

'I move to desert simpliciter, my lord,' she said.

For those not in the know, there are two ways in which a case can be deserted; either *pro loco et tempore*, i.e. 'for time and place' or *simpliciter*, which means it can never be re-raised. In this case, the fiscal wished to drop matters with all the speed of someone landed with a lapful of red-hot lava.

'Very well,' said the sheriff, turning to me. 'Mr McIntyre, you're free to go.' Collecting his papers, he rose and beat a hasty retreat from the bench.

My brother came towards me in the dock.

'We've got them by the balls,' he said, smelling blood in the water. 'D'you want them done with perjury?'

'What I want is to get out of here.'

'You sure?' he asked. 'They're all bang to rights.'

'Forget it,' I said. 'We won, they lost, just leave it at that.'

My brother, though still hot from the battle, shrugged his agreement, and so it was, the two perjuring policemen, instead of having their careers destroyed, being locked up and losing the precious pensions they'd sold their souls for, walked free. But they know who they are, so do I, and I wouldn't be one of them for the world.

If the reader recalls, this whole scenario started with the cops charging me with a minor road traffic matter from over a year ago, an offence in fact committed by the bus driver. So, why were the Crown desperate to drag me from the district court, drive me across country, lock me up for five days, and have the police commit perjury all to obtain a conviction for a trivial, non-imprisonable offence? There's a simple answer. It was all part of a larger plan, one to convict me of a far more serious matter, for which I was on bail: possession of firearms. The powers that be were desperate to prove the maroon BMW belonged to me, as it would be pointless to plant bullets in a car belonging to someone else.

51

'To have a retentive memory, and to proceed "by the book."'
— *The Murders in the Rue Morgue*, Edgar Allan Poe

The only sure way to guarantee getting off with an offence or crime is if the police don't suspect it was you; if they do, you're about as safe as a sandcastle with the tide coming in.

Evidence can exist in many ways: DNA, fingerprints, eyewitness testimony, written, aural, circumstantial, and of course, confessions and verbal evidence. The first two – DNA and fingerprints – can be planted, and confessions and verbal evidence, quite simply invented.

I was defending a client in a jury trial in Dumbarton Sheriff Court. He was a friendly guy, a big fan of cars, and unfortunately, despite being repeatedly disqualified by the court, he kept on driving. Eventually, he racked up so many convictions for this same offence, instead of sticking him on summary complaint, he was placed on indictment, hence me turning up at his sheriff and jury trial.

Briefly, the facts were these: he and his brother-in-law had been out and about with a van, with the intention of stealing some railway sleepers (apparently these were of some monetary value) when the cops came on the scene. As a result, both men abandoned the idea and took off in the van.

The brother-in-law, who happened to be the younger brother of another client of mine, was legally licensed and qualified to drive the van, but such was my client's infatuation with motor vehicles, he climbed behind the wheel, and they drove off. Once well away from the area, my client pulled the van over and both got out.

Shortly after they'd parked up, the police arrived. Suspicious the pair had been up to no good, the cops searched the van, and on finding nothing but recognising my client, decided to do him with something, so charged him with, if I recall correctly, what was then his twelfth offence of driving while disqualified. He'd been locked up for this in the past and being done again meant he'd go straight to jail, but this time, being on indictment, for a considerably longer period.

While preparing the case, I went over the evidence with my client and told him the cops claimed he'd told them he had been driving the vehicle. The Crown's case was simple, straightforward and seemed watertight. My client merely shrugged, admitted to me he'd been driving the van but stated that they were both out of the vehicle by the time police arrived; at no time had they seen him driving, and there was no way he'd admitted to being the driver.

When I asked if he'd been cautioned and charged, he told me he had, but assured me he'd made no reply.

Some months later, I turned up at Dumbarton Sheriff Court, the jury was selected, sworn in, my client adhered to his not guilty plea and the case began. The first cop was called by the Crown and stated my client had been cautioned, charged and confessed to driving the van. Satisfied, the fiscal sat back down, drawing me a look that clearly said 'why are we even doing this?' The look on the sheriff's face merely mirrored that of the fiscal; however, he turned to me with a sigh, hoping the answer would be no, but having to ask:

'Any cross-examination, Mr McIntyre?'

'I have a few questions, my lord.'

The sheriff sighed again, even more audibly, glancing at the clock as I stood and turned to address the witness.

'Officer, am I right in saying you were already aware my client was a disqualified driver?'

'Yes. That's correct.'

'And you've told the court he admitted to you he'd been driving the van in question.'

'That's also correct.'

'Would you tell the ladies and gentlemen of the jury just how did my client admit to driving this vehicle?'

'What do you mean?' queried the cop.

'I mean, the confession you claim my client made, I take it this took place after he was cautioned and charged?'

'That's correct.'

'What exactly did my client say?'

'What do you mean?'

'You've asked me twice what I mean. I take it English is your first language?'

The witness shot me a look. 'Yes.'

'Excellent. In that case, tell the court what my client said to you. What were his actual words?'

The cop hesitated, then shrugged.

'I . . . I can't recall exactly. It was my colleague who did the caution and charge.'

Something was up. I could smell it.

'Are you saying you didn't note down what my client said, but your colleague did?'

'That's correct.'

'I seem to be getting a lot of things right.' I smiled. He didn't. 'Wouldn't you and your colleague normally both note down what an accused says, in order to be able to corroborate matters in court?'

'Not always.'

'The common law caution states that what an accused person says will be noted down, does it not?'

'Yes. And my colleague noted what he said. But we both heard him.'

I decided it was time for a little goading, to put him off his stride, or at least to stop him continually saying 'that's correct'.

'So, as far as you were concerned, that part of the caution, the act of taking down in writing my client's words, was simply flung out the window!'

'No . . . No, but . . .'

That jab hurt, I could tell. I followed with a hook.

'Are you seriously telling the ladies and gentlemen of the jury you can't recall exactly what my client said, but he definitely confessed to the offence?'

'That's correct.'

'That's handy, isn't it?'

'What do you mean?'

'That's a hat-trick. Are you sure English is your first language?'

Without waiting for an answer, I sat down. The sheriff drew me a look as the fiscal announced, 'No re-examination, my lord,' and promptly called the second police witness to give evidence. This cop followed his colleague into the box, was sworn in and came up with the same story; namely, that my client had been cautioned and charged and admitted he was the driver at that time. Satisfied once more, the fiscal sat down. This time the sheriff didn't bother to look round.

'Mr McIntyre?'

I rose to my feet.

'Obliged, my lord.' I turned to the witness. 'Officer, when you came across the van, both the occupants were standing on the pavement, is that right?'

'Yes.'

'And am I right in saying you suspected that there were stolen items in the back of the vehicle?'

'Yes, that's right.'

'Accordingly, you searched the vehicle?'

'Yes, we did.'

'But you found nothing of an incriminatory nature. Is that right?'

'Yes. They must've seen us coming.'

'Try sticking to my question constable. The fact is, there was nothing stolen in the van.'

'No.'

'No, that's not the fact, or no, there was nothing stolen in the van.'

'Yes.'

I sighed. We could be here all day at this rate.

'Were there any stolen items in the van?'

'No.'

'At last, that's that settled. However, you weren't happy about that, were you?'

'What do you mean?'

With an effort, I refrained from the 'Is English your first language' line.

'We both know exactly what I mean. You recognised my client, didn't you?'

'Yes. He's well known to the police.' He smirked, thinking he was terribly smart.

I smirked back. 'Exactly, which is why, after finding nothing stolen in the van, you didn't want to leave without charging him with something, am I right?'

'Absolutely not.' And he let out a little laugh, as if finding the idea ridiculous.

'No?'

'No!'

'You've already told the court you recognised my client. Yes?'

'That's right.'

'Did you know him to be disqualified from driving?'

'Yes.'

'So, since you couldn't do him for anything else, you decided to charge him with that, didn't you?'

'Certainly not!' He glared at me, as if grossly insulted.

'I think you've been over this ground already, Mr McIntyre,' said the sheriff.

I ignored the man on the bench and continued.

'You told my friend, the fiscal, you cautioned my client before charging him.'

'That's correct.'

I turned to the fifteen good citizens of Dumbarton as I addressed the witness.

'Perhaps you'd be kind enough to advise the ladies and gentlemen of the jury of the terms of the common law caution.'

'"You're not obliged to say anything, but anything you do say will be taken down and may be used in evidence."'

'Which means that whatever the person cautioned says will definitely be taken down, but only may be used?'

'That's right.'

'So, there's no question that what an accused person says may be taken down, but only if you can be bothered to do so?'

The officer smirked again, as if I wasn't quite up on the common law caution.

'No.'

'Excellent. Then, what did my client say in reply to caution?'

'He said, "It was me who was driving the van."'

'Those were his actual words, in reply to caution and charge?' I asked.

'That's right.'

'So, obviously, you'd note his reply, in keeping with the terms of the caution.'

The cop's eyes flickered for a fraction of second. Then . . .

'Of course.'

'In that case, perhaps you'd be kind enough to read what he said from your notebook.'

Another flicker of the eyelids.

'There's no need, I know exactly what he said,' answered the witness.

'I'm sure you do, officer. However, humour me.'

'As I said, there's no need for me to—'

'Kindly hand me your book,' I cut in, 'I'd like to read the reply for myself.'

This time, there was no flicker. The witness turned to face the sheriff.

'My lord. I don't have my book with me.'

And bang! That was it! I had him. Like a fish on the hook. It was merely a matter of reeling him in.

'Where is your book?' I asked the witness, before the sheriff could respond.

The cop kept looking at the sheriff as he replied, 'My lord, I've left it in my coat in the witness room.'

The sheriff opened his mouth to speak, but I beat him to it.

'My lord, I've no objection to waiting until the notebook can be obtained. However, as this witness is currently giving evidence, I should be obliged if my lord orders he remain in court while the bar officer recovers the book.'

'Very well. I'll rise for a few minutes,' said the sheriff with a deep sigh, glancing again at the clock. The bar officer called 'court', the fiscal and I bowed, the sheriff headed to his chambers and the jury to their room. This left the clerk, my client and me in court, along with the cop who sat trying to look cool in the witness box, but I could tell he was starting to sweat.

After an awkward five minutes had passed, the sheriff was back on the bench and the jury in their box. The sheriff turned to the witness.

'I take it you now have your notebook, officer?'

'Yes, my lord.'

The sheriff turned to me. 'Mr McIntyre?'

'Now, officer, would you please read out my client's reply to caution and charge.'

'I've already told you I remember what he said quite clearly.'

'You claim he said, "It was me who was driving the van."'

'That's correct.'

'Perhaps you'd hand the bar officer your book so I can check my client's reply.'

But before the bar officer could move, the cop turned to the sheriff.

'My lord, this is my private notebook and contains matters concerning several other cases.'

The sheriff was obviously surprised at this but turned to me.

'Mr McIntyre, you heard the witness, and as the notebook is not a production in this case, I can't force the officer to hand it over.'

'My lord, I don't wish to read anything other than my client's reply, so if the witness would be kind enough to turn to the relevant page, I promise not to pry into the contents.'

The sheriff turned back to the witness, but before he could speak, the cop cut in.

'My lord, I'm not prepared to hand the defence my notebook. I know what the accused's reply was and have already given it in evidence.'

This was simply a lie. I knew my client hadn't made a reply. How did I know? Because he told me he hadn't. As Benjamin Franklin once said, 'Don't misinform your doctor, nor your lawyer.' I agree with him, plus, I'd add a priest to the list. Everyone else is fair game.

I turned to the cop.

'I'll tell you what, why don't you give the sheriff your notebook. My lord can read the reply for himself, and I shall be happy to accept his word for what's written there.'

The sheriff turned to the witness for the third time. But again before he could speak, the cop cut in, his voice nervous, squeaky, as if he'd been sucking on a helium balloon.

'I'm not giving my book to anyone. I know what the accused said and what I wrote down.'

I turned to face the jury for full effect, as I addressed the cop with my back to the witness box.

'Okay, officer, final offer. Hand the sheriff your notebook, and if my lord assures me you wrote down the reply to caution and charge, as you claim you did, my client will tender a plea of guilty, or else I will withdraw from acting immediately. I can't say fairer than that.'

There was complete silence in court. A mouse peeing on cotton wool would have made more noise. Everyone's attention was directed at the witness in the box. Even the sheriff was staring at the cop.

I smiled at the witness. 'Well, how about it? Can we wrap this up right now, and –' I pointed to the jury behind me '– let these fifteen good people go home?'

There was a long pause, as the police witness began to melt into a puddle, like a snowman after a thaw. Then . . .

'No. It's my book, and I'm not letting anyone see it.'

He sounded for all the world like a wee boy saying, 'It's my ball, and nobody's getting to play with it.' But by this time, his ball was well and truly burst.

'I see,' I said, and turned to the sheriff. 'No more questions, my lord.'

It will come as no surprise to the reader when I say my closing speech to the jury was the shortest I ever made; perhaps the shortest in history, and the time it took the jury to come back with their verdict was even shorter.

'Ladies and gentlemen,' said the clerk of court, 'who speaks for you?'

A slim woman with gold-rimmed glasses stood up. 'I do,' she said. 'On the charge on the indictment, how do you find the accused?' 'We find the accused not guilty.'

'And is that verdict unanimous, or by a majority?'

'Unanimous.'

Of course it was. People know a liar when they see one, whether he's in or out of uniform. This perjuring policeman was so used to being believed, especially by sheriffs sitting alone without a jury, he had arrogantly assumed his word would be accepted without question and hadn't bothered to write down the words he and his partner had made up.

Did anything happen as a result of the cops' clear perjury? Of course not. That would involve some sort of justice. The reader may recall the case of the Birmingham Six, whose convictions were quashed after seventeen years in prison, yet they had to wait ten more years before receiving a penny of compensation. When referring to this case, rather than call it a massive miscarriage of justice, Judge, Lord Denning, the Master of the Rolls, stated:

Just consider the course of events if their action were to proceed to trial. If the six men failed it would mean that much time and money and worry would have been expended by many people to no good purpose. If they won, it would mean that the police were guilty of perjury; that they were guilty of violence and threats; that the confessions were involuntary and improperly admitted in evidence; and that the convictions were erroneous. That was such an appalling vista that every sensible person would say, "It cannot be right that these actions should go any further." We shouldn't have all these campaigns to get them released. If they'd been hanged, they'd have been forgotten and the whole community would have been satisfied.

This statement, uttered by one of the most senior judges in the UK at the time, was quite simply evil. The judge would rather the innocent were put to death than doubt be cast on a corrupt police force. The fact is, the deck is always stacked against the defence, so it's important to have an ace up your sleeve and know when and how to play it.

52

'*Cocaine isn't habit forming. I should know. I've been using it for years.*'
– Tallulah Bankhead

In my opinion, people take cocaine in the same way they eat fish suppers, or chocolate, or have sex. Why do they do it, continue to do it, miss it if they can't, and will go to all kinds of lengths to get it. It's simple. They like it.

Don't think for an instant I'm advocating the use of cocaine. Far from it. Cocaine is both physically and psychologically bad for you. Yes, it is habit forming, but in my view, as I've already said, that's because people tend to continue to do the things they like to do, things they get a hit from, a buzz, whatever; but, at least in my experience, it's not like alcoholism or gambling, or addiction to heroin or nicotine. You can stop taking coke with very few side effects, other than your wallet gaining weight again.

To the best of my knowledge and experience, taking coke's not like shooting up, chasing the dragon, or smoking cigarettes, where a physical dependency develops. Yes, cocaine can take over your job, family, life, but you can stop without having to suffer the heebie-jeebies, the delirium tremens, the flu-like sickness that occurs when trying to come clean from booze or the brown powder. Don't get me wrong, crack is a whole different ball game. I've seen people on it, seen the state they get into, been offered it many times, and refused. You want my advice, these days? Don't touch drugs!

The first time I ever took a line of cocaine, I was twenty-six years old. The youngsters of today may consider that to be ancient, but I'm talking about back when MDMA, or ecstasy, was a multi-coloured powder sold in cigarette wraps. No pills had yet been produced for the mass market, and the MDMA was pure. Now ecstasy is produced illegally either by chemists out to make a few quid, who know what they're doing, or at the other end of the spectrum, made by someone stirring some mad cocktail in a pail in a shed. Back in the day, ecstasy wasn't cut with ketamine, rat poison, or any other junk the makers could get their hands on.

How my first line came about was as follows. I had a client, who originally hailed from Maryhill, Glasgow. When he was fifteen years old, he'd been convicted of murder at Glasgow High Court, and sentenced to Her Majesty's pleasure, which is the equivalent of a life sentence, and the maximum given to someone of that age age. Eleven years later at the age of twenty-six or twenty-seven, he'd been released and moved to Edinburgh. The first time I met him, I warmed to him immediately. He had a way of walking, a sort of swagger, and was certainly not afraid of anyone. He was about my size, but broader, and each time I saw him he wore a suit with an open-necked shirt.

JJ had been charged, along with his girlfriend, with possession and intention to supply heroin from a property in the east end of Edinburgh. The situation was the drug squad had burst into the top-floor flat, but by the time they managed to break in, the drugs, if indeed there ever had been any in the flat, had allegedly been disposed of. So, when the DS finally forced entry, there was nothing to be found.

However, it transpired that, according to the DS, fearing drugs may be disposed of during their surprise raid, a few officers had apparently had the foresight to take up a position at the very bottom of all the back gardens of the tenement, some hundred yards or so away, in case anything was thrown from a window. The fact is that due to the distance, there was less chance of spotting this happening than there was of Ian Paisley joining the IRA.

However, the cops said that was what happened, and though cases like the aforementioned Birmingham Six, the Guildford Four, and many others show they can be the biggest bunch of liars one ever came across, their evidence must be taken into consideration, and for some reason is valued by judges as more credible and reliable than anyone else's, leading to them being believed in order that the accused can be convicted, and the public's faith in the police continue, when the fact is that ship sailed a long time ago.

Lo and behold, the DS stated that during this raid, they not only had undercover cops positioned in the back greens who had seen someone open a bathroom window, fitted with heavily frosted glass, and drop a bag down into the garden, but were able to positively identify my client as being the person who had been in possession of the drugs. The powers that the police apparently possess, particularly when it comes to any of the five senses, are truly exceptional: I say truly, but truth has nothing to do with it. In any event, my client and his girlfriend were both arrested and charged with the possession and supply of a Class A drug, namely diamorphine hydrochloride, or heroin, under the Misuse of Drugs Act.

It was obvious to me from the start that the cops were hard at it. If they truly believed they'd catch the occupants of the flat by surprise, why did they expect anything to be flung out of a window? Secondly, as stated, there was no way anyone could be identified at that distance, especially when the window opened to a maximum of forty-five degrees, meaning the most one could ever see was somebody's hand dropping something or other.

The truth is, one would have required binoculars, or a telescope, to identify anyone at that distance, plus the small window would have had to be open full ninety degrees for the person's face to be seen at all.

My dad, who was a doctor with the Scottish Office, had once been asked by a young man to be given a reference as he wished to join the police force. Knowing the person and his family well, Dad gladly gave him the reference and so it was that Freddie became a member of Lothian and Borders Police. I seem to be digressing again, but stick with me; it's relevant, I promise.

Some years later, Freddie advised me that on one occasion he was on points duty in Princes Street, Edinburgh, when he received a call on his radio to assist in the pursuit of someone suspected of shop-lifting. Having been so directed, Freddie left his post and assisted in the chase, which resulted in the culprit being captured in Waverley train station and dragged into the back of a police van. After the cops arrested the suspect, they proceeded to kick seven shades out of him as Freddie looked on, stunned and disgusted by what was happening.

The two arresting officers then charged the suspect not only with theft, but also various police assaults in order to cover their own actions and the marks left from beating up the accused. Now, I fully realise there will be people who will find it quite understandable that police handed out their own justice on the spot, but the fact remains the man was merely a suspect, nothing had been proved against him, and it was purely because the police had had to chase him that he was getting a kicking: that and the fact some cops enjoy doing so, as I heard them admit when I was banged up in the cells in Edinburgh High Street.

Forgive me for digressing yet again, but all these so-called reality shows on TV, documentaries about cops tackling criminals, recorded on camera, arresting them, placing them in police custody are, in my experience, purely for public consumption to portray the police in the best possible light.

Shortly after, at the charge bar, Freddie was asked by the duty sergeant about this event, and he explained, in detail, what had gone down, stating he would not be corroborating any statement by the other officers as far as the police assault charges were concerned. This man may well have been the thief, but it was he who had been battered in the back of the van by Freddie's colleagues.

When the sergeant heard this, he advised Freddie if he was going to work on the force, he had to go along with what the other officers said in their statements, whatever had happened, or else nobody would ever work with him, because that's just the way things were. Freddie was by no means a goody two-shoes, but he wanted nothing to do with fitting people up for offences they hadn't committed.

Freddie told me years later that there and then he realised there was no future for him in the force, no way he could hope to climb the ladder if this was how things went down and he resigned the following week. Freddie became a social worker, retiring recently from a very senior position after many, many years of helping a huge number of people.

However, what interested me in the case wasn't only Freddie's past as a policeman, but his abilities as an amateur photographer. I asked him if he could bring his camera equipment to the locus where these drug offences were alleged to have taken place. Freddie duly arrived, set up and took several photos from both inside the bathroom looking out and from the bottom of the garden looking back, with me acting as a model, opening the window and dropping a bag out of it.

As I thought, Freddie confirmed the frosted-glass window could only have been opened a fraction of the way, and nobody's face could have been seen at that angle; plus, his photographs proved even if the window had been forced open a full ninety degrees and a bag of drugs dropped from it by someone, it would have been impossible to identify who the person was due to the distance from the back of the communal gardens to the building.

As the case was being heard in the High Court, I had instructed Senior Counsel to act for my client, and a rather pug faced QC named Dawson was appearing for the co-accused. I was advised by Dawson, in a rather high-handed manner, that if my client was prepared to plead guilty to all the charges, then his client, my client's girlfriend, would have all the charges dropped against her. It's nearly always the same old story where a man and woman are charged: the woman is often offered an out, an avenue of escape, provided the man throws his hands up and pleads guilty, but it's never the other way about. So much for equality of the sexes.

Dawson clearly assumed that I'd take the deal, but my client was currently out on life-licence, and a plea to anything would've put him back in prison for years. Accordingly, however unchivalrous, I advised my client to turn down the deal and told Dawson we were going to trial. This decision left Dawson hopping mad, in the metaphorical sense that is, as the man would've found balancing his body on only one leg more difficult than most.

Apart from the fact Freddie's photographs demonstrated without doubt that no-one could be identified dropping anything from the bathroom window at the distance stated by the drug squad, I was also counting on his testimony in the witness box to the effect that the police were perfectly prepared to perjure themselves, and he himself had personal experience of this from a professional point of view, causing him in fact to leave the force.

I'm delighted to say the jury paid close attention to Freddie's photographic evidence, and were impressed, even shocked, by his oral testimony that he'd felt morally obliged to leave the force. As a result, both my client and his co-accused were acquitted on all charges.

I would stress at this stage that to me the matter wasn't whether or not my client and his girlfriend took drugs, possessed drugs, or sold drugs; it was the fact that the evidence being used to convict them had been manufactured by the police, and that client, like everyone else, was entitled to be acquitted by the jury of the charges based on what happened and not what the police had invented.

Tom Dawson went on to become Solicitor General, the second most senior prosecutor in Scotland, and was later elevated to the bench, where he went on record as being the judge to have had more appeals upheld against him than any other judge in the history of Scots law. For a kick-off, getting a case in front of the Court of Appeal is far from easy, and having an appeal upheld happens once in a blue moon, as their lordships require to decide whether their fellow judge erred in his charge to the jury, or that there had been insufficient evidence to convict. Either way, this tends to indicate that the trial judge had allowed an accused person to be wrongly convicted on his watch, which raises questions as to the way these people are picked to prosecute others and sit in judgment on their fellow man.

I went on to defend the same client again in a sheriff-and-jury trial. He had been charged along with a co-accused, who was being represented by George More. Both our clients had been arrested by the police and appeared on seven charges of assault against bouncers at the door of a public house. Charges of assault on bouncers always amuse me as they usually involve someone being beaten up, then, as in police assault charges, after receiving a good kicking, they're charged in order to cover up the incident and the person's bruises.

There was CCTV footage that the defence were allowed to view, which involved a blurry account of a stramash taking place at the pub door, with blows and kicks being exchanged, and some unidentified person lashing out with a heavy chain. Kenneth MacIver, a senior procurator fiscal depute, who the reader will recall was playing golf while I was locked up in the High Street cells, appeared for the Crown, and it was clear he was out to get my guy.

The Crown evidence was led, the video played, after which it was the turn of the defence to lead evidence. George More thought that the bouncers and Crown witnesses would be believed anyway; however, I had an idea which I thought would make my client's evidence more credible. I told George, on this occasion, my client had nothing to lose by going into the witness box, and when he did, I was going to ask him about his previous conviction for murder. George nearly fell off his seat; he called me insane. But in my view, it was a matter of nothing ventured, nothing gained. In Scotland, the law is, or at least was then, that an accused person's previous convictions cannot be led by the Crown, unless the defence have first attacked the record or reputation of a Crown witness. This rule has since been ridiculously extended in favour of the Crown, but still, I was banking on telling the jury that my client did not require to go in the witness box, nor have his previous conviction revealed, and that he had chosen to do so, basically betting on this making my client seem more believable.

Accordingly, I put my guy in the box, and he gave his version of what happened at the bar that night. During my speech to the jury, I explained that my client had not needed to give evidence, nor disclose his previous murder conviction, asking them to accept the fact he had as proof that his evidence was truthful, or that at least it raised a reasonable doubt.

The jury retired to consider their verdict, came back, and convicted the co-accused, but found my client not proven on each charge. The twist in the tail of this tale is that the co-accused was sentenced to eighteen months' imprisonment, meaning he would serve nine, yet my client, despite being acquitted on all charges, was arrested for a parole violation, mixing with known criminals and sent back to prison for a full two years. True, had he been found guilty he would have doubtless been remitted to the High Court for sentence and received a far longer time; still, it all goes to prove that if the powers that be want you, they'll get you, one way or another.

Anyway, it was after this success I went back with my client to a flat to have a few drinks and celebrate our victory. It was there that he put out a few lines of cocaine and invited me to try some. I remember some years later seeing Al Pacino being interviewed on television and saying that after taking your first line of cocaine, every other line was merely an attempt to recapture the memory of that first hit. He was right.

The use of cocaine is a common practice in the film and TV industry, plus, as I've stated before, I know solicitors, advocates, procurators fiscal, QCs, sheriffs, High Court judges who've done the same, though I won't mention any names. However, I've never understood this nonsense about being an officer of the court. In my view when you take on a case to defend a client, then you do everything you can to get them acquitted and they are your primary and only concern, not the court. So, if a defence agent or counsel chooses to smoke a joint or snort a line, while committing a statutory offence they're not, in my opinion, breaching any moral code.

However, again, as I've stated before, there is clearly a difference when it comes to prosecutors and judges, those prepared to prosecute, judge and convict others of doing exactly what they are doing are obviously hypocrites in anybody's book.

However, let me make it crystal clear: I would never advise anyone to take any illegal drug. They say cocaine is God's way of telling you that you have too much money. But the truth is cocaine doesn't care who you are, and is never your friend. As someone else once said, 'The rich take drugs because they can afford to, while the poor take drugs because they can't.' The simple fact is, nobody can afford to, and only a few are fortunate enough to learn that lesson before it's far too late.

53

'Give a man a fair trial, and then hang him.'

– Judge Jeffries

Okay, so, we've had a look at some of the ways the legal system in Scotland works, and more often doesn't work, but it's time, dear reader, we returned to where we kicked off and cast our minds back to the beginning of this book, when I was arrested by an armed response unit, and banged up for possessing a couple of pistols and ammunition. But bear in mind all I've said about the hypocrisy and the carryings-on in court, because it's all about to become relevant.

Eventually, after eighteen months on bail, fighting the forces of the Crown, the day of my trial for possession of firearms and ammunition, along with the seven or so other charges the Crown had stuck on for good measure, rolled round. My case was called in Edinburgh High Court of Justiciary, situated on the left-hand side at the top of the Mound, on the corner with the High Street, which used to be the old Edinburgh Sheriff Court.

The old Sheriff Court had rather resembled a giant Victorian toilet with marble everywhere from floor to ceiling but since the building's elevation to the High Court of Justiciary, to accommodate their hugely important lordships, the place had been completely overhauled, new courtrooms built, each fitted out with the latest high-tech equipment, screens, recording machines, computers, the works.

My young brother William and I entered the court. He took a seat beside my senior counsel while I sat in the public benches. After a few minutes, the judge, Lord Marnoch, was ushered onto the bench by his macer, and my case kicked off. I won't bore the reader by rehashing the routine evidence given during that first morning and afternoon nor go into what took place the evening prior to my arrest. Those who know, know, and have my respect. Those who don't know, don't need to know. Instead, I'll merely mention my movements, as I made for home in the early hours of the morning on the day in question.

As mentioned at the beginning of the book, I'd been making my way along the High Street and was passing the alleyway down which Oliphant Bakers have their bakehouse. It was about five o'clock in the morning, and I caught the delicious aroma as it came wafting up the close. I decided to get something to eat for the walk home, ventured into the bakehouse, bought a mince round and bit into it. As I did so, some of the gravy from the mince gushed out, ran down my chin and spilled down the front of the grey suit I was wearing.

It's highly likely many of my readers will not be au fait with the layout of Linlithgow, so let me explain briefly. Linlithgow is a royal burgh and a ribbon town, with a long main street that runs its full length, while the railway and Union Canal run parallel with it. Various side streets, avenues and other smaller roads lead off the main thoroughfare to the south, while others lead to the loch on the north side.

If you cross over from Oliphant Bakers (in my opinion, makers and purveyors of the best pies in Linlithgow) you'll find a narrow, steep street running at a right angle to the main road named Lion Well Wynd, which heads uphill for a hundred yards or so, and at the top splits into two. The left-hand side leads you to a little bridge which crosses the railway, then along Strawberry Bank to another bridge over the canal, and onwards up Manse Road to Friar's Way, which is where I was staying at the time with my girlfriend.

The route I've just described was by far the quickest way home but being in no rush to arrive back and receive a rollicking for coming in at five in the morning, happily munching my mince-round, I took a left out of Oliphant's close and headed east, along the High Street. I passed the flats known as the Vennel on my left, crossed the main road and walked on until I reached Linlithgow post office, which is now a large and popular public house.

When I came to Linlithgow in 1962 the town's population was the same as it had been when Mary, Queen of Scots was born here, namely four thousand people. There was a large post office, four banks and three building societies. Today the town has a population of approximately 17,000 people, there is a tiny post office which doubles as a gift shop, one bank and no building societies. Such is progress. But I digress.

As I passed the post office, I noticed several people standing on the pavement holding banners beside a uniformed policeman. I stopped, still munching on my mince round, and asked the cop what was happening. He advised me this was a demonstration for higher pay by post office staff, at which point I shouted, 'Up the workers,' and carried on.

I walked on to the end of the High Street, under the railway bridge and took a hairpin right turn up Station Road, approaching the bridge over the canal from the opposite direction I would have, had I taken the shorter route previously described.

As I was walking up onto the bridge, I pulled the semi-automatic from my pocket, pulled back the slide, to check there wasn't a bullet in the chamber, and was in the process of putting the gun away, when I saw the young lady who was delivering newspapers coming down over the bridge.

The reason I go into this at some length is that the route I took home was by far the longest one I could have chosen. Had I taken the one the police apparently thought I'd taken, both the time it took and the direction I came from would have prevented me from passing the protesting post office workers, the policeman on duty, and meeting this witness.

However, later it would become important that the investigating authorities were able to corroborate my possession of the guns and ammunition in some fashion. Apparently, whoever was called upon to carry out investigations into my case had clearly, though wrongly, assumed I'd have taken the shortest route home, up Lion Well Wynd.

I'm told that, surprise, surprise, when this shorter route was searched, several 0.22 bullets were found to have been accidentally 'dropped' in that area, despite the fact I'd been nowhere near there and had chosen the route referred to above.

This leads one to conclude either there was another gunman on the loose that night, or the bullets were planted to provide proof of possession of the ammunition by me on my way home. It never seemed to dawn on the donut-munchers that if I'd come from the direction where they claimed the bullets were allegedly found, the vital witness would never have seen me with the gun. Unfortunately, the cops never have to worry about getting things correct, as the Crown and the courts allow the police to add two and two together and pretend it makes five.

During the Crown evidence, one of the cops speaking about ballistics was asked if he believed the bullets they'd found could be fired. I knew the ammunition was damp, and so couldn't be considered live. However, this expert witness, encouraged along the path by the judge, stated *if* the bullets were first taken apart, then *if* the powder was removed and dried, then *if* the powder was placed back into the shell and *if* the bullets were then reassembled, it would be possible to fire them, therefore they would be live. As my old mum would say, 'If we had bacon, we could have bacon and eggs. If we had eggs.'

I don't intend to dwell on the rest of the Crown case, except to mention that, at the close of the day my counsel made a motion to the court that there was no case to answer on the majority of the charges. These other charges included driving a motor vehicle recklessly, while under the influence of drink or drugs, despite the fact no evidence was ever led by the Crown that I'd driven any vehicle, taken any drink or drugs, or been breathalysed.

Another of the charges was I had brandished a firearm and by so doing had frightened the sixteen-year-old witness who had been delivering papers that morning. This was, of course, completely invented by the Crown, as was proved when this witness gave evidence, and very honestly stated that she first thought I had been holding a mobile phone, and it was only as she drew closer realised it was a pistol.

The witness went on to state she had not been frightened in the slightest, and in fact told the court that as soon as I spotted her, I had smiled and politely wished her a very good morning before carrying on up the road.

In view of the fact there was no evidence whatsoever for the road traffic charges, and contradictory evidence about pointing the gun, my counsel's motion was granted, and all but two charges were dropped due to the complete lack of evidence for any of them. Of course, in view of this it had been highly improper to put the charges on the indictment to begin with, but the Crown was determined my case would be heard in the High Court, in order that if convicted (and the cops made sure of that) I would receive a more severe sentence than would have been imposed in a lower court, and so included charges they knew perfectly well would, and indeed could, never be proved.

The two charges remaining on the indictment were the simple possession of the two pistols and a quantity of ammunition without the necessary firearms licence.

At the end of the Crown case, I gave my evidence and explained my reason for having the firearms, namely, that they had been given to me by a client so that I could hand them into the police the next day, which was only a very short time after an amnesty had been held for the handing in of such weapons.

After I gave my evidence, my counsel called the initial solicitor I had asked to be contacted by the police when I was first arrested and held in the cells in Livingston police station awaiting court on the Monday. During this witness's evidence, he was asked by the Crown if he, as a solicitor, would ever have accepted guns from a client to hand to the police at any time, to which question he answered, 'No, I wouldn't, but James would.'

I'll assume, rather generously giving him the benefit of the doubt as he didn't elaborate or assist me further, that he was trying to state that, while it was out of the ordinary for a solicitor to act in that fashion, that I would have done so believing it to be in order. Either way, he was as much help to my defence case as a handbrake on a canoe.

After I gave my evidence my main defence witness was called. He was a very close friend of mine, and I was best man at his wedding and godfather to one of his three boys. He was initially warned that he was not required to answer any questions which may incriminate him. Yet despite this fact, the witness went on to state that he had handed me the guns, with the intention of having me pass them over to the police, so leaving himself wide open to prosecution later, whether or not I was convicted of the offences. The guy had more guts than anyone I ever met. The name of the witness was Michael Joseph Patrick Lavin, known by everyone as Paky (short for Patrick).

Before the trial took place, something happened which Michael would later laugh about and relate to others, and I write it out of respect for him and his carefree, cavalier self.

As I mentioned, I'd been remanded in Saughton prison in Edinburgh, and my mind was working overtime. I was very aware the cops were trying to pin everything they possibly could on me and had been told by pals of mine that the police had pulled up people who had outstanding charges, promising them if they gave evidence against me their charges would be dropped. This may be true. I believe it, and certainly wouldn't put it past them. That mob were so desperate to tuck me away, they could taste it.

I also was advised that the family of the girl who had identified me as having the gun on the bridge over the canal had been told by the police that they were in danger for giving evidence against me and that one of them could be found in a skip. I have no idea whether, or not, what I was told was true, but in my view if it is, it was merely with the intent of getting the witnesses to help the police and rely on their protection as much as possible.

What I do know is my best friend from Glasgow, the head of what was the largest organised crime family, approached me and told me that they would find out places the father of the girl frequented and have a word with him, make it crystal clear that it wasn't in his best interests that I should be identified in court by his daughter. It was already known to the defence where this witness and her family lived.

I realised that my friend's offer was made out of kindness and respect to me as a member of his 'family' and had this been a different type of case and completely innocent people not involved I may have come to a different decision; but, on this occasion, I advised my friend that I didn't want this done on any account. The girl and her family weren't grasses, but rather civilians doing what they considered correct, and that they should not be approached, spoken to, or leaned on in any way whatsover in connection with this. I fully believe that the result of the trial was in God's hands, and since then He has blessed me more than I can ever say. All that remains for me to add is that I respect what the girl and her family did, as civilians, and harbour no ill feeling towards them whatsoever.

However, I knew the cops were very keen to get hold of Michael, to get his version of what had happened that night, and I was equally keen the defence spoke to him first, as he'd be my witness. While on remand, I rang up and told Evelyn, in as few words as possible, for all calls on prison phones are recorded, to take Michael through to Glasgow and tell some friends of mine to take care of him. Evelyn did exactly as I requested. She and Michael drove to Springburn in Glasgow, he was put in a safe house provided by some of the family and supplied with food and drink for the duration of his stay.

Later, Michael told me that one night, he was lying on the sofa, half asleep when he was suddenly aware of someone hovering over him. He woke, now fully alert and noticed the person had a measuring tape in their hand and was stretching it along him. Michael sat up quickly, asking the guy what he thought he was doing. The person gruffly answered he'd been told to take care of Michael. At this point Michael, who could fight for fun, realised the message had been misinterpreted, and told the guy to back off, explaining I'd asked the family to 'take care of him' by making sure he was looked after, and not to 'take care of him' in that way. Only Michael would have found that funny, as he was very capable of handling anybody trying to 'take care of him' in that fashion.

Shortly after, Michael moved to another hideout, provided by another friend of mine, and was placed in a flat used as a safe house for people who supported 'the Cause', across the water. In this way, we legally avoided Michael from being questioned by the cops before he got to court.

I write these words today smiling, yet with a heavy heart as Michael has since passed away after battling a long and serious illness. He was one of the bravest men I ever met, certainly the most game, loyal, and will be very much missed by his family, and many, many other friends among whom I am honoured to be numbered. May eternal light shine upon him, and through the mercy of God may he rest in peace.

My counsel closed the case, speeches from both sides were heard, and the judge gave his charge to the jury, telling them that, in his view, the fact that I was in possession of the guns, and the reason given, meant they had a choice of two verdicts: guilty and guilty. Either I was guilty of possessing the guns for the reason I gave, and the defence evidence led, in which case they could add a rider that leniency be shown to me, or I was guilty of possessing the guns for my own purposes. However, although the judge omitted to say this, not a single, solitary shred of evidence had been led at any time by the Crown to support that the guns were in my possession with the intention of committing any criminal act. The jury were then requested to retire and consider their verdict.

The jury returned a short time later. The clerk of court asked if they had reached a verdict, at which point the foreperson of the jury stood and replied, 'Guilty.'

The clerk then clarified matters by asking them if they meant guilty with leniency, or guilty without leniency. 'Guilty, with no leniency.'

I remember looking at this heartless shower, one of whom had been sound asleep during the whole trial, yet their verdict was unanimous. Obviously, someone must have woken him up to tell him which way to vote. I'd accepted possession of the two pistols from the start, there was with no evidence there had been any assaults (even the young girl wasn't frightened by me), no harm, nothing, but this bunch of low brows weren't satisfied with that, they wanted to see me punished as much as possible. However, looking back at what in my opinion was a sorry bunch of saddos, I realise their punishment was just being themselves.

After the verdict, the judge announced he would require social inquiry reports before delivering any sentence and my counsel moved that I be released on bail, as I had a very busy legal practice and required to tidy up various office and staff related matters, including ongoing cases over the next month, in which I was already involved.

However, Marnoch, in his infinite wisdom, refused my counsel's motion and remanded me in custody in Edinburgh prison for the next month, for no good reason other than, in my opinion, sheer bloody-mindedness, as there was no possibility of me being a flight risk and trying to leave the country. So, on 30 October 1997, I was off back to prison to await sentence in four weeks' time.

54

'Punishment. The justice that the guilty deal out to those that are caught.'
– Elbert Hubbard

One month to the day later, I arrived at Glasgow High Court for sentence. I'd been convicted in Edinburgh High, but the case was being sentenced in Glasgow purely to fit in with the plans of His Lordship, who happened to be sitting on the bench in No Mean City. Accordingly, no matter the cost to the public purse, every arrangement was made to suit him.

My case was called, I was brought up from the cells below, where senior counsel appeared for me, while my brother William and Evelyn sat with my dad, and his friend, Peter. Sadly, neither my dad nor Peter are with us now, but I have no doubt my father's prayers for me are still heard in heaven, and I continue to need every one of them.

My QC put forward a number of mitigating factors, reminding the judge that all but two of the charges had been dropped from lack of evidence, and that the judge himself had directed the jury to clear me of aiming the gun at anyone or terrifying any witness. Also, the court was reminded that the two remaining charges of not possessing the relevant firearms licence for a period of two hours at most, and both pistols were found by the police in a locked drawer, in a locked garage, in a locked house.

True to form, the judge, despite having had four weeks to think about matters, read the social enquiry report, and had allegedly noted down everything my counsel said, decided he still needed to go away and think about it, and I was sent back downstairs to the cells as he ruminated.

Before long, doubtless having checked there was no further work which would be given to him that morning, the judge returned to deliver his sentence:

'Being in possession of lethal firearms and ammunition for which the only possible use is the furtherance of crime can't be other than a very serious matter. You, as an officer of the court, must have been well aware of that.'

As I said before, there was, of course, not a single scrap of evidence to support what the judge decided to tack on when sentencing me; nothing to suggest the only possible use of the guns was the furtherance of crime, nothing to suggest any alternative reason for me possessing the guns at all, other than the one I had given, but the judge had to come up with something to justify jailing me for three years, and so at the same time he thought, ruin my career, the only thing I was trained to do.

The charges did not involve any question of dishonesty, embezzlement, fraud, fiddling clients' accounts (as a criminal defence lawyer I had no client account), there had never been any question of a breach of client confidentiality, on which my reputation was and still rests, but in my opinion, and that of my counsel, the establishment was clearly looking for a way to get me locked up. I don't state this as some sort of vague conspiracy theory, but have good reasons to suspect this, which I'll get to in a moment.

Now, don't get me wrong. Twenty-five years down the line I'm not complaining about my sentence, and since my release from Betty's Guest House, God has blessed me more than I can ever say. In fact, as my long-suffering mother (now in her late nineties) said to me, quoting Joseph's remarks to his brothers in Genesis, Chapter 50 v 20: '*They (in this case the court) meant evil against me, but God used it for good.*' God certainly did, and I can never be thankful enough.

The reader will be used to me digressing by now, but in support of my theory that the court was determined to lock me up, I'd offer the following.

The firearm offences for which I was charged took place some considerable time before any mandatory prison sentence was imposed by statute. As far as I understand there's only been one other solicitor in Scottish history ever charged with the possession of firearms. That was a gentleman named James Wright. Interestingly, or not, after the various Jacobite rebellions in the eighteenth century when certain Scottish clans were prohibited from using their tartans or surnames, the McIntyre clan were among that number.

As it happens, the name McIntyre, in Gaelic, is rendered Mac-an-T'saoir, which means 'the son of the carpenter'. The word 'wright' is an old word, used to describe a carpenter, or joiner, a worker in wood, such as a wheelwright, shipwright, etc., and it transpired that many of the Clan McIntyre adopted the name Wright as a secret, hidden meaning of their true hereditary identity. Accordingly, it could be suggested that the name of the only other solicitor ever charged with possession of firearms was also called 'James McIntyre'.

When one contrasts the two cases, in mine, the most the Crown could prove was that I had possession of the two guns and ammunition, for whatever reason, for a period of about two hours before the police raid. However, in the case of James Wright, he had pled guilty to carrying a sawn-off shotgun and a loaded pistol, in his briefcase, for a period of more than one and a half years, in various public places, and he stated as his defence that he feared he was going to be attacked by certain persons and required them for self-defence.

In Scots law it is illegal to carry any item whatsoever if the reason for carrying that object is to defend oneself in case of an attack. Consequently, in the case of James Wright, the reason given for carrying the guns over such a prolonged period, in various public places, was by his own admission to use said weapons if attacked, which clearly added to the severity of the offence.

However, notwithstanding all this, the powers that be decided to deal with Mr Wright not in the High Court, as they did in my case, but rather held it in the sheriff court, where he was merely fined the sum of £300, and permitted by the Law Society to continue to practise as a solicitor.

But (as Irish comedian Jimmy Cricket used to say) there's more.

In 2001, four years after I was convicted, after I had served my time, at a time when gun crime was being taken even more seriously, especially if connected to the possession and supply of class A drugs, a former pupil from what the newspapers referred to as the 'exclusive George Watson's College in Edinburgh' (I won't reveal his name, as I have nothing against him) appeared before the same judge that sentenced me, Lord Marnoch.

This privileged young man had been captured by the cops while in possession of a 9mm semi-automatic pistol, six bullets, and £16,000 of heroin, which class A drug could be cut down to street level and sold for many times that amount. This student clearly wasn't an idiot nor a dupe but storing the drugs, gun and ammo for a prostitute he'd become infatuated with. Yet the same judge, who sentenced me to three years' imprisonment, allowed someone guilty of possession of a semi-automatic pistol, capable of firing not 0.22, but 9mm ammunition, and in possession of thousands of pounds of a class A drug, to walk out of court completely free with only a reprimand; whereas he ordered that I lose my liberty, my career (which the judge specifically stated during sentencing), spend a sentence behind bars, even denying me bail in order to organise matters at my office, for the sake of my clients, during the four week remand between conviction and sentence.

'Boo hoo,' I hear some of you say, 'stop whining, you got what you deserved.'

I don't agree, but even if I did, surely all things should be equal. As demonstrated in the cases mentioned above, others charged with more serious offences lost neither their liberty nor their employment. I didn't go to private school, I attended the local one in Linlithgow, but I learned one lesson from Lord Marnoch, and later the Law Society. As long as you're not a criminal defence lawyer, fighting hard against the forces of the Crown, or if you went to a posh public school, and you're caught with firearms and ammunition, suddenly the sole reason for being in possession of this gun is no longer 'purely for the furtherance of crime', as Marnoch told me, but merely forms part of a 'most unusual case'.

As for possession of £16,000 worth of smack, apparently that's okay too, providing you're looking after it for a prostitute you're infatuated with, who, going by the quantity, is likely holding it for a drug dealer.

I've seen poor, hopeless drug addicts, men and women taken away in handcuffs, their kids put into care, while they were banged up for possession of a tenner bag of smack for their own use. But these people came from places like Pilton, in Edinburgh, or Easterhouse, or Barlanark or Castlemilk in Glasgow, large sprawling housing estates, where the percentage of people attending George Watson's or some posh school is absolutely zero.

I stood in the dock seconds after being sentenced, completely ignoring the nonsense about the furtherance of crime, my mind working overtime. I calculated that out of the three years, if I behaved myself (that was a big IF) I'd only serve half that time, and as I'd already spent a month on remand and the sentence had been back-dated, I could be out of prison in seventeen months, just under a year and a half.

The truth of the matter is, my QC, knowing me, knowing the court, knowing the cops and knowing the score, had said if convicted I should expect about four years. So, when I was given three, I quickly performed the calculation referred to, and a feeling of relief swept over me. I turned towards Evelyn in the public benches, winked, blew her a kiss and trotted down the stairs to the cells, before the cop could even catch up with me.

I was in the cells below Glasgow High Court for about ten minutes when my brother came in with my QC to see me. I remember William looking at me, tears filling his eyes. I felt very touched and joked, 'I don't know what you're crying about, it's me going to jail,' which made my brother smile. He and my QC had done everything they could, the jury were just a heartless bunch of buffoons and with the establishment determined to lock me up, this result had been pretty much on the cards.

Shortly after this, the cops came, cuffed me, and I was placed in a prison van and driven to Saughton prison to start my sentence; one which, though it would alter my life to a great extent, I would learn a lot from.

55

'Honor is the gift that a man gives himself.'

– Rob Roy MacGregor

I have a younger brother and two young sisters, none of whom have had so much as a parking ticket. It's true, the police had no love for me, and did everything in their power to lock me up, but at the end of the day, I was the one who gave them the chance. They could never have managed it all by themselves.

The van I travelled in from Glasgow High Court to Edinburgh eventually arrived at its destination, and Saughton prison opened its gates to welcome me. When you go to jail at first as a convicted prisoner, they take you to a hall where you're locked up for the night, and next day you attend induction. Induction basically involves some officer telling you what the prison rules are, none of which involve going home very soon. Nobody pays the slightest bit of attention, many have been there on numerous occasions before, and after an hour or so sitting in a very uncomfortable plastic seat you're allowed to return to your cell.

I recall the first few minutes of my arrival in C Hall, which was the induction hall at the time. The cell I was allotted was already occupied by a young man, who greeted me in a friendly fashion. I noticed that he had a small transistor radio (this was the nineties) sitting on the lower of the bunkbeds and that the news was on. Suddenly I heard the newsreader announcing:

'Top criminal lawyer James McIntyre was jailed for three years today at Glasgow High Court for possession of two guns and ammunition.

The .22 pistols were found in a drawer of McIntyre's garage on 30 August last year. The solicitor was arrested after police armed with sub-machine guns surrounded his home while a police helicopter kept watch overhead.'

As I said earlier, surreal is a hugely overused word, often incorrectly; however, I found walking into the prison cell, at the very moment these words were being spoken by the newsreader, a very surreal experience indeed.

After spending a couple of days in C Hall, I was transferred to Forth Hall, also known back then by some inmates as Vietnam. As I walked in, escorted by an officer, I heard someone calling my name from an open cell door. I walked over and the guy got off the bed he was lying on, handed me eight phone cards and said, 'The McGoverns say hello.'

At the time, phone cards cost £2 each, and the standard prison wage was around £8 per week, so I was being handed two weeks' worth of phone cards, three more than the number you were allowed to carry, which was five. This act of kindness enabled me to get in touch with my family right away without having to wait until I had earned money to buy anything from the canteen. Also, the cards did not require to be replaced as they were a gift.

Let me be clear, the cards were in no way some sort of payment for keeping my mouth shut. As I've said earlier, the guns I was convicted of possessing had absolutely nothing to do with the McGovern family. Now, some twenty-five years after my arrest, there's no point in me lying. I'm out. I gave my reasons for having the guns and at no time did I, nor my defence, nor the Crown lead any evidence or suggest in any way whatsoever that the guns came from that family. They didn't.

The involvement of the McGoverns was, as usual, totally made up by the tabloid press. Some journalists who write for these rags think that because they cover various crime stories, they're somehow in the know about what's going on in the underworld, when in fact they know nothing and wouldn't last ten seconds in that environment. Rather, they prefer to sit at their desks inventing headlines they hope will catch the public's attention.

One of the first things I discovered when entering Forth Hall was that the place contained more drugs than a chemist's shop, though the service was a lot faster. Prison management make a big deal about the fact they drug test prisoners, which indeed they do. However, they mostly test prisoners who they know for a fact don't take drugs: that way they get a large percentage of negative results, which makes it look as if they are successfully fighting the drug problem, when in fact they're merely fiddling with the statistics.

In my experience, people who are known to be regular drug users are rarely tested, otherwise the statistics would show the problem of drugs in prison to be the very big one it is. The fact is, many people are in prison for drug-related offences, and drugs are necessary to keep a lid on things and prevent the violence from spilling over. This means a blind eye is often turned towards those who are taking drugs.

Drugs are smuggled into prison in a variety of different ways; however, as I'm not an informer I'm not going to list how this is done but will select only one example. In prison people regularly received newspapers and magazines sent in by families and friends. Heroin could be smuggled in by spreading the powder out over the crossword puzzle in a newspaper and then an identical crossword puzzle cut out from another newspaper would be placed over the first crossword puzzle, the edges pasted down and ironed flat, sandwiching the heroin between the two layers. In this way, the newspapers passed a cursory inspection, and the drug was successfully smuggled into the prison.

The reason that heroin is the drug of choice is because cannabis can remain in the bloodstream, in the body, nails, hair, etc. for weeks after it has been taken and therefore anyone being tested that has smoked cannabis will be found positive. Accordingly, many prisoners who enjoy a joint instead end up chasing the dragon, and so smoke smack instead because they know that they can drink litres and litres of water during the night, which will flush the drug from their system, so they can pass a drug test if pulled the next day.

So it is that many people who have taken soft or recreational drugs and gone to prison for one reason or another have ended up addicted to heroin; an addiction which has, in cases I know about personally, proved fatal.

I've referred earlier to the fact that back in the nineties there were no toilet facilities in some of the halls, and Forth Hall was one of these. You were required to use a plastic potty, and do so in front of your cellmate; also there were no facilities for washing your hands after doing so. Accordingly, prisoners with no toilet facilities in their cells would squat down and do the business onto a sheet of newspaper, turning the saying that the tabloids are full of shit from a metaphor to a reality, use another piece of newspaper to clean themselves, then fold the whole lot, origami style, into a small package, open the cell window a fraction (that's as far as they open, one of Lowry's matchstick-men would be lucky to squeeze though the space) then push the parcel out between the bars, causing it to drop with a plop to the ground below.

Next day, these little bundles of treasure would be collected by a con the screws had picked on for some trifling offence and placed on 'bomb patrol'. His job was to go around picking up, bagging and disposing of newspaper-wrapped number twos.

By the time I arrived in Forth Hall, having already spent a month in custody, I was fairly familiar with how things went down, so collected my gear from the guy who doled out the sheets, duvets and pillows, and headed for the cell appointed me. I introduced myself to my cellmate, one of a number I had during my stay, then made up my bed on the top bunk, and put away the few belongings I had in the square wooden box the prison provides for this purpose.

My cellmate was a quiet, pleasant guy, serving a very short sentence for something I can't remember, and after collecting my dinner on a plastic plate with the plastic knives and forks prisoners are provided with, I took the food back to my cell, where I ate and soon after fell into a sound sleep.

Our cells were opened the next morning for a head count at 7.00 a.m., then again for breakfast at 7.30 a.m. I've described before what 'le petit déjeuner' in prison was like. There was always a plentiful supply of porridge (hence 'doing porridge' being the term for serving a sentence), which truth be told was excellent, as it was made in a giant pot, the type missionaries are put in and boiled in cartoons. The porridge was so thick, that, if poured onto a plate and left on the windowsill for a day, it hardened into a type of salty flapjack.

However, porridge was the highlight. The rest of breakfast consisted of a selection of cereals which passed, only just, for Rice Krispies or cornflakes, after which you were given a roll with either a piece of black pudding, or square sausage or a canned plum tomato, but each of these appeared singly, and never arrived together as in a proper breakfast.

'And why should you have a proper breakfast?' I hear someone shout. 'You were in prison.' True, I was in prison, but down the years I paid a lot of money in tax, and so was entitled to a lot better fare than the kind being offered during my stay in Betty's Bed and Breakfast.

Not long after finishing breakfast on my first day in Forth Hall, an officer came to my cell and announced I was required at the agents' visits block. I asked the time, to be told it was 9.00 a.m. This struck me as strange. Agents' visits didn't start until 9.15 a.m. However, I thought my younger brother might have managed to call early, maybe to check how I was getting on before the other agents arrived.

Anyway, I followed the officer from the hall and, on arriving at the agents' visits area, instead of my brother, I found three of the top brass from the prison sitting on the other side of a table in one of the cubicles, apparently waiting for me. Accordingly, I took a seat and faced them.

'Really, it's rather late for a welcoming party,' I said. 'I'm already settled in.'

This remark met with a wall of silence and after an awkward moment, the officer with the most scrambled egg on his peaked cap leaned slightly towards me, resting his forearms on the table in front of him, his fingers entwined.

'I'll cut to the chase. You know a great many of the prisoners in here; some of them, their fathers, brothers, uncles, cousins have been your clients.'

He paused, looking hard at me.

'And?' I ventured.

He glanced round at his fellow top brass, and back to me.

'As you're doubtless aware, we have a big drug problem, especially with heroin.'

I looked at the three of them.

'Have any of you considered rehab?' I asked.

The man evidently had no sense of humour, and continued. 'People are always devising new ways to smuggle it into the prison. So, we thought we could perhaps come to an accommodation.'

'You can come to my accommodation any time you like,' I said, 'but you'll find it rather cramped, as I already have a roommate.'

Clearly, scrambled-egg-cap man was becoming tired with my repartee.

'I'm talking about coming to an arrangement.'

'Really?' I said. 'What kind would that be?'

'Your past employment has always involved an element of strict confidentiality and therefore the cons are naturally far more likely to confide in you, or at least converse in your presence about matters, than they are with any of the staff. So, we considered that, when you are mixing with the other prisoners, you could use your status among them, your past relationships with them, their families, to find out what's going on, what's being done drug wise, and who's doing it. If you are prepared to help us in this way, we'll put you straight into E Hall, and your job will be something like making tea for the governor, working in the office, something like that.'

Things will doubtless have changed dramatically by now, but back then there were various halls housing different categories of prisoner. As I said earlier, C Hall was for induction, Forth Hall was where I'd been placed, which was a dirty madhouse. D Hall (as it turned out later) was an incredibly clean and shiny place, run in a regimental style and housing prisoners doing longer sentences.

However, E Hall was a whole different scenario. This was normally where non-violent prisoners were put, after they had proved they could be trusted. The cells were considerably more spacious, consisting of square rooms with wooden walls, far more comfortably fitted out, and a prisoner could leave his cell to visit the bathroom day or night, and was relatively free to roam around as he wished.

While I was locked up in Forth Hall, another lawyer arrived in Saughton. He'd been convicted of defrauding deceased clients, stealing money from their estates as the executor, depriving numerous children's charities and others out of huge sums of money. However, he wasn't a criminal lawyer, had never appeared for the defence in a criminal trial, never 'got anybody off' in court, annoyed the Crown or the cops, so his dishonesty didn't really concern the powers that be. As a result, despite the large amount of money he'd swindled, he received the incredibly lenient sentence of two years, and on his arrival in Saughton, was sent to E Hall as a trusted prisoner.

I stared at the prison officer who was leaning towards me, as the others looked on to gauge my reaction. They didn't have long to wait.

'So, the bottom line is, you want me to find out what I can, and report back to you: in other words become an informer?'

'We'd appreciate your assistance and reward it accordingly.'

'Basically, you want me to grass on people I've acted for, or whom I know?'

'I wouldn't refer to it as grassing, rather as helping us to solve a serious situation, a real problem, plus of course, as has been said, you'd benefit personally in the process.' He paused a second, smiling. 'So, what do you say?'

I smiled back and said, 'I've a much better idea.'

The officer's face brightened.

'Why don't you take me back to Forth Hall, and save us both any further embarrassment?'

I stood, turned, and left the room, the officer who'd brought me, hurrying to catch up. The request made to me by the prison authorities indicates the type of persons they were in several ways. Firstly, it displayed their incompetence, the fact they required to rely on a prisoner to solve what was in fact their problem. It's a prison, they're in charge, they make the rules, but simply can't cope.

Secondly, had I been willing to rat out people for my own benefit, they were quite willing to risk my safety in prison should my complicity come to light.

But, thirdly, and most importantly by far, it was obvious these people had no sense of honour, and assumed I'd bite their hand off for a chance to make my time inside easier.

Of course, one can argue what they were doing was perfectly legal; trying to enlist my assistance, as I was in a better position to find out what illegal activity was going on, but there comes a point, in some cases, very quickly, where legality and morality part company, indeed are diametrically opposed to one another, and you need to decide which side you're on. In a situation where it comes down to them against us, if you started on the side of us, and change it to them, merely to suit yourself, then you're morally bankrupt.

However, the authorities had their petty revenge. Despite the fact I behaved impeccably, didn't touch drugs, attended Mass religiously every week (on reflection, religiously is the only way one should really attend Mass), reading the lesson, still the top brass made sure I peed into a potty in Forth Hall for many months more than was appropriate for a prisoner serving my length of sentence. But then, I had the satisfaction of knowing I wasn't a rat: never was, and never will be.

56

'Another day down, another day closer to the door. Do us both a favour. Try to behave yourself.'

        – Evelyn McIntyre (extract from letter to me in prison)

I don't intend to go into any great amount of detail about my time in Edinburgh prison. Readers who have never been to jail will already know a fair bit of what they look like from various film and TV dramas. I spent a good deal of time giving legal advice to convicted prisoners who were appealing their sentence or conviction and was treated with a great deal of respect by the other inmates.

The weeks passed, and often people counted them by the number of cheese and jams they still had to go. For anyone who's never been banged up, this was because on a Saturday there was a skeleton staff of screws, so after lunch we were all locked up until dinner time, then let out to collect our jam, cheese and bread to make sandwiches, as there was no hot meal that day. Bread was in plentiful supply, piled up on the counter of the serving hatch. Brown bread was a big favourite, as it had the highest yeast content, so could be used to make hooch.

However, the cheese was the cheapest of the cheap, masquerading as cheddar, and though yellow had the taste and texture of candlewax. The jam came in a bucket, which was plonked down in the middle of the bottom flat by a prison officer, with a huge spoon stuck in it, for everyone to partake. What flavour the jam was remains a mystery to me to this day. The only certainty is that no type of fruit known to mankind had ever been used in the making of it. There was a strange smell emanating from the bucket when the lid was removed, and this gelatinous mass wobbled about daring you to taste it, which I did once, but never again. It had an antiseptic smell which suggested that a bucket of said red gel would have been put to better use cleaning Forth Hall floor than being eaten.

After spending far too many months in that dirty dump, I was moved to D Hall. As I said earlier, this was a far cleaner place, spotless in fact, and prisoners and officers alike took a pride in keeping it that way. However, it was more regimented, and housed prisoners who were serving sentences of more than just a few months or so, meaning a lot of the rockets that fly in and out of prison a couple or three times a year weren't running about like lunatics, looking for gear.

I can't be sure of the situation now, but back in the nineties, prison visits were ridiculously short – thirty minutes per week – so I'd save them up and have my girlfriend, Evelyn, and my sons, Scott and Sam, visit me once a fortnight for an hour. I only allowed my daughter, Mhairi-Clare, and my mum to visit me on one occasion, even then not until I'd made it to the semi-open nick. My daughter (now a mother with her own kids) was still at primary and, thinking I was working away, living in an hotel, would send me pictures, and scribble little letters. My unwillingness to let my mum or daughter visit me may seem sexist, but I'm old school and believe the prison environment is no place for women if it can be avoided; that includes those women who are serving sentences.

In my opinion, far too many women are locked up, especially for drug or drug-related offences for which they should be receiving treatment, rather than being separated from their children and families. The problem of poverty in the deprived areas these women (and men) come from needs to be properly addressed rather than the empty promises made by politicians seeking election, which they have little intention or interest in keeping once in office.

Being sent to prison is a different experience for men. Don't get me wrong, it's far from being a barrel of laughs, but many look on their jail time as an occupational hazard, and doing their jolt as something macho; then they come out as if having done a bit of bird merits some kind of badge, which they wear with pride, while the fact is it's their womenfolk who've had to hold the family together the whole time the men have been behind bars.

On the other hand, many women who are locked up feel ashamed both while inside and after their release; they're looked down upon by society as failures, bad mothers who couldn't take care of their kids. You hear about men who, after serving a sentence, are rehabilitated and have become artists, sculptors, journalists, writers, and turned their lives around. When was the last time you heard about a woman leaving prison and being seen as any sort of a success?

While in jail, I was visited by several people, many of whom put money into my property: Joe and his crew from Springburn; John Lynch whose bar I referred to before in London Road and had strong connections across the Irish Sea; Hugh Gemmill, a friend of John's, but whose cultural and religious background was the total opposite. But hey, that's Glasgow.

I was also sent several books by two solicitors, Roy Harley, and Duncan Hughes, both good guys, and other lawyers, such as Dick Whyte, would grab a quick word with me, offering their best wishes if I bumped into them during an agent's visit with my brother. One elderly solicitor, Keith Bovey, sent me a different postcard every month during my stay in Saughton, with an inspiring message on each one. I still have them. This kind gentleman has now gone to his reward; however, I'll never forget his thoughtfulness during those dark days. When you're in the nick you certainly find out who your friends are.

I got a job working in the prison kitchen, and began on washing-up duty, cleaning dirty dishes for seven hundred or so prisoners three times a day, then moved on to help cook the meals.

However, the main aim anyone has while working in the prison kitchen is to steal as much as they can from the stockroom, conceal it on their person and successfully smuggle the booty back to their cells, where they can distribute it to their mates in return for tobacco, phone cards or other commodities. Believe me, if you hadn't stolen before, you started stealing now. This proved easier than one would have thought, as paradoxically, the prison officer in charge, whose presence was meant to prevent this behaviour, knew perfectly well what was going on.

At the end of a shift, he'd pat each prisoner down very lightly as we left the kitchen but was never thorough. If you weren't totally tearing the backside out of it, he'd pretend not to notice various bulges in our clothing, so as to keep the peace and ensure everything ran smoothly.

Some guys made their own hooch, so I received a lot of requests to bring back as much sugar as possible, to turn into alcohol. During my time in the kitchen, I must've pinched an entire plantation's worth. A mate of mine, Eddie, known as 'Fast Eddie', liked to brew his own booze. He'd use any fruit he could get hold of, plus sugar and water, put everything in a large plastic bucket which had once held the jam for the entire hall, add a couple of loaves of brown bread for yeast, mix this up and stick it under his bed. Somehow, he managed to manufacture a valve from an empty plastic tub of Brylcreem and a Biro, which served to let the air out of the bucket. It also served to let out an awful stink. How the screws never caught on was a marvel, unless, which is likely, they let him carry on as it kept him out of other mischief.

I was a year into my sentence before the powers that be decided I was trusted enough to be moved to E Hall. The fact is, they'd deliberately delayed sending me there, holding me in the other halls for as long as possible. E Hall was the paradise the prison authorities had promised to send me to immediately on my arrival, provided I snitched on my fellow prisoners. After my rather blunt refusal, instead of day one, it was around day three hundred and sixty-five that the knobs in the top brass moved me. Still, it was worth every day. Honour knows no price.

While in E Hall, I continued to work in the kitchen, bringing back various goodies for snacks with my cellmate, Stewart, who was about my age, a hotel owner from Dunfermline, and a friendly, funny guy. He and his son were serving three months for stealing thousands of pounds' worth of computer chips. E Hall was a far more relaxed regime than the rest of the nick; everybody came from and went to work with no hassle and spent their spare time as they pleased. I became mates with two boys from Bathgate: Big Sandy, who's sadly no longer with us, and Paul McFaulds, with whom I remain friendly today.

However, E Hall was in Saughton, and Saughton was very much, and still is, a closed prison. For me the next step was to make it to the semi-open, situated at Castle Huntly, near Dundee, which I heard great things about, and where I hoped to complete my sentence – hoped being the operative word as things turned out. Consequently, I continually harped on and on at two of the officers, called Phil and Neil, about being moved, until at last my name was placed on the list for transfer.

On one of the last days I spent working in the kitchens while waiting to leave for Castle Huntly, contemplating what I considered would be at least partial freedom, I was talking to a guy who'd just been sent back from the semi-open after having been caught smoking smack. I recall sympathising with him, while simultaneously thinking, what a rocket! How crazy can you be, managing to get out the closed nick, only to make a complete cock of it, get caught doing something stupid and be banged up again behind bars. Ah, gentle reader, as it is written, 'Judge not, that ye be not judged.'

Okay, so it wasn't freedom, but it felt very close to it. One thing was certain: where we were headed was a whole lot better than being behind bars in Saughton.

At last, the big moment arrived. The van came to pick up those who'd been put on the list for the Open: the prison, not the golf tournament. I was as excited as a kid at Christmas. Indeed, Christmas was only a month and a bit away when we arrived in early November, and we were all so busy chatting in the back, I can remember nothing of the journey north.

Castle Huntly is now used as a semi-open prison, some seven miles from Dundee. It might not be Balmoral, but it beat being banged up in Saughton by a long way. Of course, it's not actually a castle, but rather a big building with turrets that houses the administrative centre and the governor's office, plus prison visits are held in a large

L-shaped room there. The living quarters, areas for education and the workshops are situated at the bottom of the hill from the castle and prisoners aren't kept in cells, as they would be in a closed prison, but live in dormitories, each of which, if I remember correctly, can hold up to six people. Outside are grassed areas, green spaces with plenty of places where friends and family can drop contraband off, tuck things out of sight behind trees, and put bags under bushes, to be collected later by whichever of their loved ones was serving a sentence.

There were education classes, music classes and workshops, where prisoners could make things under a certain amount of supervision. Some chose to make chairs and coffee tables. I had a bash at that, but metalwork was never one of my strong points at school and ended up making chess sets, the boards consisting of wood and the pieces made from plaster of Paris, having been set in rubber moulds, before being painted. Some prisoners were even taken to work in people's gardens and fields but to me that smacked rather of being part of a chain gang and I preferred to stay in the workshop whiling away the time perfecting my chess pieces.

Every night, I'd phone my girlfriend and we'd chat and count down the days until Christmas. At Christmas each prisoner was allowed to take leave and go home for five full days to enjoy the festive period with his family, so both of us were very much looking forward to this. However, Christmas was still a few weeks away and I discovered that it was possible to have a single day's leave if a prisoner required to see his lawyer for legal advice.

As a result, I decided to have a go at getting a day out, requested to see the governor and went up the steps to the castle, where I was shown into his office. It happened that the governor, a charming, elderly gentleman, was a client of my younger brother's firm, and I explained to him the necessity of seeing my lawyer in order to sort out certain legal matters. To my surprise the governor took very little convincing, and it was arranged that one day in the following week, I was to be picked up by my girlfriend at seven o'clock in the morning and returned to Castle Huntly prison for seven o'clock that evening.

Clearly, my request about requiring to visit my solicitor was a barrowload of BS, but I thought I'd better touch base, to be on the safe side, in case some busybody bothered to check. I'd chosen as my solicitor for this day out my good friend and former legal partner Paul. At the time he had his own practice in Leith Walk, Edinburgh, and I'd called him in advance to mark his card about what I was up to.

All went like clockwork. On the appointed day, Evelyn picked me up early doors at Castle Huntly, and we shot down the road. We pulled up outside Paul's office and I ran inside, spent all of ten seconds saying 'Hi' and 'Goodbye' to my mate, got back in the car, and headed home at the speed of light. The kids were all at school, so the opportunity was there for a long-awaited roll in the hay before lunch. The children came home, and I spent some time with them. I remember as soon as my son Sammy saw me, he burst into tears; I like to think of joy at seeing me out, not at the fact he thought I may be back for good.

Tired, but happy, we took off back to Castle Huntly, where Evelyn dropped me off, and I made it back inside by the skin of my teeth. However, someone wasn't a happy chappy about the fact I'd enjoyed a day out: that someone was the deputy governor.

For some reason he'd got his tights in a bunch simply because he considered I'd used the system, which of course I had, and would encourage anyone who finds themselves in an open prison to act accordingly. It was no skin off his nose, but he'd clearly marked my moment of happiness, disapproved greatly, and had it in for me.

57

'Remember that time is money.'

– Benjamin Franklin

It's customary when seeing a client in custody, or consulting in the office on a criminal matter, to complete legal-aid forms for advice and assistance, and, if there was to be a trial, other forms for full legal aid, and have them sign the same. The difficulty was if you had several clients appearing from custody on any given morning, they were not brought into the sheriff court cells from the various police stations around the city, or from prison, until shortly before they were due to appear in court. This left very little time to fully complete all the necessary forms before the clients signed them, and if they did, lawyers risked being late for court and found in contempt.

However, normally the client was a regular and his or her details, address, income, etc. were well known to you already and it was common practice to have them sign the form, take their instructions and then move on to the next client before court started; then, later, at court or back in the office, the form could be properly filled in without the client requiring to be present, plus there was a good chance he or she had been returned to custody.

A clear sign the Law Society were after their pound of flesh, and gunning for me and my firm, was that while I was in prison, representatives of the Scottish Legal Aid Board raided my office in the Saltmarket, Glasgow and took away bundles of documents containing green forms, which they stated had been signed and not completed, complaining therefore that this was evidence of fraud and that clients were signing blank forms in connection with legal advice on criminal matters which they never received.

This was, of course, nonsense. I had cabinets full of clients' files and didn't require to invent imaginary ones or pretend to give advice to people who didn't ask for it, or even exist.

However, SLAB had the bit firmly between their teeth and were desperate to prove that something illegal was going on. As I said, I was only advised of this while I was serving my sentence and my partner and assistant at the time were both accused of the same thing. However, both had consulted with counsel and so had expert legal representation at the forthcoming hearing in Edinburgh before the disciplinary tribunal.

I received very little information in prison about this hearing and had virtually no opportunity to prepare. SLAB had produced mountains of photocopied forms and documents for everyone, including my partner and assistant, both counsel, the representatives of the Scottish Legal Aid Board, plus each of the members of the tribunal, and who knows what proportion of the rainforest had been chopped down in order to supply the paper for this. The only person who had no opportunity to read any of this documentation was me.

Nor was I able to instruct counsel to come up to Castle Huntly, consult and represent me, as I wasn't earning as a lawyer, and doubted that the prison wage of approximately £8 a week would quite cover their fees. As a result, I required to defend myself. I was taken in handcuffs down from Castle Huntly to Edinburgh and brought before the tribunal alongside my partner, assistant and their respective counsel.

I was granted a short time to sit handcuffed in the Signet Library to look up some law books, which were of absolutely no use at all in this case, and realised that, though an unusual approach to adopt, telling the truth may well be the proper defence to this matter.

SLAB clearly reckoned on this hearing taking some considerable time, thinking all the documentation would require to be gone over, perused in detail, studied at length, and explained before the members of the tribunal came to a decision. In fact, the opposite was the case.

The tribunal hearing began, but before the opposition opened their case, I advised the members of the tribunal that this was simply a waste of their time and of mine. I told them about the difficulties mentioned, about completing legal aid forms for several clients in custody, minutes before they were due to appear in court, and that the details, if not already known, could be jotted down, the forms signed and then properly filled in at a later stage back at the office. Sometimes, the forms would be sent off to SLAB, at other times if the case was going no further or something else intervened, the form would not be sent in, but at no time were the forms signed with any intention of submitting them fraudulently for advice which was not given or representation for clients who did not exist.

At this point one of the members of the tribunal asked if this was in any way common practice. Whether or not the person was being facetious, or it was a genuine remark, I replied that it was incredibly common and in fact solicitors such as Joseph Beltrami, and several other well-known defence agents who regularly appeared in the criminal courts, especially when on duty, required to do the same due to the limited timescale involved.

The members of the tribunal asked counsel for my colleagues if this was in fact the case and were assured that it was. This now pushed the SLAB representatives into a corner. They had no intention of going after certain other solicitors, thus opening a can of worms, but were interested solely in the ones they'd picked out to prosecute in this particularly unfair fashion. Accordingly, after floundering about like fish out of water for a while, they closed their case, and the tribunal retired to consider its verdict.

The tribunal were out for barely enough time to have a cup of tea, before they returned and stated neither I, nor my colleagues, had acted improperly or inappropriately in any way whatsoever, and found the Scottish Legal Aid Board liable for the costs of the case, plus the defence expenses, which ran to the tune of over £100,000. I had not been able to instruct counsel, was still banged up, and it would have been stretching things a bit to send myself a bill for legal services. However, the costs involved preparing for this ridiculous witch-hunt meant that SLAB, while refusing legal aid in more deserving cases, required to fork out a small fortune for their own, only to watch it go down the tubes. Despite the fact I was locked up, still they were desperate to get me for anything else they could, even if in the end it was the taxpayer who had to pay for their pathetic, petty little plot.

58

'*Return'd so soon?*'

— *The Comedy of Errors*, William Shakespeare

One of the good things about Castle Huntly, apart from the food, which was far better than anything ever cooked up in Saughton, was that unlike the Edinburgh prison, there was no chapel in which to hold Mass on a Sunday. I don't say that because I wanted to miss Mass, far from it, but because someone from the local parish was appointed to pick up any prisoner who wanted to go to church and drive them there and back. What's more, there was no prison escort.

As it was a semi-open prison, very few prisoners wished to take advantage of a trip out of the prison on a Sunday as they were free to roam around the grounds, perhaps searching for the contraband planted in previously arranged places by friends and relatives. In fact, my mate Eddie, one other person and I were the only cons keen to go.

I had attended Mass without fail every Sunday in Saughton, often reading the lesson. While there, I noticed that when the officer came into the hall on a Sunday morning to shout out that it was time for the Catholics to go to chapel, he would yell 'RCs for Mass' but slur the words in such a way to make it sound like 'arses for mass'. I noted the hall governor had a southern Irish sounding surname, hazarded a guess at which foot he kicked with, and asked to see him. During our discussion I discovered my guess had been correct and advised him of what was going on. As a result, he brought the matter to an abrupt halt and thereafter the offending officer was forced to annunciate very clearly, 'It's now time for Roman Catholics to attend Mass.'

Anyway, my reason for wishing to attend Mass at Castle Huntly was entirely genuine, though the fact that we were driven to and from the service did offer us another opportunity, and it seemed a shame to look a gift horse in the mouth. Sunday on the way back from chapel we would ask the driver to stop at the local newspaper shop so we could buy some sweets, newspapers, etc., and this kind gentleman always complied. He shouldn't really have allowed us to leave the car, but he did, and this small corner shop also doubled up as an off-licence, where we would buy half bottles of vodka to smuggle back into the prison. I'd only buy a half bottle, and stuff it down the front of my jeans. But Eddie would have bottles down his trouser legs, up his sleeves, and secreted all over his body, so that on our return to Castle Huntly he would walk in, his limbs stiff and straight, robotic, clanking like the Tin Man from *The Wizard of Oz*.

How Eddie managed to get the booze into the place and never be pulled up was a measure of the man's confidence in the ineptitude of those in charge of the prison system.

As I said earlier there was a large workshop where prisoners could manufacture various objects from wood, metal and other materials, which they were allowed to pay for and take home at the end of their sentence. I had been working on a chess set, but after painting the various pieces I got bored and decided to make a toy for one of my sons, who was only six years old at the time.

Without really thinking it through, I decided to make him a wooden gun. Dear reader, if ever you find yourself imprisoned for possessing firearms, the worst thing you can do is to make yet another one in the prison workshop, even if it is merely made from wood. Take it from me, it doesn't go down well. Call me crazy, many have, I never gave it a moment's consideration and carried on regardless.

My woodwork skills, as my teacher at school would happily have attested, left a great deal to be desired. However, I had a bash, and with the use of a bandsaw cut out the shape of a revolver. I then split a thin rod of doweling and placed the two halves on either side of the flat wood to form a barrel, split a thicker piece of doweling in half and stuck that on either side to look like the chamber of the gun holding the bullets. I was still engrossed in my task when it came time for lunch, so I stopped and left the unfinished project in a vice on the bench, in full view of everyone, and headed off to the dining hall.

After lunch I returned to discover the wooden gun was missing. Very shortly after that I was pulled up and told the deputy governor wanted to see me. Until this meeting took place, I was locked in a room and left to sweat for over an hour. Eventually, an officer came and brought me into the presence of this little dictator, who sat staring at me like the cat who'd got the cream.

He laid the wooden revolver down on the desk in front of me. 'What have you got to say to that?' he said.

I looked at the offending article.

'The workmanship's rather rough, but to be fair it's not finished yet, and . . .'

'I mean what are you doing making a gun in my prison?' he cut in, pronouncing the words 'my prison', as if the place belonged to him.

'It's not a gun, it's just a toy, and I was making it as a Christmas present for my son.'

'So, you say.' He spat the words out like bullets. 'You could have painted this wooden gun black and used it to escape.'

'If I wanted to escape,' I spat back, 'I'd catch the bus at the end of the road. Your prison (I emphasised the word 'your') is a semi-open one, or hadn't you noticed?'

Dear reader, I can hear you saying, why didn't you just shut up, rather than goad the man? And you're right. Clearly, I wasn't sounding nearly repentant enough for this clown, but by now I'd realised I'd crossed the Rubicon, not that this rocket would have known what that meant. However, he now had the excuse he'd been dreaming about, all the ammo required to send me back down the road to Saughton. And this he did without further ado.

I was given ten minutes to pack my stuff, and when I asked, was told to leave behind the chess set I'd made. As a result, I thought it pointless to ask if I could keep the gun.

Just before we left for Edinburgh, an officer allowed me to make a very quick phone call to Evelyn, who was due to come for a visit that evening, to save her the journey. As I said before, I was due five days' leave at Christmas, and we'd been talking about it since I'd arrived at Castle Huntly. Now that I'd completely cocked things up, there was more chance of Santa coming down the chimney than me arriving home for Christmas day, so it wasn't a phone call I relished making.

At first, Evelyn thought I was joking. Then she thought this was an excuse, part of some dastardly plan I'd come up with so I could spend Christmas somewhere else. It simply didn't dawn on her that what I was saying was true, and that I'd been daft enough to do what I did. However, eventually she believed me, and I vaguely recall her screaming down the phone, 'How can you have been so stupid?'

I was trying to figure that out for myself, but before I could answer, she hung up on me, I was cuffed and led to a waiting car for the journey back down to the capital.

As with the journey to the open prison, I don't recall any of the return journey, my mind was jammed full of thoughts, but not the happy ones they had been before.

Looking on the bright side, my return to Edinburgh prison could have been worse. At least my woodwork activities in Castle Huntly had not lost me any days for my lack of good behaviour, plus no charges had been brought for conspiracy to escape from an open prison with the use of a partially made wooden pistol. After a day or so of sleeping through the induction in C Hall, I was brought back to D Hall, where I'd been a couple of months before. As I walked in, a prisoner who was leaning on the railing on the first flat above me shouted out, 'Hey, look! Jimmy Two Guns is back!'

This was the first time I'd been referred to by that nickname. I felt like shouting back, 'Actually it should be Jimmy Three Guns,' but it didn't have quite the same ring, so I left it, and the name stuck.

It was late December, and my release date was the last day of April, meaning I'd just over four months of my sentence left to serve. In jail, prisoners do various jobs. Some work in the paint shop, others in what was originally 'the mailbags' but now where white forensics suits were stitched together, some worked in the kitchen, others in the prison gardens, which were kept in perfect condition. However, some prisoners stayed in the hall, employed as passmen.

This job involved sweeping and tidying up but had the advantage in that you were allowed out of your cell when others were locked up. During my previous time in Saughton, I'd worked in the mailbags checking the white suits for any faults, and in the kitchens, but shortly after my return, one of the passmen was released and I asked for the position – and rather surprisingly was granted it. I spent the next few weeks wandering up and down the landings, or sometimes being allowed to sit in a cell with another prisoner for a cup of tea. I had several cellmates during my time in D Hall, including Paul Kerr, brother of Jim Kerr from Simple Minds; David Donnell from Paisley; a great wee guy called Tufty from Fife; and I was very friendly with Jimmy Emslie, a steel erector, and Big Rod MacLean, who'd been handed twelve years for his part in allegedly importing five tons of cannabis into the country, which sentence was reduced to eight years on appeal.

As I said earlier, the food in Castle Huntly had been very good, and I'd scoffed a great deal of it. As a result, on my return to closed conditions in D Hall I was weighing in at about sixteen stone. For someone who's five feet nine inches in height, that's way too much to be carrying, and I decided it was time to do something about it.

Big Rod was a judo expert, very keen on training, and started me on a regime requiring me to do sit-ups, push-ups, squats, plus step aerobics in my cell, at 6.30 every morning before breakfast.

In D Hall there was a pantry where the cooked food was brought three times a day in large trolleys, which also served to smuggle sugar for hooch, or perhaps a special order for a prisoner from a pal working in the kitchen, plus notes called 'stiffies' could be passed from hall to hall this way. I'm not giving away any secrets here, as this was common knowledge; if it wasn't, I wouldn't be saying a word.

Meals were dished out to the prisoners who queued up at a large hatch to collect their plastic plates, knives, forks, and food. Each landing, or flat, took it in turns to be called first for meals, meaning everyone got an equal chance to choose from the menu, while there still was a choice. After a few weeks working as a passman, a vacancy became available in the pantry, and I was granted permission to take over the position. This was the easiest job going, and by far the best. It even beat working in the gardens, as pantrymen had sole access to all food entering the hall, including the fruit, which was always highly sought after.

I worked in the pantry with Jimmy Emslie. One day while dishing out dinner, one guy said he wasn't happy with the number of chips he'd been given. Jimmy had been fair, but this person who was serving a sentence for violent crime tried to pressurise him into piling more onto his plate, meaning there'd be fewer for everyone else. Accordingly, Jimmy told him he'd had all he was getting, and to move on.

At this, the guy leaned into the hatch, towards Jimmy, thumbing his own chest and said, 'Do you know who I am?'

Jimmy turned to me with a dry smile. 'Hey! Check this guy out. He doesn't know who he is.' And turning back to the queue called, 'Next?'

Jimmy's cool response, together with the fact he was totally unruffled by the apparent threat, caused the guy complaining about his chips to back off and we continued with service. The whole time I worked in the pantry I continued training hard, getting up every morning at 6.30. I was eating porridge and boiled chicken and exercising constantly. As a result, in only four months I dropped from sixteen to eleven stone.

Every night before being banged up, I'd phone Evelyn. The trouble was phone cards cost £2 each and my weekly wage meant I only had enough money to buy four. Since all my cash was used up, I had to do without crisps, sweets, or anything else from the canteen. At the time, I was receiving a codeine-based tablet from the prison doctor, due to a sore ankle I'd got during my training, and came to a deal with a couple of other guys to swap my tablets for two phone cards each week, but that only took my count up to six; the cards didn't last long and I did a lot of talking.

One thing I found out quickly during my first weeks in prison was to never ever give anyone a phone card no matter how dire or desperate they claimed their need for one was. Whatever they told you, it was a lie, and you'd never receive the card back. After all, the place was full of crooks.

The problem I faced was how to acquire enough cards for my frequent phone calls. Fortunately, a fellow inmate had a solution to the matter. I arranged for Evelyn to take some cash from my stash on the outside and give it to my mate's friend, who then deposited the money into my mate's bank account. He was running a racket in jail, the details of which we needn't go into, but the result of this transaction was that I received twenty-five cards per week, plus the two for my tablets, and my own four, if I chose to use my legit wage.

However, this presented a new problem. Each prisoner was only allowed five cards at any one time, and a search of your cell could result in the cards being found and confiscated. Phone cards were green on one side, with SPS in silver letters, standing for Scottish Prison Service, but the flip side was plain, black shiny plastic. Some prisoners collected used phone cards which they stuck to the wall in their cells with Blu Tack, black side facing out, to make patterns. One of the guys who did this was a mate of mine called Dougie, serving the same sentence as me.

Dougie was old school, and his 'Peter', as he called it, was always spotless; curtains at the window, pot plants on the sill, a rug on the floor, and his cell was rarely searched. When I got my weekly supply of cards, I'd give them to Dougie, who'd flip them over and create a pattern on the wall with them, the difference being these cards weren't duds. Every time I made a call, which was at least once a day, Dougie gave me a couple of cards from his wall, I'd use them, then the duds would be put back, to be replaced with live ones as they arrived.

My cell was on the top landing or flat at the far end, next to where the phone hung on the wall. Each night before bed, I'd phone Evelyn for a chat, as we were arranging to get married the day I got out, and I'd always be the last man standing when everyone else had been banged up for the night. The screw on duty on my flat would shout, 'McIntyre, for the last time get off that fecking phone.' But I'd keep right on chatting until he had walked the full length of the landing and was only a few yards from me before I'd hang up and head back to my cell, whistling cheerfully. It was sheer bravado. But still the weeks were going in.

59

'Woe to you, teachers of the law and Pharisees, you hypocrites ... you have neglected the more important matters of the law—justice, mercy and faithfulness.'

— Gospel of Matthew, Ch. 23 v 23

Eventually, after being back in the closed prison for a couple of months, it dawned on the Law Society my sentence was drawing to a close, and soon I'd be let loose to continue the fight against the Crown and the forces of darkness. Accordingly, they decided the time had come to drag me in front of their disciplinary committee, with the clear intention of having me struck off.

So, one morning, I was handcuffed, placed in a prison van and driven to appear before the above-mentioned tribunal, which on that occasion consisted of seven or so members, from a variety of backgrounds, including a lawyer, a doctor, a social worker, and people from other professions. On arrival, my cuffs were removed, and I was taken to the committee room, where my senior counsel was waiting to represent me, which he did free gratis and for nothing.

There was a tall, skinny guy representing the Law Society who assumed the matter to be clearly an open and shut case, claimed that as I had been in possession of these two pistols and some ammunition and was sentenced to three years imprisonment, I should be struck off. End of story.

My counsel explained to the tribunal that both the guns I was found guilty of were 0.22 millimetres, a very small calibre, the period of possession was extremely short, they'd both been found in a drawer, in a locked garage, adjacent to a locked house, inaccessible to anyone, no person had been injured, threatened, frightened, or in any way affected, all but two of the original charges on the indictment had been dropped due to a total lack of evidence, and I had not been convicted of a breach of client confidentiality or any type of dishonesty whatsoever. The offences simply involved the failure to hold a firearms licence, and that for a very short time, full stop.

The tribunal members listened to both sides, after which the chairman advised us that they intended to retire to consider matters. The tribunal had several options open to them. Starting at one end of the spectrum, they could admonish me, or fine me, or fine me and restrict my practising certificate, meaning I'd be required to work as a solicitor under supervision, or suspend me from practising for a specified period, while at the other end, they could order my name to be removed from the roll of solicitors.

After about half an hour's adjournment, we took our seats again and the disciplinary tribunal returned with their decision, stating in their opinion I'd been punished enough, and as I had not breached client confidentiality, nor acted dishonestly, they chose to simply admonish me, and I could return to practise immediately on my release from prison.

To say I was over the moon at that moment would be an understatement. I turned to look at the long drink of water representing the Law Society, who stood staring, shaking his head in utter disbelief, his bottom jaw hanging down, like one of those clowns at the fair, whose heads swivel from side to side, as people throw ping pong balls into their open mouths.

As I said, he'd assumed matters were cut and dried, would go through on the nod, that I'd be struck off, then dragged back to jail to finish my time. Now he had to report to his superiors that he'd, at least in their eyes, managed to snatch total defeat from the jaws of what should have been a certain victory.

However, my delight at the tribunal's decision was short lived, as very soon after the Law Society did something that it had never done before in its entire miserable history. Such was their desperation to stop me from practising, from doing my best for my clients, without cow-towing to the Crown, and going along with the sheer nonsense of a defence lawyer being an officer of the court, the Law Society decided to appeal against the Law Society! Yes, in a last-ditch attempt to have me struck off, they threw their own to the wolves, and asked the Court of Session to give them a second shot at me, something that was totally unheard of.

So, it was that some weeks later, again represented by counsel, I appeared before a certain high court judge and former law officer, who, I foolishly thought, may have deemed that as I had already been punished and paid my dues by serving a prison sentence, I deserved a second chance. Who was I kidding?

After kicking the Law Society round the court for some considerable time, roundly criticising their incompetence, he agreed to play the game with them, and gave in to their request, sending my case back to the disciplinary tribunal in order that they could have another boot at the ball, the ball being me and my future as a defence lawyer.

I was advised by a friend of mine, now retired, but formerly a senior clerk in the Court of Session and High Court, that on one occasion many years ago, he had entered a courtroom in Parliament House early one morning to sort out some documents, a few hours before proceedings began that day. However, he was shocked to discover the very same judge who had let the law society off the hook, then an advocate, had already begun his own proceedings, with a female advocate. On clocking this, my friend beat a speedy retreat.

While not pointing the finger at the judge for using the courtroom in this fashion, again, one would have thought, being aware of his own behaviour, he may perhaps have proved more likely to treat his fellow man more mercifully, but it wasn't to be, and back to the tribunal I went.

My second disciplinary hearing was to be held in the Advocates Library in Parliament House. As I arrived there that morning, I briefly bumped into a solicitor I knew, a good guy, and one who was well up on the machinations of the Law Society, who managed to warn me in a whisper that, 'I'm afraid that lot have really stitched you up this time.'

As counsel and I entered the room where the tribunal was to be held, it suddenly became apparent what my friend had been talking about as he passed me. This time around there were not seven or eight members on the board, nor had they been picked from a variety of different professions. No. This allegedly impartial tribunal consisted entirely of what I'm told were five past presidents of the Law Society, all primed in advance for the occasion, with one result in mind. After a mere pretence of listening to my counsel, without any need to adjourn to consider matters, they passed sentence, and instead of admonishing me, went directly to the other end of the spectrum and announced that my name should be removed from the register of solicitors.

In the course of his speech, the chairman of what appeared to me to be clearly a kangaroo court pronounced that: *'Recent events have raised the public awareness of any offence involving a breach of the Firearms Acts.'*

Clearly this public awareness was completely overlooked by Lord Marnoch, when, some years after my case, at a time when firearm offences were being taken even more seriously, he allowed the former Watsonian pupil to walk out of court a free man, despite being convicted of possessing a semi-automatic pistol, live ammunition and large bag of heroin.

The chairman went on to state that: *'The public expects that members of the solicitors' profession shall maintain a high standard both in connection with their actings as a solicitor and in their private life.'*

What the chairman failed to point out was that I did not commit any act of dishonesty when dealing with a client, however, numerous solicitors have, and continue to commit acts of clear dishonesty when dealing with clients yet are not brought to book. Of course I can't confirm the accuracy of the following, but merely quote from *A Diary of Injustice* published in June 2010, which claimed that the Law Society of Scotland covered up complaints to protect rogue lawyers, and alleged that solicitors siphoned off tens of millions of pounds a year from wills and executry estates in Scotland and got away with doing this because the Law Society continually whitewashed complaints made by families, beneficiaries and sometimes even charities.

An example was given where one elderly client was charged £1,000 for a straightforward will in a non-inheritance tax estate and even driven to her bank by the will writer to withdraw the money in cash to pay the fee. In another case, a client merely wanting a simple will drawn up was apparently sold specialised services they didn't require, and others still were persuaded to pay up to £2,400 when £150 would have sufficed.

This same excellent publication lamented the lack of protection to the public from these civil lawyers, who, to use the words of Michael Corleone, steal more with a suitcase than anyone can with a gun. The report goes on to give several examples, some of which follow.

A solicitor was ripping off a dead client and their family after an elderly man had left his house, possessions and all his investments to his wife and family in what he'd thought was a straightforward will, but made the mistake of appointing this particular solicitor as his executor. This solicitor promptly opened up three accounts with a bank he himself dealt with on a personal basis, then took three years to process his dead client's estate, while squirrelling away almost £30,000 in interest for himself. Apparently, when the deceased's widow was told that three-quarters of the investments mentioned in her husband's will had vanished, she had a careful investigation carried out and discovered the investments had been changed at the solicitor's own discretion, rather than being realised and handed to the family as per the instructions in the will. However, it seems the Law Society backed the solicitor against the family, despite a £250,000 loss in the deceased's investments, and the loss of title deeds to the house in which the widow lived, while apparently the solicitor's personal wealth had increased greatly, and he was able to purchase three top of the range cars.

In yet another case, a solicitor acting as executor for a deceased soldier nicked over £30,000 from a trust the client had set up for his children. The solicitor seemingly cashed in the trust and paid off his own substantial gambling debts, and guess what happened to him. That's right: absolutely nothing. And on and on it goes . . .

I don't quote the above examples to in any way excuse what I did. I leave it to the reader to decide if my sentence was fair, when one considers that nothing happened to the solicitors mentioned in the examples above, and that both the solicitor before, and the student after me, convicted of more serious offences, walked free from court. My point is merely to illustrate what nonsense the chairman of the tribunal spouted when he'd the brass neck to state in my case that the criminal offence of which I was convicted was of a personally disgraceful character.

Apparently, the public would be much more upset by a criminal defence lawyer being convicted of possessing two pistols and some dud ammunition without the necessary licence, in a locked drawer, in a locked garage for a couple of hours, than they would be by a solicitor carrying a pistol and sawn-off shotgun in public, for his own protection for eighteen months, or a student possessing a 9-millimetre pistol, live ammo, and a large haul of heroin, or of solicitors putting together premeditated plans to plunder tens, or even hundreds of thousands of pounds from innocent clients and their families, who not only did not face prosecution or prison, but were actually and actively supported by the Law Society. The hypocrisy is disgusting.

The apparently hand-picked puppet, who was chairing what in my opinion was clearly a kangaroo court/tribunal, concluded by saying that the trust and respect between solicitors and the court had been compromised because I was convicted of a serious offence (in his opinion), and thus, according to him, I was no longer a fit and proper person to remain on the roll.

I must confess that I had to stop myself from bursting out into laughter at this point. I wasn't asking anyone to love or like me, but I'd been busy working for eighteen months while on bail awaiting trial, acting in dozens of cases, dealing with other solicitors, procurators fiscal, advocates, QCs and clients, never breaking client confidentiality, or my word to anyone in the business. The idea that other criminal defence agents, or anyone I dealt with on a day-to-day basis, suddenly would no longer be able to trust and respect me, was absolute rubbish.

Never one to give up till the bell rings, I had one last pop, and appealed this tribunal's decision to the Court of Session. However, the judges on the bench bent over backwards to uphold the decision and referred to the part where Lord Marnoch stated that the sole reason for my possession of these guns could only have been for the furtherance of crime.

There had not, of course, been a single, solitary scrap, not one iota of evidence, led by the Crown during the court case to establish anything of the sort. Lord Marnoch had quite simply, in my opinion, plucked this idea out of the air, as something serious to say when passing sentence, which was then latched onto by the judges, and accordingly they refused the appeal on the basis of a totally unfounded and spurious premise. But, hey, what's new?

I realised then that if these people, in my view a bunch of hypocrites, were the sort of persons who presided over my profession, then I was probably better off out of it and doing something different that didn't involve dealing with them.

60

'Let's all cry peace, freedom and liberty!'
— *Julius Caesar*, William Shakespeare

At last, 29 April 1999 arrived. I was due to be released next morning, the last day of the month, and the plan was that my brother would be picking me up from prison, then I'd be met by my friend Joe McGovern, and marry Evelyn later that morning. Joe was to be my best man and was later one of the godfathers to my three kids.

I deliberately didn't invite my younger brother William or his lovely wife, Gillian, to the wedding, nor one of my younger sisters, Margaret, and her husband, Peter. This was not due to any fall-out – we were and are all still very close – but my brother had been best man at my previous wedding, and along with my sister Margaret remained firm friends with my first wife, Alicia. As a result, I felt very conscious of the fact it may look like I was rubbing my ex-wife's face in things if I invited my brother and sister. As it happens, Alicia and Evelyn are now the best of pals, and even holiday together, clearly united in their high opinion of me.

The whole event was designed to be a very low-key affair, with just family and a few friends, and the reception was arranged to take place in the Barnton Hotel, Edinburgh, for the manager was an old friend of Evelyn's. However, as it happened, somehow the press found out I was being married on the morning of my release, and a journalist from one of the Sunday papers contacted Evelyn; how they got her phone number we don't know, but anyway, she hung up on them. (She's an expert at that, after practising on me so many times while I was in prison!)

However, the press visited Evelyn's mother's house before finally tracking her down at the flat. The journalist offered Evelyn several thousand pounds (she refused to tell me how much) plus stated the paper in question would pay for our honeymoon abroad, provided we gave them an exclusive about our forthcoming wedding, everything that led up to it, and our past together in general.

I found out about this during one of my phone calls to Evelyn from D Hall and thought it a great idea, plus it would save me having to put another dent in the little money I'd left to pay for the forthcoming nuptials. However, Evelyn thought it was a dreadful idea, and point blank refused to even entertain it. I assumed at first this left us in a bit of a predicament, with one vote each, until Evelyn advised me, as chairperson, she had the deciding vote in the matter. I still can't quite recall the process by which she was elected to that position, but she assured me it was the case, and I'd better get over it. Strangely enough, she still holds the same post. In any event, there was no way she was having our pictures put in any Sunday rag, or some scumbag (her view on journalists isn't the highest) inventing a pack of lies about us. I'd rather have fenced with Zorro than fight with Evelyn, and so the newspaper's offer was declined.

Because of all the workouts I'd been doing in my cell and the weight I'd lost, there wasn't a single suit at home to fit me for my wedding. Evelyn had to buy me one and bring it into the prison for me to try on in advance. Taking off and putting on a pair of trousers in front of an audience of dozens of guys on a visit isn't for everyone; but needs must, and I found the wolf whistles encouraging.

As the saying goes, all things come to those who wait, and at last the evening before I was due to be released rolled round. During recreation that night, I was getting some things together for my imminent departure when there was a tap on the door. A former client of mine, at the time serving a ten stretch, asked me to come downstairs to his cell, which was directly below mine.

Puzzled, I followed him, to find two other prisoners I was friendly with already there. My client pointed to the table. On top of it lay several lines of cocaine and speed, and I was told to help myself, as this was a going-away present from them. I confess to feeling touched at the fact they'd not only remembered the date but thought enough of me to share their stash to mark the occasion. At the same time, I was terrified.

I hadn't touched any type of drug during my sentence, though tested more times than a lab rat, but if I partook now and got pulled, Evelyn's anger at me making a wooden gun would be nothing compared to her wrath if I did not turn up at my wedding the next day.

I explained my position to the lads, who told me to relax, advising me even if I was tested and came up positive, all I had to do was appeal it and, as it took seven days for the results to come back, I'd already be out the door and therefore untouchable. I told them I knew this normally to be the case and thanked them sincerely for their kindness; but they didn't know Evelyn, and over the years I'd grown attached to my testicles, so it just wasn't worth taking the risk.

To my relief, they all understood, didn't take my polite refusal as any lack of respect, and I left them to enjoy the party they'd arranged for me as I headed back to my cell on the top flat. As I reached my landing, it was just about lock-up time, and Eddie who coincidentally was also being released the next morning, having served half his two-year sentence, met me at my cell door. Glancing around, checking the coast was clear, Eddie slipped me a plastic bottle which had once contained Kia-Ora orange juice, and was now filled to the brim with Eddie's home brew.

'That'll make sure you get a good sleep; see you in the morning,' he said and winked.

I thanked him for his thoughtful gift, wished him goodnight and went into my cell. As soon as the door closed behind me for the night, I opened the bottle of booze and poured it down the toilet. It's not that I wasn't grateful, I was, but once again I wasn't taking any risks about the next day and, after saying goodnight to Tufty, who was my cellmate at the time, I climbed into my top bunk, and several hours of tossing and turning later, eventually I entered the land of nod.

61

'I beat the prison dust off my feet as I sauntered to and fro ... and I exhaled its air from my lungs.'
　　　　　　　　　　　　　　　　　– *Great Expectations*, Charles Dickens

Day was breaking behind the bars and the first fingers of dawn reached through the window to waken me. In five minutes flat I was down from my bunk, washed, shaved, dressed and teeth brushed. The rising sun saw me fully packed and pacing the floor impatiently. I didn't have a watch to check the time. For some reason you're not allowed a watch in prison; at least you weren't back then.

When I arrived, I'd been wearing a Rolex, bought by instalments with my wages as an apprentice, which back then was £40 a week. It had a stainless steel and gold band, a black dial, and was my prized possession. However, as I was getting married the morning I got out, I'd previously had it released from my property and sold on the outside to a jeweller, to pay for Evelyn's engagement and our wedding rings, which we still have. Sounds romantic, but I recall how little I got for it and realise I was robbed. I got a little revenge for that matter further down the line, but that's another story.

As early each morning I'd followed a rigid training regime, I could tell it was only around 6.00 a.m. I sat staring at the door, got up, paced again for a bit, sat back down and stared at the door some more. It didn't move. No tell-tale sounds could be heard from outside in the hall. The seconds ticked by slowly. They say a watched kettle never boils. Try waiting for a cell door to open. I climbed back onto the top bunk and lay staring at the ceiling this time, but this proved to be no more interesting than the view before.

Then suddenly I heard it. A quiet sound at first, as if coming from far away, but I recognised the rattling of keys in doors. I'd heard that noise for 545 days in a row.

The screws had started the morning head count from the other end of the hall, opening each cell, checking each prisoner was present, making sure no one had magically turned into a mouse, made themselves so small they'd managed to slip between the bars during the night.

Normally, after an officer had checked the prisoners in a cell, he'd lock the door again and open it once the count was completed, but on this occasion, the screw opened the door wide, looked at me standing there and said, 'James McIntyre.'

I'd never been so happy to hear my own name before.

'Ready?' he asked.

The question was both rhetorical and ridiculous, but the man was smiling, and this was no time for witty repartee, or sarcasm. I nodded returning his smile.

'Yep.'

'Okay, let's go.'

I lifted my bag and gave my cellmate in the bottom bunk a shake, to say goodbye. I can't remember what I said to Tufty, but if he ever reads this, I'm sure he'll forgive me for forgetting. He was a good guy, great company, and fantastic at making all sorts of cards for me to send out to Evelyn, and I hope things went well for him after he'd done his time.

I'd said my farewells to friends the night before, so followed the officer from the top flat to the bottom floor, out of the hall, over to the part of the prison where I'd pick up my property before being released.

It must've been about 7.30 a.m., I was packing my property and the other items I brought with me from my cell into a cardboard box when it struck me, I hadn't seen Eddie, who was getting out that same day. I looked around, couldn't spot him, but assumed as his cell would've been opened before me he must've got a head start, so thought no more about it.

I later discovered Eddie's home brew had done exactly what he'd said it would, at least for him, and ensured he got a good night's sleep. So good, rather than being released that morning, it was around lunchtime before the screws managed to wake him and carry him bodily from his cell, insisting he leave the prison as his sentence had now been completed and it was illegal to keep him any longer.

I left the property office, carrying my cardboard box, and five minutes later found me standing behind the large electric gate of the prison, waiting, watching as it rose at an agonisingly slow rate. At last, the gate stood open, my sentence was served, and I stepped out into the spring day.

My young brother William was waiting for me in the prison car park. I always enjoy seeing him, but never so much as I did then. He knew and totally understood about the wedding arrangements and the plans I made and drove me home to my mum and dad's in order that I could get dressed in the new navy-blue suit my future wife had bought me, then headed off to work.

My father had visited me a couple of times while I was in Edinburgh prison, but I'd only seen my mother once during my short stay at Castle Huntly. Our meeting was emotional, and I remember feeling guilty for the first time; not for any offence or crime I may or may not have committed, but for all the worry and upset I put her through, not just on this occasion, but all through the years. As Rudyard Kipling once wrote:

'If I were hanged on the highest hill,
Mother o' mine, O mother o' mine.
I know whose love would follow me still,
Mother o' mine, O mother o' mine'

They say there is no love like a mother's and as I write this, I'm extremely blessed to still have my mum, who's now in her ninety-eighth year.

Speaking of mothers, one of the stories recorded in the Gospels particularly fascinates me and was partially responsible for my conversion to Catholicism. It's found in St John's Gospel, Chapter 2, where we read:

> On the third day a wedding took place at Cana in Galilee. Jesus' mother was there, and Jesus and his disciples had also been invited to the wedding. When the wine was gone, Jesus' mother said to him, 'They have no more wine.' 'Woman, why do you involve me?' Jesus replied. 'My hour has not yet come.' His mother said to the servants, 'Do whatever he tells you.'

As we all know, Jesus then turned the water into wine. However, I think we often see this simply as Jesus' first miracle and miss an important point. As we know, in those days, wedding celebrations involved the whole community, lasting several days, and the wine running out would've been humiliating for both the bride and bridegroom, and their respective families. Clearly, Jesus' mum was aware of the embarrassment which would ensue and felt compassion for the couple. But this also begs the question, why would Mary, a guest, immediately bring the matter to her son's attention? The answer can only be that she knew in advance Jesus could do something about it and she expected him to sort it out. I always envisage Jesus smiling when he asks his mum what the wine running out has to do with them, and it's interesting to note his mother doesn't answer him, nor plead or persuade him, but rather, like all mums, assumes he'll do what he's told, and tells the waiters to, 'Do whatever he says.'

This makes one wonder what other things Jesus had done in his mother's presence during the thirty years he spent with her before his public ministry began.

Anyway, back to my wedding day. I got myself suited and booted, and before long my best man Joseph McGovern arrived in a white stretch limo to pick me up. We drove from my parents' house to Evelyn's, then with my wife-to-be and her sister Julie, we carried on to Queensferry, on the banks of the River Forth to get married. After the ceremony the limo took us to the Barnton Hotel where Evelyn's friend was the manager and had booked a private sitting room and dining room for twenty people. By this time, I'd have been out of prison for four hours and the whole experience had a dream-like quality about it.

After the meal was over, the four of us climbed back into the stretch limo and drove through to Glasgow, where Joe had booked the whole top floor of one of the city centre's top hotels for the weekend, and we partied like it was 1999 (because it was) for seventy-two hours straight.

Monday morning came, and it was time to leave the hotel and head home. Two weeks later my wife and I caught a plane to Crete, where we spent a fortnight on honeymoon in a beautiful little hotel on the beach. Used to getting up early, I rose at dawn each morning and watched as the sun came up over the horizon, looking like a pink tennis ball, which after a few seconds suddenly burst into flame, shining its light across the water to where I sat on the balcony looking out and contemplating the future.

On the first day of the trial, the Crown had dropped all but two of the nine charges on the indictment against me, due to a lack of evidence, evidence they knew perfectly well they didn't have despite serving the indictment on me, to ensure my case was heard in the High Court.

In the end, I'd been convicted of possessing two small calibre pistols without the relevant licence. Both guns had been in a locked drawer, in a locked garage, adjoining a locked house. I'd caused no harm, no injury, committed no act of dishonesty, nor breach of client confidentiality. Yet the Law Society, not satisfied with me having spent a significant period in prison, furious their own disciplinary tribunal had admonished me and allowed me to practise my profession, had taken the historical step of appealing their own decision, determined by hook or by crook to deprive me of doing the only thing I was qualified for, and loved to do: defend people. How could my conviction affect that? I'd been practising throughout the whole year and a half while I was on bail, and it hadn't made the slightest difference to the way I was treated by my fellow lawyers, clients, or the court. The Law Society's decision (the second time round) to remove my name from the register of solicitors (I'm still a lawyer) had nothing to do with my legal abilities, or the protection of the public – indeed confidentiality was of key importance to my clients and I'd proved I considered that sacrosanct – but was rather what I would call the petty revenge of a bunch of pathetic, pen-pushing nonentities whose sole purpose in my opinion is to perpetuate a system that pretends to care about the service the public receive from practitioners, but in reality is bothered only about protecting and covering up for those who belong to their brotherhood.

So it was, I sat staring out over the Aegean Sea, thinking only a couple of weeks ago I'd finished a three stretch and started a life sentence with Evelyn. But what would I do for a living? How could I take care of my wife, bring up my three children? What lay ahead for me and my family? Those were the big questions, and I was going to need some big answers.

62

'Life can only be understood backwards; but it must be lived forwards.'
— Søren Kierkegaard

I'd been back from abroad about a week when there was a knock on the door. I opened it to find Alan, one of my clients, a friend and international fraudster, leaning against the bonnet of a blue Bentley parked outside. He handed me a fat envelope.

'Here, that'll help get you back on your feet.'

I thanked him, and moments later he bundled the kids, Evelyn and me into the car and drove us to Glasgow for a beautiful meal washed down with bottles of pink champagne. What company Alan had copping for that bill is anybody's guess.

Of course, my friend was going out of his way to help me financially, without making me feel like a charity case. I soon realised things couldn't carry on this way much longer. I needed to have a serious think about what I was going to do.

I mentioned earlier that long before I embarked on a career as a criminal lawyer, I'd wanted to be a journalist, but my dad had other ideas. I'd always enjoyed writing, but how could I make a living out of that at the age of forty-two? As I said before, I had some big questions, but thank God, he had the big answers.

About a month or so after my return from honeymoon, Moray, my mate from university who'd studied law but after graduating moved to London to become a writer/actor, got in touch with me. He wanted to know if I fancied writing a script with him, about a legal practice with two partners, one a straight-laced lawyer, and the other more like me.

They say if you're going to write, write what you know, and the criminal law world was one I had first-hand experience of, from both sides of the barbed-wire fence. I jumped at the chance, and Moray and I wrote a script entitled *Guilt-Edged*, which we sent to the executive producer of SMG. The script was well received, though in the end due to scheduling and other reasons, it was never greenlit, but we were paid for our writing, and paid well. This prompted me to keep an eye out for any further possible work as a screenwriter.

At the time *River City*, the BBC Scotland soap, had recently started production and was running a shadow script scheme for writers, to see if they were up to scratch for the show. Nothing ventured, nothing gained, I submitted a sample. The original entries were whittled down to sixteen writers, then cut down once again to a final two. I was fortunate enough to be chosen, along with one other. So started my career with *River City*, a show for which I'm proud to have written consistently for these past twenty years. I've also penned episodes of *EastEnders*, *Taggart* and *New Street Law*, a legal series created by a close friend of mine, Matthew Hall, produced by Red Productions, in conjunction with the BBC. As a result, to date I'm credited with around seventy hours of prime-time television.

Okay, I hear you say, we get the picture, stop bumming, but I assure you I don't mean to. I admit to having committed many sins, but make no mistake, this book is not about some Damascus Road experience. God has guarded me all my life and I thank Him for each of His blessings. I very much repent of the hurt I caused my parents and those close to me; however, the sins for which one day I'll be judged (as indeed we all will) are not those that got the Law Society's tights in such a bunch.

Many years ago, when I was eight, there was a girl in my class who for some reason the other pupils didn't speak to. I know now she'd had a hard home life, but as a boy all I cared about was being popular and joined the others in ostracising her. One day in class I leaned over and tried to jab her leg with a sharpened pencil; however, I held it the wrong way round, with the result (quite rightly) I stuck the pointed end into my hand. As I write this, fifty-eight years later,

I still have the tiny tip of lead that broke off lodged deep in my right palm.

As if what I'd tried to do wasn't nasty enough, I invited everyone in my class to my house for my eighth birthday party, but deliberately left the girl out. The following day, on the way to school, we happened to meet, and she handed me a little bunch of flowers she'd picked, wishing me happy birthday. Not inviting that girl, going along with the way others treated her, in my opinion ranks among the greatest sins I ever committed, and over half a century later I still lie awake at night and feel guilty for the way I acted. If she ever reads this and remembers, I beg her to please forgive me, because believe me, I'll never forgive myself.

As for my career as a criminal lawyer, I make no apologies. I fought for my clients against the forces of the Crown, using the same weapons they used. If I crossed the line, so did they. But as I've said before, the dice were always loaded, the deck stacked in their favour, so in my opinion, like *Rollerball*, there were no rules. 'In the jungle there is only one law. Don't die.'

There are many more stories I could tell, and hope to, plus many I can't, but one thing is certain: were it not for God, I wouldn't be here to tell any of them. I don't say this in any sort of sentimental way, but state it simply as a fact. Today, I have a wonderful wife, three lovely children, five fantastic grandchildren (so far) and I'm blessed to work as a writer. I give God all the glory and am grateful to Him for guarding and guiding me, and pray He continues to do so. After the Law Society got their second kick at the ball, and booted me out, I was at a loss what to do on my release. I remember writing to my mother (she wrote to me almost every day) and she replied with the well known words found in the book of the Prophet Jeremiah, Chapter 29 verse 11: 'For I know the plans I have for you,' declares the Lord, 'plans to prosper you and not to harm you, plans to give you hope and a future.' And, as usual, my mother was right.

Acknowledgements

Firstly, I wish to thank my wonderful wife and family for putting up with my artistic temperament throughout the writing process, and my friends, Paul Ferris, Matthew Hall, Sergio Casci, Des Mulvey and Neil D. Murray KC, for their support, advice, contributions and encouragement.

Huge thanks are also owed to my publisher, Campbell Brown, for reading my speculatively written manuscript and seeing potential where others in this fearful age saw reasons for rejection. Also, many thanks to Clem Flanagan for all her patient work in editing and navigating between the Scylla and Charybdis of modern sensibilities and the cold hard truth that needs be told.

Finally, a big shout-out to the Law Society of Scotland, who strove so tirelessly, with varying degrees of success, to have my name struck from the roll. Had they not eventually succeeded, I doubt this book would ever have been written. I may briefly bask in the satisfaction of having the last word for now, but I assure you, what happens at the last trumpet matters far more to me.